I0054797

Advanced Snowflake

Processing Data, Developing Applications, and Deploying ML Models at Scale

Muhammad Fasih Ullah

O'REILLY®

Advanced Snowflake

by Muhammad Fasih Ullah

Copyright © 2026 Muhammad Fasih Ullah. All rights reserved.

Printed in the United States of America.

Published by O'Reilly Media, Inc., 141 Stony Circle, Suite 195, Santa Rosa, CA 95401.

O'Reilly books may be purchased for educational, business, or sales promotional use. Online editions are also available for most titles (*http://oreilly.com*). For more information, contact our corporate/institutional sales department: 800-998-9938 or *corporate@oreilly.com*.

Acquisitions Editor: Andy Kwan	**Indexer:** Ellen Troutman-Zaig
Development Editor: Shira Evans	**Cover Designer:** Susan Brown
Production Editor: Katherine Tozer	**Cover Illustrator:** José Marzan Jr.
Copyeditor: Liz Wheeler	**Interior Designer:** David Futato
Proofreader: Miah Sandvik	**Interior Illustrator:** Kate Dullea

October 2025:   First Edition

Revision History for the First Edition

2025-09-25:   First Release

See *http://oreilly.com/catalog/errata.csp?isbn=9781098170219* for release details.

The O'Reilly logo is a registered trademark of O'Reilly Media, Inc. *Advanced Snowflake*, the cover image, and related trade dress are trademarks of O'Reilly Media, Inc.

The views expressed in this work are those of the author and do not represent the publisher's views. While the publisher and the author have used good faith efforts to ensure that the information and instructions contained in this work are accurate, the publisher and the author disclaim all responsibility for errors or omissions, including without limitation responsibility for damages resulting from the use of or reliance on this work. Use of the information and instructions contained in this work is at your own risk. If any code samples or other technology this work contains or describes is subject to open source licenses or the intellectual property rights of others, it is your responsibility to ensure that your use thereof complies with such licenses and/or rights.

978-1-098-17021-9

LSI

Table of Contents

Preface

Six years ago, I first encountered Snowflake while looking for a better data warehouse replacement at my previous company. What started as a technical assessment quickly turned into an exciting journey that continues to this day. Since then, I've watched Snowflake evolve from a cloud data warehouse into a comprehensive data cloud platform, releasing innovative features at a pace that both thrills and challenges data professionals.

As a Snowflake Data Superhero, I regularly connect with practitioners at meetups and conferences. Time and again, I hear the concerns around one theme: Snowflake is moving so fast; how do I keep up with everything? Features like Snowpark, Native Apps, and AI/ML capabilities are transforming how we think about data platforms, but the rapid pace of innovation can feel overwhelming.

This challenge inspired me to write *Advanced Snowflake*. While basic Snowflake resources are plentiful, there wasn't a comprehensive guide that could distill the platform's advanced features into digestible, actionable insights. This book fills that gap by focusing on three game-changing areas: Snowpark for programmatic data processing, the Native Apps and developer ecosystem for extending platform capabilities, and Snowflake's expanding AI/ML functionality.

Beyond these core topics, I explore exciting developments like Iceberg tables, dynamic tables, advanced SQL functions, including window functions, and Snowflake's geospatial capabilities—all the features that showcase Snowflake's versatility and power. While I touch on the latest Summit announcements like Openflow and AISQL, I've focused primarily on mature features you can implement today.

My goal isn't just to explain these tools, but to show you how to think creatively about applying them to your unique challenges. Through hands-on exercises and practical examples, you'll discover new approaches to familiar problems and unlock capabilities you might not have considered. Whether you're a data engineer, analyst, or architect looking to elevate your Snowflake expertise, this book provides the knowledge and practical experience to help you harness the full potential of the data cloud. Let's explore what's possible when you move beyond the basics and embrace Snowflake's advanced capabilities.

Who Should Read This Book

This book is designed for data professionals who are already familiar with Snowflake and databases in general, and are ready to explore the platform's advanced capabilities. If you can navigate Snowflake's web interface, write SQL queries, and understand basic database concepts, you're prepared for what lies ahead.

The ideal readers include data engineers looking to leverage Snowpark for complex processing workflows, data scientists wanting to operationalize machine learning models within Snowflake, data analysts seeking to expand beyond traditional SQL, data architects evaluating advanced features, and technical decision makers understanding the art of the possible with Snowflake's evolving capabilities.

This book assumes working knowledge of Snowflake fundamentals. While I start with basic concepts for advanced features like Snowpark, I don't cover Python programming fundamentals. I jump directly into implementation after setup. If you're new to Snowflake entirely, I recommend starting with *Snowflake: The Definitive Guide* by Joyce Kay Avila (O'Reilly) before diving into this advanced material.

Navigating This Book

This book is designed with flexibility in mind. While the chapters flow logically from foundational concepts to advanced implementations, you don't need to read it cover to cover; feel free to jump directly to the features that excite you most.

The book follows a progression from understanding to action. Chapters 1 and 2 set the theoretical foundation, exploring Snowflake's evolution and architectural principles. Chapter 3 introduces advanced SQL capabilities with practical examples to bridge theory and practice. Then we dive deep: Chapters 4, 5, and 6 are where the magic happens, featuring comprehensive, hands-on exercises for Snowpark, Snowflake Native Apps, and Snowflake for AI and ML, respectively. Finally, Chapter 7 looks toward the future of the platform.

Each hands-on exercise is completely standalone. You can tackle Snowpark today and Native Apps next month without missing a beat. When concepts from other chapters are relevant, you'll find clear cross-references and links to guide your exploration.

In a way, the book is structured like a "choose your own adventure" book. Curious about building applications? Jump straight to Chapter 5. Eager to explore machine learning capabilities? Chapter 6 awaits. The beauty of Snowflake's ecosystem is that these advanced features can work independently or together, and this book reflects that flexibility.

I've focused on features with stable core functionality while linking to Snowflake's documentation for areas likely to evolve. This approach ensures you're learning skills that will remain valuable even as the platform continues its rapid evolution.

The setup requirements are covered in Chapter 1, so start there for your environment preparation, then chart your course through Snowflake's advanced capabilities.

Conventions Used in This Book

The following typographical conventions are used in this book:

Italic
Indicates new terms, URLs, email addresses, filenames, and file extensions.

`Constant width`
Used for program listings, as well as within paragraphs to refer to program elements such as variable or function names, databases, data types, environment variables, statements, and keywords.

`Constant width bold`
Shows commands or other text that should be typed literally by the user.

`Constant width italic`
Shows text that should be replaced with user-supplied values or by values determined by context.

This element signifies a brief Q & A.

This element signifies a general note.

This element indicates a warning or caution.

Using Code Examples

Supplemental material (code examples, exercises, etc.) is available for download at *https://oreil.ly/advanced-snowflake-repo*.

If you have a technical question or a problem using the code examples, please email *support@oreilly.com*.

This book is here to help you get your job done. In general, if example code is offered with this book, you may use it in your programs and documentation. You do not need to contact us for permission unless you're reproducing a significant portion of the code. For example, writing a program that uses several chunks of code from this book does not require permission. Selling or distributing examples from O'Reilly books does require permission. Answering a question by citing this book and quoting example code does not require permission. Incorporating a significant amount of example code from this book into your product's documentation does require permission.

We appreciate, but generally do not require, attribution. An attribution usually includes the title, author, publisher, and ISBN. For example: "*Advanced Snowflake* by Muhammad Fasih Ullah (O'Reilly). Copyright 2026 Muhammad Fasih Ullah, 978-1-098-17021-9."

If you feel your use of code examples falls outside fair use or the permission given above, feel free to contact us at *permissions@oreilly.com*.

O'Reilly Online Learning

For more than 40 years, *O'Reilly Media* has provided technology and business training, knowledge, and insight to help companies succeed.

Our unique network of experts and innovators share their knowledge and expertise through books, articles, and our online learning platform. O'Reilly's online learning platform gives you on-demand access to live training courses, in-depth learning paths, interactive coding environments, and a vast collection of text and video from O'Reilly and 200+ other publishers. For more information, visit *https://oreilly.com*.

How to Contact Us

Please address comments and questions concerning this book to the publisher:

O'Reilly Media, Inc.
141 Stony Circle, Suite 195
Santa Rosa, CA 95401
800-889-8969 (in the United States or Canada)
707-827-7019 (international or local)
707-829-0104 (fax)
support@oreilly.com
https://oreilly.com/about/contact.html

We have a web page for this book, where we list errata and any additional information. You can access this page at *https://oreil.ly/AdvancedSnowflake*.

For news and information about our books and courses, visit *https://oreilly.com*.

Find us on LinkedIn: *https://linkedin.com/company/oreilly-media*.

Watch us on YouTube: *https://youtube.com/oreillymedia*.

Acknowledgments

Writing a book about a platform as dynamic and evolving as Snowflake requires more than individual effort. It takes a community of passionate practitioners, thoughtful reviewers, and unwavering support. If you find value in these pages, it's because of the remarkable people who shared their expertise, time, and encouragement throughout this journey.

My deepest appreciation goes to the technical reviewers who ensured accuracy and clarity: Nadir Doctor, Fernando Brito, Angela Harney, and Sudheer Lagisetty. Your meticulous attention to detail and thoughtful feedback shaped every chapter. To Joyce Kay Avila, a fellow Data Superhero and author of *Snowflake: The Definitive Guide*, thank you for your wisdom and encouragement. Your pioneering work paved the way for books like this one.

I'm grateful to the Snowflake Community leaders, Elsa Mayer, Amilee Alesna, and Howard Lio, for helping me navigate the correct course throughout this journey.

My Snowflake journey began thanks to Per Enell, Amina Taghaboni, Jesper Grip, and the rest of the Swedish Snowflake team. Without your introduction to this incredible platform six years ago, this book wouldn't exist. I'd also like to thank Simon Wessberg, whose enthusiasm and support reminded me why this platform captivates so many of us.

To my professional mentors who shaped my career: Björn Idren, Magnus Dahlbäck, Lisa Bruzelius, Fredrik Hjelm, and Rahman Amandius. Your guidance and trust gave me the foundation to explore, experiment, and eventually share knowledge with others.

The O'Reilly team made this vision a reality. Special thanks to Shira Evans, whose editorial expertise guided this project from concept to completion, and to Sara Hunter for her support.

To the global community of Snowflake Data Superheroes—you inspire me daily with your innovation, collaboration, and dedication to pushing the boundaries of what's possible.

A big thank you to my friend Talha Chattha for his encouragement, support, and most importantly, spinning up the resources when I needed them for Openflow. Even though the details didn't make it to the book, it was fantastic testing them out.

To my incredible circle of friends: Hassan Iqbal, Daniyal Awan, Maaz Musa, Fahad Shafi, M. Hanif, Okasha Razzaq, Faiq Chaudhary, Ahmed Aleem, Raghas Naveed, Ammar Khan, Saad Waqar, Hamza Shafique, Hazim Malik, Sumsam Khan, Hassam Riaz, Hamza Zaib, M. Ahsan, Haseeb Mazhar, and Umar Sajjad, thank you for reminding me that there's a world beyond Snowflake warehouses.

Finally, to my family: my wife Zainab, whose patience and support made the late-night writing sessions possible; my parents, whose belief in education and perseverance shaped who I am today; and my sisters Rohma, Irha, and Raaem, who always encourage my pursuits and cheer for me no matter what. And to my daughter Ayana, who may not understand SQL yet but has already mastered the art of perfectly timing her adorable interruptions during my most important tasks; your giggles are worth every rewritten paragraph.

This book exists because of your love and support.

## CHAPTER 1

Getting Started and Setting Up the Environment

Kudos to you for starting this book and taking the next step in your Snowflake journey. In this chapter, I will go through the new Snowflake UI and explain more about all the different sections. I'll then show you how to set up the environment you'll need in order to follow the examples presented throughout this book.

To follow along, I recommend having a working Snowflake account or trial account (*https://signup.snowflake.com*). If you are a student, you can create a 120-day Snowflake trial account (*https://signup.snowflake.com/?trial=student*).

Introduction to Snowflake's New UI (Snowsight)

Snowflake has had two different UIs in recent times. The legacy classic UI (Figure 1-1) is no longer available for new accounts, and Snowflake recommends moving to the new UI called Snowsight (Figure 1-2).

Figure 1-1. Snowflake classic UI

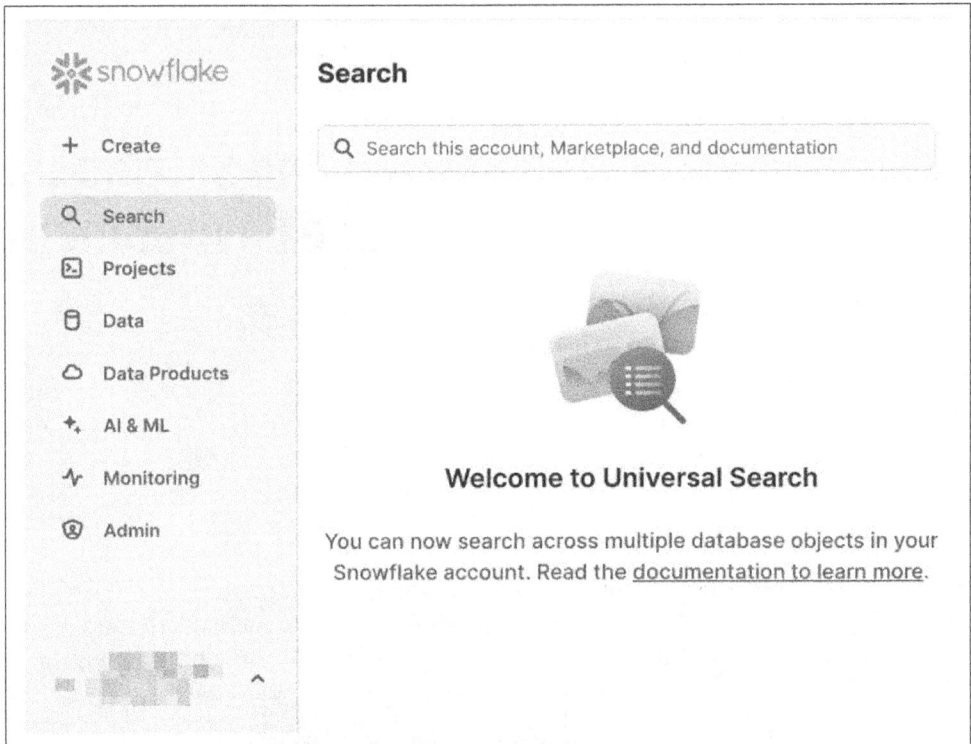

Figure 1-2. Snowsight (new Snowflake UI)

Snowsight, the new Snowflake UI, recently got an upgrade, and several new sections were added, which are available for all Snowflake customers. Snowflake also announced the much-awaited "dark mode" on Snowsight during the Snowflake Summit 2024. Figure 1-3 shows Snowsight in dark mode and highlights the steps to switch from the default light mode to the dark mode.

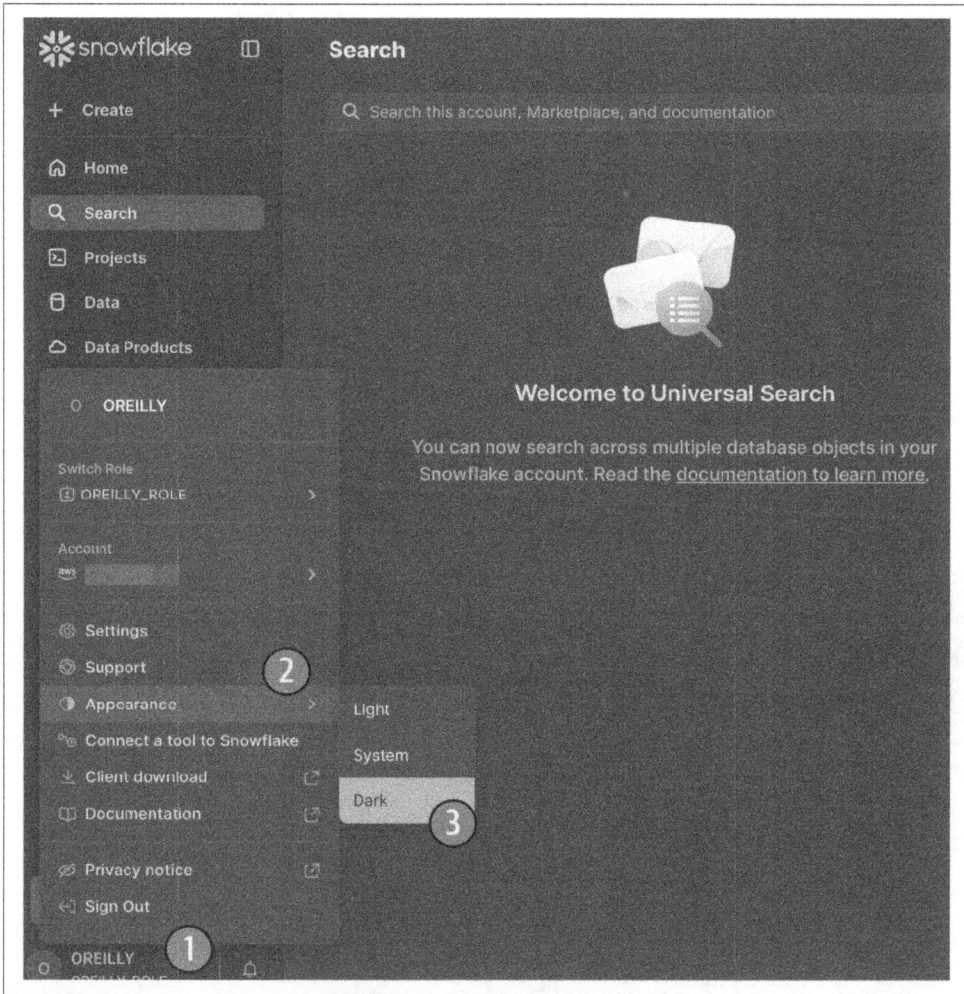

Figure 1-3. Snowsight in dark mode

Once you log in, you will be welcomed by a sidebar similar to Figure 1-4. You will see several new sections and subsections. Let's go through them now.

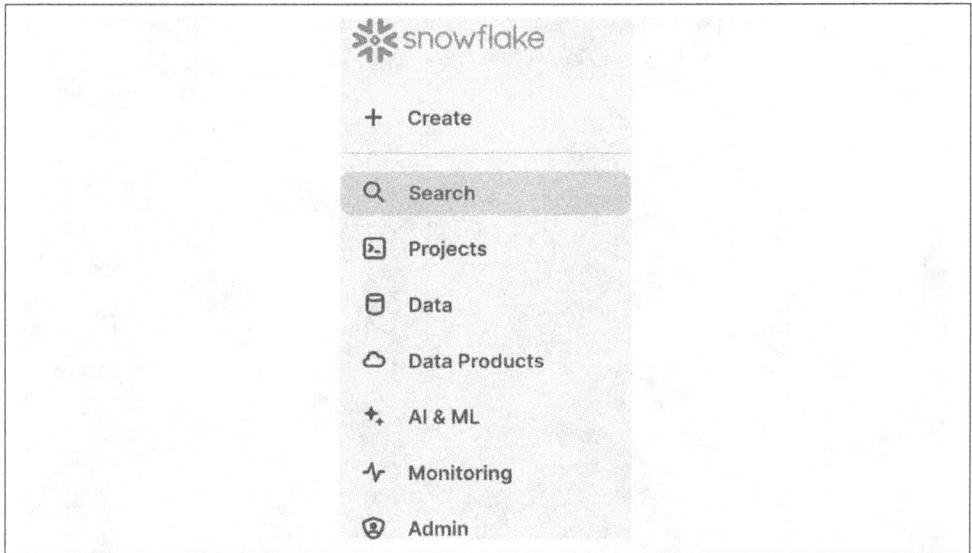

Figure 1-4. Snowsight sidebar

Search

Universal Search enables a global search across your account (Figure 1-5). You can search across several Snowflake objects (databases, schemas, tables, views, procedures, functions), Snowflake Marketplace, and the Snowflake documentation.

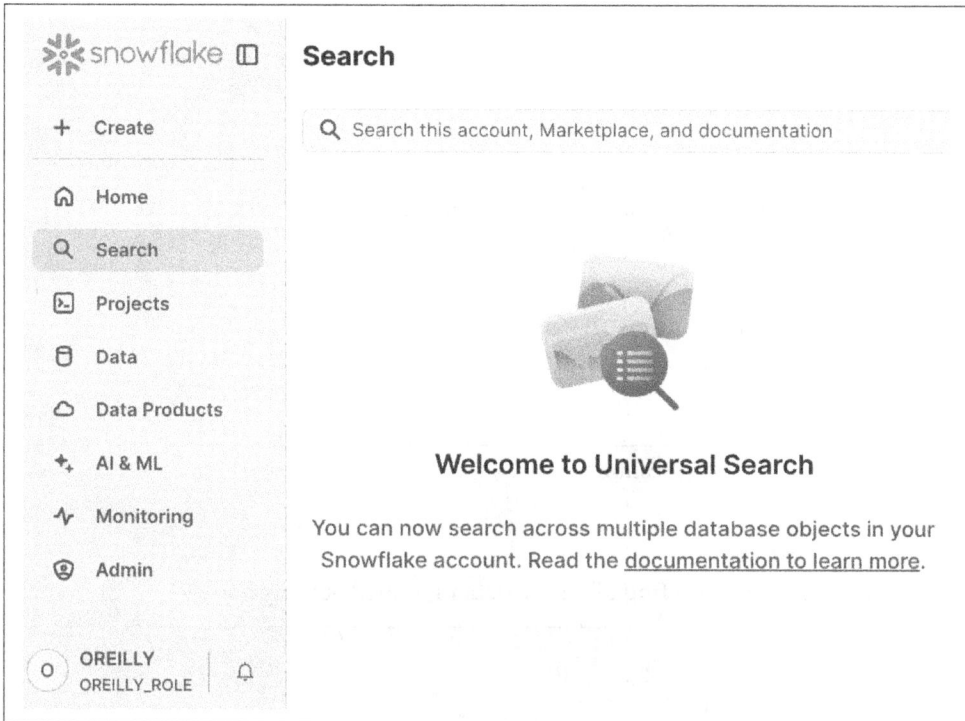

Figure 1-5. Search tab

Projects

The Projects tab comes with a few subsections, as Figure 1-6 shows:

Worksheets
Here you can find the collection of all our workbooks (SQL and Python) and the folders.

Notebooks
Here you can find all your Jupyter notebooks. You can create a new one within Snowflake, import them from a repository, or import an *.ipynb* file. Snowflake Notebooks allow you to run Python and SQL code in separate cells consecutively without switching the interface.

Streamlit
This is the place to organize all of your Streamlit apps.

Dashboards
This is a tab where you can keep all of your Snowflake dashboards.

App Packages
  Here you can build and maintain all of your application packages.

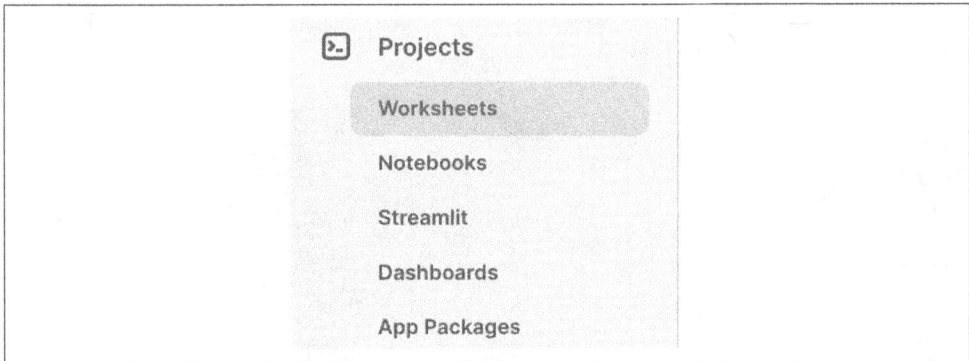

Figure 1-6. Projects tab subsections

Data

The Data tab is where you find all of the data in Snowflake (Figure 1-7).

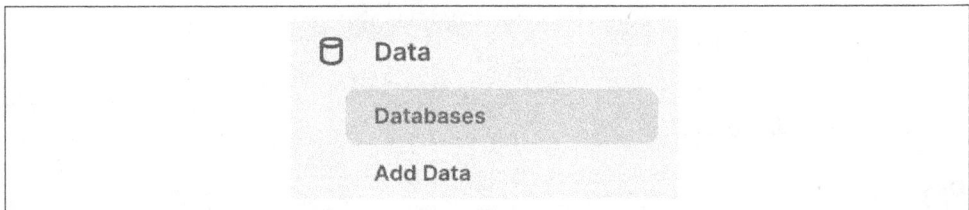

Figure 1-7. Data tab subsections

The first subsection is the Databases section, where you can find a list of all your databases, including the ones shared with you. The second subsection is the new UI for data loading. It provides you with multiple options for loading data into your Snowflake environment (Figure 1-8).

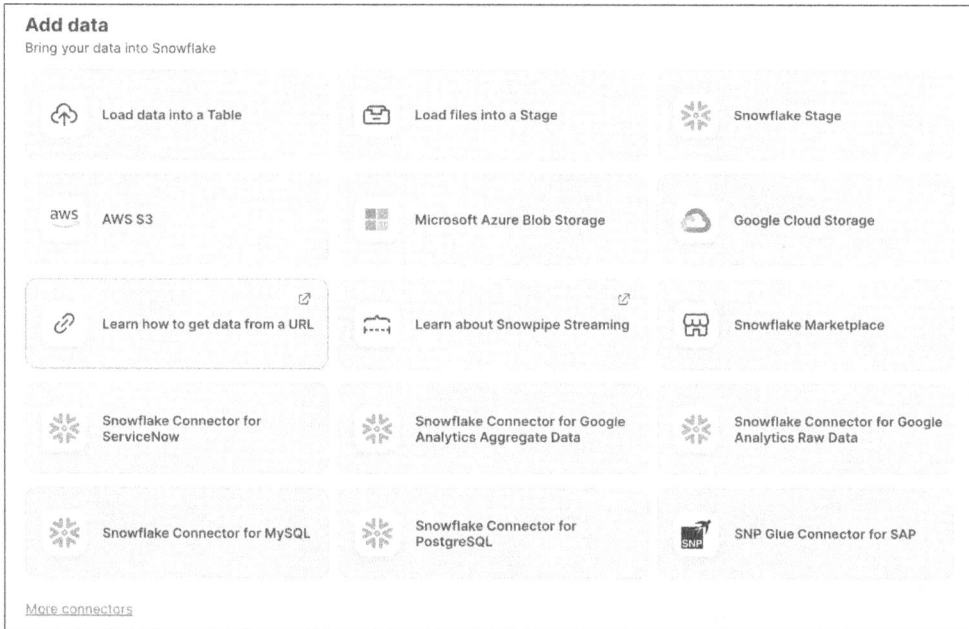

Figure 1-8. Add Data options (see this screengrab in full size) (https://oreil.ly/adsf_0108png)

Data Products

The Data Products section of the menu (Figure 1-9) is all about different data products you can connect to or are using in your Snowflake account. A data product can be a dataset, an application, or an agentic product:

Marketplace
> This is where you can find all data products listed by different companies on Snowflake Marketplace.

Apps
> Here you can find the apps you are using.

Private Sharing
> In this subsection, you can see all the inbound and outbound data shares, e.g., if you have an inbound data share from a partner company.

Provider Studio
> Just like YouTube Studio, if you want to or you already share your data products with other Snowflake customers, this is where you will see them. You can also see the usage analytics of such data products.

Partner Connect

Partner Connect allows you to seamlessly create trial accounts with select Snow-flake partners and integrate them within your Snowflake environment.

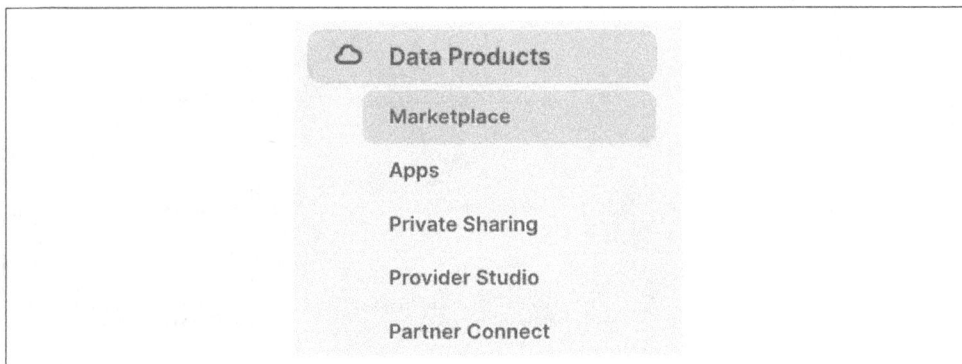

Figure 1-9. Data Products subsections

AI & ML

AI & ML (artificial intelligence and machine learning) is a new section at the time of writing, and all the subsections are preview features for now (Figure 1-10):

Studio

Also known as Snowflake AI & ML Studio, this is where you see the summary of what Snowflake AI & ML Studio can do and where you can quickly create a model (Figure 1-11).

Models

All the models logged into the Snowflake Model Registry will be listed in this section. Models created in the AI & ML Studio will automatically be registered and shown here.

Document AI

Snowflake Document AI uses a proprietary large language model (LLM) called Arctic-TILT to extract data from documents. This is where you will see the Document AI model builds.

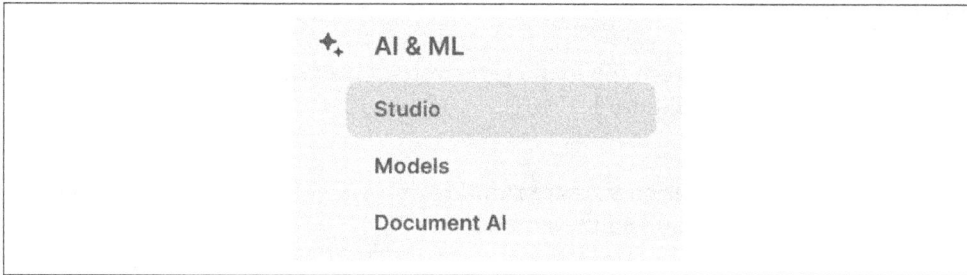

Figure 1-10. AI & ML tab subsections

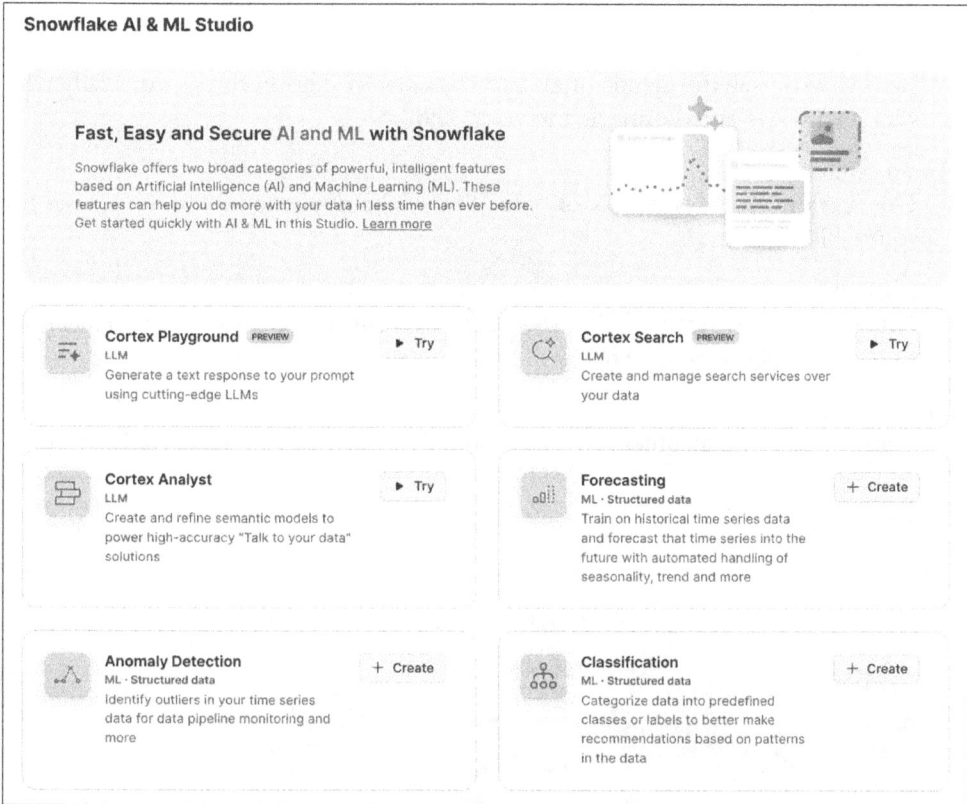

Figure 1-11. Snowflake AI & ML Studio overview (see this screengrab in full size) (https://oreil.ly/adsf_0111png)

Monitoring

The Monitoring section from the menu gives you an overview of what is going on in your Snowflake account (Figure 1-12):

Query History
> Here you can see what queries are running on your account. This includes queries from all the users and all the systems.

Copy History
> This subsection contains load info for all the `COPY INTO` commands running, e.g., how many rows are being loaded, the size of data being loaded, status, etc.

Task History
> Here you can see the details of all Snowflake tasks. This becomes especially relevant if you have apps connected to your account.

Dynamic Tables
> This section provides details on your Snowflake dynamic tables configured for your table.

Trust Center
> This is a preview feature. This section scans your account for potential security risks and displays them all here.

Governance
> Here you can find all objects with tags and their defined row access policies.

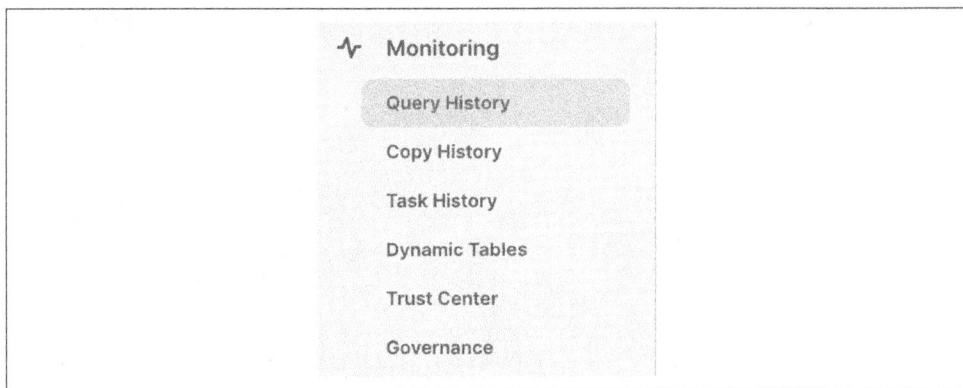

Figure 1-12. Monitoring tab subsections

Admin

The Admin section (Figure 1-13) is only available if you have extended privileges granted to your user or you have admin roles:

Cost Management
> In this tab, you have an overview of the costs for your account. You can see day-over-day costs, credits consumed, and cost trends. You can also set up resource monitors and budgets for your accounts here.

Warehouses
> Here you have the list of all the warehouses configured for your account. You can add new warehouses and maintain your warehouses here.

Users & Roles
> Here you have the list of all the users and roles configured for your account. You can add new users and remove or disable current ones in this tab.

Accounts
> If you have multiple accounts under your organization, this is where you can see them.

Security
> All the network policies and network rules are defined and listed here.

Contacts
> Here you can list the email addresses to receive notifications on from your Snowflake account.

Billing & Terms
> In this section, you can see the different terms and conditions applicable to your Snowflake account, add payment methods, and review billing documents.

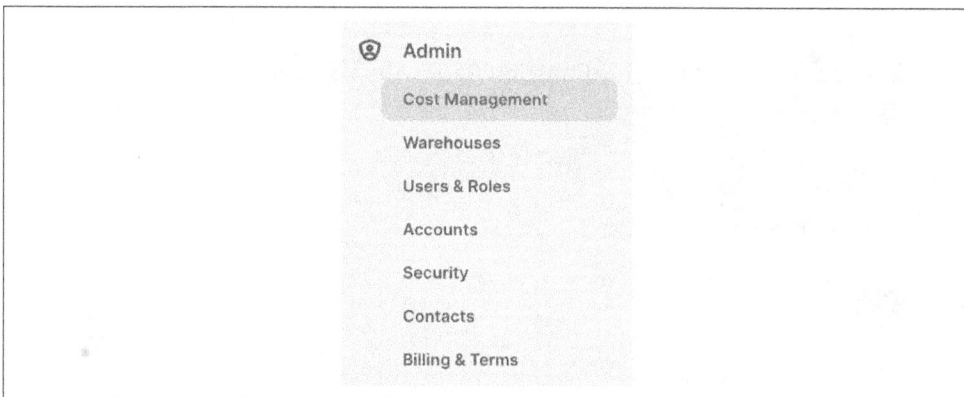

Figure 1-13. Admin tab subsections

Introduction to Snowflake Worksheets

Worksheets are the core components of the Snowflake UI. They are the integrated development environment (IDE) where you can write your code and interact with the Snowflake platform and your data. You have options to create two different types of worksheets: SQL and Python.

SQL Worksheets

Let's recap and take a look at the different sections of an SQL worksheet (Figure 1-14):

1. *Context setting:*
   Here you'll find a drop-down menu to select the database and schema for the worksheet.

2. *Settings*
   Here you will find the editor settings, e.g., highlighting.

3. *Role*
   This button opens a drop-down menu to select a role for the worksheet.

4. *Warehouse*
   Here you'll find a drop-down menu to choose a warehouse for the worksheet.

5. *Share*
   From here, you can share your worksheets with other Snowflake users within your organization.

6. *Run*
   This button can be used to run the Snowflake command or a query in the worksheet.

7. *SQL editor*
   Here you will find the SQL editing interface within Snowflake.

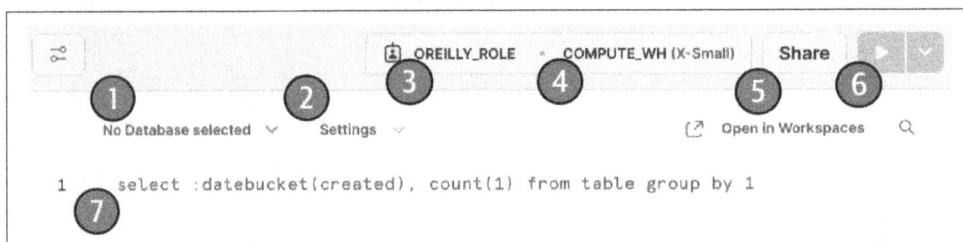

Figure 1-14. Snowflake SQL worksheet

Python Worksheets

Let's walk through the different sections of a Python worksheet (Figure 1-15):

1. *Context setting*
   Here you'll find a drop-down menu to select the database and schema.

2. *Settings*
   Here you can set the handler function, return type, line wrapping, and linting.

3. *Packages*
   Here you'll find a drop-down menu to select the packages to load for this worksheet.

4. *Role*
   Here you'll find a drop-down menu to select a role for the worksheet.

5. *Warehouse*
   Here you'll find a drop-down menu to choose a warehouse for the worksheet.

6. *Share*
   From here you can share your worksheets with other Snowflake users within your organization.

7. *Deploy*
   From here you have the option to deploy the Python function as a stored procedure in the database and schema chosen in context settings.

8. *Run*
   You can execute the script using this button.

9. *Main function*
   This is the main body function. It is also the default handler function, i.e., the function that will be executed first when you press Run.

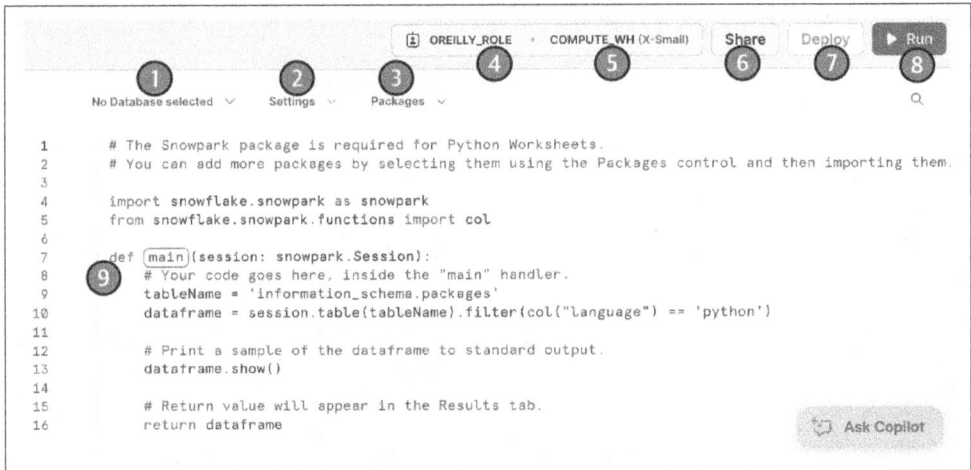

Figure 1-15. Snowflake Python worksheet

Setting Up the SQL Environment

In the SQL examples in this book, I will be using the sample datasets (*https://oreil.ly/EGO_r*) already available in Snowflake. If I use a different dataset for some examples, I will ensure that I provide you with the necessary data.

To follow along with the code examples, you will need a Snowflake user with access to an active warehouse and the sample database. More specific environment settings will be shared with code examples if required. We will be creating our custom roles and users using the `ACCOUNTADMIN` role in the trial, just so no one ever runs into access control problems, but I must highlight here that it is not a recommended practice; you should always use proper designated roles to create users and roles and grant privileges. To stay updated with access control best practices, you should refer to the Snowflake documentation (*https://oreil.ly/oPsf9*).

Once you have successfully created the trial account, you can run the script (`initial_setup.sql`) to set up a new user, `OREILLY`, and a new role, `OREILLY_ROLE`. You may log in to a Snowflake instance with this new user, and you should have everything available to you to follow along in the later chapters.

Setting Up the Snowpark/Python Environment

A good practice while learning new tools is to always work in isolated environments to minimize the risk of messing up anything in production. The database that we have created in the preceding section will remain our playground for Snowpark and Python-related tasks, too.

The only thing we will set up in this chapter is a local Python environment. To do that, you will use conda and the environment file (*https://oreil.ly/advanced-snowflake-repoch1*) to install all the packages you will need. The first step for you is to download the latest version of conda (*https://oreil.ly/87gbF*) on your local machine if you haven't already. Once that's done, you can create a new environment from the given environment file using the following command in your terminal:

```
conda env create -f environment.yml
```

> Make sure you run this command from the folder where *environment.yml* is present.

Conda will read the file, download all the necessary packages, and create a new environment with the specified name; in our case, OREILLY. Now run the following command to activate the environment:

```
conda activate oreilly
```

Once activated, you can verify that everything is installed correctly using the following command:

```
conda list
```

And voila! You should see all the packages listed in the *environment.yml* file on your terminal. Lastly, to deactivate the environment, you can simply run the following command:

```
conda deactivate
```

Summary

In this chapter, you got a quick overview of the Snowflake UI. You saw the different menus, different options, and where to find the features while navigating the platform. A great conclusion to this chapter from your end would be to create a Snowflake trial account and set up the user and the sandbox environment you will need for the following chapters.

Now let's move on to Chapter 2 for an overview of Snowflake's architecture.

Snowflake Overview

This chapter provides an overview of Snowflake, including an explanation of the multilayered Snowflake architecture and a short introduction to Snowflake objects.

Snowflake Architecture

The Snowflake architecture is multilayered, with the following three layers at its core: the optimized storage layer, the elastic multi-cluster compute layer, and the cloud services layer (Figure 2-1).

Storage Layer

The Snowflake storage layer, also known as the cloud storage layer or database storage layer, is a hybrid columnar database storage that allows for fast and seamless access to your data. It enables elasticity and infinite storage scaling using the power of the cloud. It uses micro-partitions to cluster and arrange the data in the background to provide top-notch performance while accessing the data.

Compute Layer

Snowflake's elastic multi-cluster compute layer, also simply known as the compute layer, is the core layer where all the data processing occurs. It is responsible for query execution. The biggest advantage of it being separate from the storage layer is the isolation of resources. Like the storage layer, the compute layer can scale infinitely using cloud resources. It uses Snowflake warehouses to process the data.

Cloud Services Layer

The cloud services layer is the layer responsible for managing the metadata across your account. It also provides access control, security, infrastructure management, and query optimization. When a query is run, the cloud services layer is responsible for parsing it, optimizing it, generating the query plan, and checking security and access before passing it over to the compute layer to execute it.

Cloud-Agnostic Layer

The cloud-agnostic layer is the base Snowflake layer that allows you to run your Snowflake instance on the cloud provider of your choice. You can choose from Amazon Web Services (AWS), Google Cloud Platform (GCP), or Microsoft Azure. This eliminates the hassle of managing and securing multiple environments. As a result, everything built on Snowflake, including native applications, is cloud agnostic.

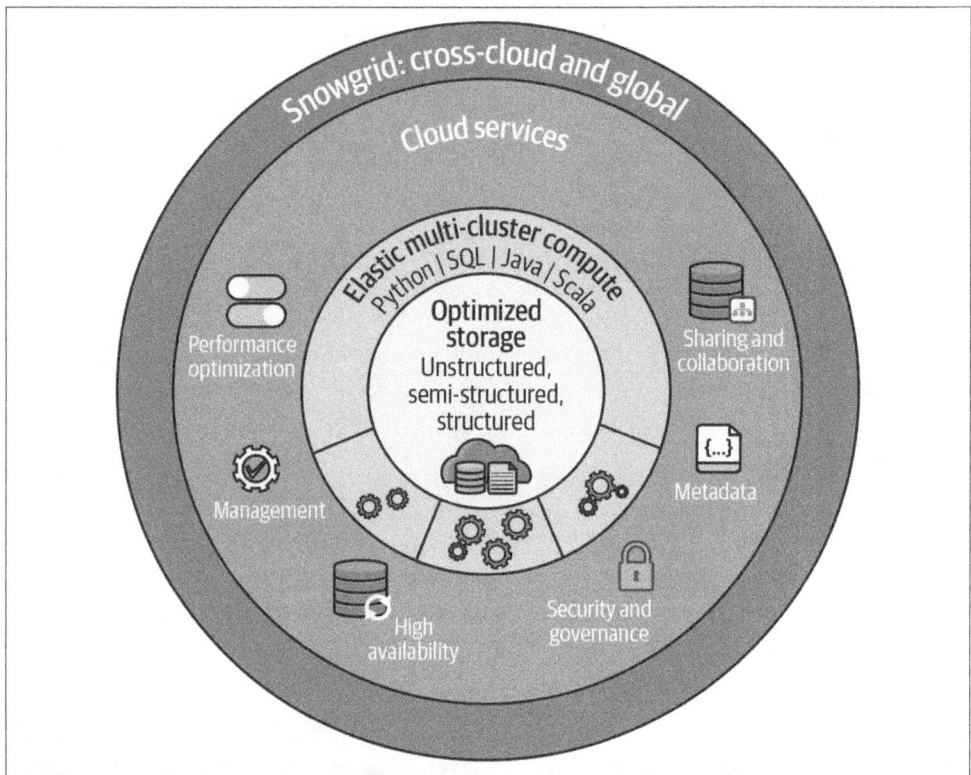

Figure 2-1. Snowflake's multilayered architecture (source: Snowflake (https://oreil.ly/eSvDp))

Optimized Storage Layer Features

You have already learned a little about the optimized storage layer. Let's now have a quick look at the different features of this layer.

Compression and Micro-Partitions

Snowflake stores all your data in micro-partitions. Unlike traditional warehouses, which rely on static table partitions, Snowflake uses micro-partitions, which are contiguous storage units containing 50 MB–500 MB of uncompressed data. This data is stored in columnar format, and the data in micro-partitions is managed automatically by Snowflake. The biggest advantage of such partitions is the data pruning that happens during the query optimization done by the cloud services layer. The cloud services layer also has the metadata on each micro-partition, including the ranges of values stored within the partition, min, max, count, number of distinct values, etc. Snowflake uses this information to include/exclude entire partitions during query execution. This is one of the primary contributors to what makes Snowflake query execution so fast.

Semi-Structured and Unstructured Data

Snowflake provides native functionality to query and store semi-structured data; i.e., any data that does not abide by a pre-determined schema and within which objects can differ from one another, e.g., a JSON array. It is usually hierarchical, i.e., the objects have a parent-child relationship, and multiple objects can coexist. The following code shows a semi-structured object with one record and no hierarchy:

```
{
    "trip_location": "Stockholm, Sweden",
    "trip_start_date": "2024-04-01",
    "trip_end_date": "2024-04-20",
    "trip_budget": 2000
}
```

This next block shows semi-structured data containing two nested hierarchical objects:

```
{
"trip_country": "Sweden",
"trip_start_date": "2024-04-01",
"trip_end_date": "2024-04-20",
"trip_budget": 2000,
"trip_locations": [
    "Stockholm"
    "Uppsala"
    "Gothenburg",
    "Gotland"
]},
{
"trip_country": "Spain",
"trip_start_date": "2024-05-01",
"trip_end_date": "2024-05-10",
"trip_budget": 2500,
"trip_locations": [
```

```
      "Madrid"
      "Cordoba",
      "Malaga"
      "Sevilla"
  ]}
```

Similarly, you can have records with multiple hierarchies. Snowflake natively supports the following semi-structured data formats: JSON (JavaScript Object Notation), XML (Extensible Markup Language), Parquet, Avro, and ORC (Optimized Row Columnar).

This data in Snowflake is stored in a data type known as VARIANT. It can hold both arrays and objects.

Unstructured data does not conform to any predefined model or schema. There are many types of unstructured data, including audio, video, and large text objects, as well as industry-specific formats, like the variant call format (VCF) (genomics), knowledge definition format (KDF) (semiconductors), and hierarchical data format (HDF5) (aeronautics). Snowflake supports loading unstructured data through stages (more on them in "Stages" on page 33). This data can further be used in machine learning models and coupled with other data in Snowflake, eliminating the need to move any data outside of Snowflake to run any machine learning models.

Time Travel

Time Travel is a feature provided by Snowflake to provide a means of quickly addressing accidental deletes and updates by restoring tables and databases to a particular point in time. It is available by default on all Snowflake accounts with a default retention period of 1 day and the period going up to 90 days on the Enterprise Edition, for data that is stored in Snowflake. You, as a Snowflake administrator, can change the retention duration at the database, schema, or table level. It is important to know that enabling Time Travel will incur additional storage costs. Figure 2-2 shows different Time Travel options available for Snowflake customers.

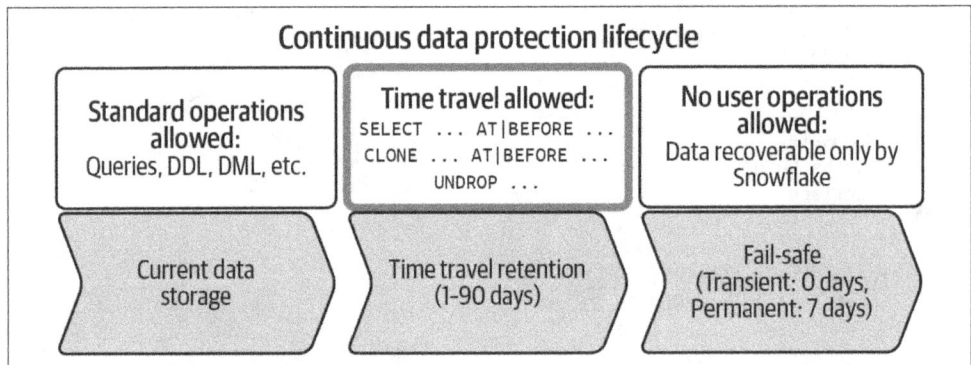

Figure 2-2. Snowflake Time Travel

Zero-Copy Clone

Snowflake also provides a feature to create clones of your Snowflake objects without physically duplicating the data. When you create a clone of a database, the new database is made to point to the original data. Unless the data changes in any of the databases (original or cloned), no additional storage costs are incurred for creating clones. It is a very handy feature to promote dev environments without having to manage heavy-duty data replication jobs. It gets you up and running within a few lines of code.

> The cloned tables point to the underlying source objects and, thus, the source tables are briefly locked when data definition language (DDL) or data manipulation language (DML) changes are made to the source object. Read more about this in the Snowflake documentation (*https://oreil.ly/FOPqA*).

Compute Layer Features

The compute layer is the layer responsible for running queries and DML operations. It can be considered the actual working force behind Snowflake. It uses virtual warehouses to carry out different workloads. Snowflake offers two different types of warehouses: standard and Snowpark-optimized. Let's take a quick look at both of those.

Standard Virtual Warehouses

Snowflake standard warehouses, now also known as Snowflake Generation 1 (Gen1) warehouses, come in different sizes. You can scale them vertically (in size) as your workload requires, and you can also scale them horizontally (in numbers) if you want to run many concurrent queries. Snowflake charges you for the resources when you're running a virtual warehouse depending on the size of the warehouse and the concurrent warehouse clusters. It uses Snowflake credits to measure how many resources you consumed.

A Snowflake credit is a unit of measure and is consumed when Snowflake resources are used. The monetary cost per credit is determined by your type of contract with Snowflake, the region you are running your Snowflake account in, and the cloud provider you're running your Snowflake on. Table 2-1 summarizes different warehouse sizes and how much they cost in credits.

Table 2-1. Mapping of Snowflake warehouse sizes with credit consumption

	X-Small	Small	Medium	Large	X-Large	2X-Large	3X-Large	4X-Large	5X-Large	6X-Large
Credits/hour	1	2	4	8	16	32	64	128	256	512
Credits/second	0.0003	0.0006	0.0011	0.0022	0.0044	0.0089	0.0178	0.0356	0.0711	0.1422

When it comes to Snowflake warehouses, it is important to keep in mind that they are charged per second, with an initial setup fee of 60 seconds. For example, if you start and suspend your X-Small warehouse for 30 seconds or 45 seconds, you'll be charged for the whole 60 seconds. If a virtual warehouse remains on all the time without being suspended, you will be charged for its entire duration, regardless of whether it is used. Snowflake has an option to configure "auto-suspend" for virtual warehouses, which monitors whether they have been idle for a certain amount of time (in minutes) and then automatically suspends them. It is important to consider the workload and the size of the warehouse while configuring auto-suspend features, i.e., you lose the warehouse cache when a warehouse is suspended, and if your queries are coming from a business intelligence (BI) system where users are more likely to run similar queries, it might be beneficial to keep the warehouse on for longer.

Snowpark-Optimized Warehouses

Snowpark is a collection of the most commonly used libraries and runtimes that allows Snowflake users to develop and manage their Snowflake workloads in Python and other programming languages. More on Snowpark in Chapter 4.

With Snowpark, one can write and deploy user-defined functions (UDFs) and user-defined table functions (UDTFs) in Python, and when you have access to Python within your Snowflake environment, the possibilities are endless. It enables you to run machine learning models all within Snowflake. Workloads like these require more memory than what the standard warehouses can offer. This is where Snowpark-optimized warehouses come into action. These warehouses start from size Medium, and they consume a few more credits than the standard warehouses. Snowpark-optimized warehouses are 1.5 times the cost of standard warehouses. These specialized warehouses are equipped with extra memory to handle working with the APIs and more memory-intensive workloads. Table 2-2 shows the credits-per-hour breakdown for these warehouses.

Table 2-2. Credits consumed per hour for Snowpark-optimized warehouses

	X-Small	Small	Medium	Large	X-Large	2X-Large	3X-Large	4X-Large	5X-Large	6X-Large
Credits/hour	n/a	n/a	6	12	24	48	96	192	384	768

Cloud Services Layer Features

The cloud services layer is the management brain for your Snowflake account. It is responsible for tying everything together within your Snowflake account. From authentication to metadata management, from provisioning and scaling warehouses to sharing data, everything is managed by the cloud services layer. Let us look at some of its features.

Metadata

I talked about how each micro-partition's data is stored in the cloud services layer. It organizes, manages, and maintains the metadata across all your data. It is constantly updated upon any changes in the table, and the cloud services layer is responsible for managing that without any external intervention from the user.

Metadata management is not limited to the data loaded into Snowflake, but it can be extended to the data available in different Snowflake stages. You will see the Snowflake stages in depth in the following sections.

Optimization

The cloud services layer stores the metadata that plays an important role in query optimization within Snowflake. It parses the query and generates the query plan. It then uses the micro-partitions metadata to understand which partitions to filter and process and which ones to skip. Data from the filtered micro-partitions is brought to the warehouse for processing the query. This is at the core of Snowflake query optimization.

Infrastructure Management

This layer is also responsible for making sure you have enough resources available to execute your Snowflake workloads. I talked about Snowflake virtual warehouses and that they can be scaled horizontally. The cloud services layer monitors the load of each warehouse and spins up additional clusters if necessary. As a Snowflake user, you don't need to worry about infrastructure management; it's automated.

Security and Governance

Authentication and access control within Snowflake is also managed by the cloud services layer. Each Snowflake user has a set of assigned roles and grants that determine which data objects they are allowed to see and interact with. The cloud services layer is responsible for managing that and ensures that the rules are enforced consistently across your Snowflake account. This also applies to all the data stored in Snowflake. All the data is encrypted by default, and the keys are rotated automatically by Snowflake.

Sharing and Collaboration

Your Snowflake data products can be shared with external users and organizations using Snowflake's secure sharing feature. When working with data and creating data products, you will often need to share them outside your account. Snowflake's secure data sharing solution comes into play here. The cloud services layer ensures data is shared and changed properly once it has been set up.

Serverless Features

The cloud services layer is also responsible for all the serverless activity that goes on within your account. If you have seen your Snowflake invoice, you might see "Cloud services credit usage," which refers to these serverless activities that go on in the background. The list of serverless features that Snowflake mentions on its website is as follows:

- Automatic Clustering
- COPY FILES
- Data quality and data metric functions (DMFs)
- External tables
- Hybrid tables
- Logging and tracing
- Materialized views

- Query acceleration service
- Cross-cloud replication
- Search optimization service
- Snowpipe
- Snowpipe Streaming
- Serverless alerts
- Serverless tasks

All these tasks are executed by stateless computing resources that are highly available across all the regions. Snowflake automatically manages these services, and it is also responsible for making sure enough resources are available to carry out your workloads without having to wait for resources.

Snowflake Objects

Any entity created within Snowflake is known as a Snowflake object. This includes databases, schemas, tables, views, stages, functions, procedures, etc. All these objects have their own set of grants and privileges, which the user must have in order to interact with them. Let's take a quick look at what they are and dive deeper into the newer objects introduced in Snowflake.

Databases

A database is the core object in Snowflake, and it holds all the other objects. I won't go into any further details about creating databases or cloning them, as it's outside the scope of this book.

Schemas

Schemas are logical subdivisions of your databases. They define how your data is segregated within a database, e.g., a database for an ecommerce store can have schemas for orders, warehouses, staff, etc. Each of those schemas can then host the relevant objects, like tables and views.

Tables

A table is a fundamental storage unit of a database, and Snowflake offers multiple types of tables for its customers. Some newer types are limited to certain regions only:

Permanent tables
> These are classic tables when created, and they remain in the database until explicitly dropped. This is the default table type in Snowflake. Permanent tables can be recovered via Time Travel and are retained with the fail-safe policies of Snowflake.

Temporary tables
> Temporary tables, as the name suggests, are temporary and expire as soon as the Snowflake session expires. They are handy tables for performing the quick data movement of smaller and reusable datasets, but are not recommended for any data that you would like to persist for longer.

Transient tables
> Transient tables are like permanent tables in the sense that they remain in the database unless explicitly dropped, but the big difference is their lower level of data protection. They only have one day of Time Travel and are not recoverable during disaster recovery. They are great for loading intermediate data during the extract, transform, load (ETL) process. Even though the data is permanently stored, the transient tables remain lightweight; they're great for cases where data is often replaced. Overall, my recommendation is not to store any critical data in transient tables.

Table 2-3 summarizes all table types and their functions.

Table 2-3. Snowflake table types

Type[a]	Persistence	Cloning (source type => target type)	Time Travel retention period (days)	Fail-safe period (days)
Temporary	Remainder of session	Temporary => Temporary Temporary => Transient	0 or 1 (default is 1)	0
Transient	Until explicitly dropped	Transient => Temporary Transient => Transient	0 or 1 (default is 1)	0
Permanent (Standard Edition)	Until explicitly dropped	Permanent => Temporary Permanent => Transient Permanent => Permanent	0 or 1 (default is 1)	7
Permanent (Enterprise Edition and higher)	Until explicitly dropped	Permanent => Temporary Permanent => Transient Permanent => Permanent	0 to 90 (default is configurable)	7

[a] For details on different editions, see the Snowflake docs (*https://oreil.ly/e1MXz*).

Dynamic tables

Dynamic tables are a new table type Snowflake introduced to simplify data engineering tasks. They were launched in 2024 and are becoming quite popular in the data engineering community. Dynamic tables are automatically updated based on either a set schedule or based on downstream modifications. Snowflake automatically manages the processing of dynamic tables (performing either an incremental or a full refresh) based on change data capture (CDC) information from the source table. Snowflake takes that complexity away from the engineers.

The four biggest advantages of dynamic tables are as follows:

Simplified pipelines
    Build data pipelines with just SQL statements—no more complex coding required.

Automatic refresh
    Snowflake takes care of keeping your data up-to-date.

Incremental updates
    Only process new or changed data for better performance and lower costs.

Chained tables
    Create complex workflows by linking dynamic tables together.

Figure 2-3 shows how different tables can come together into a dynamic table. Dynamic table A is created by querying base tables A and B, whereas dynamic table B is created by querying base table B and dynamic table C.

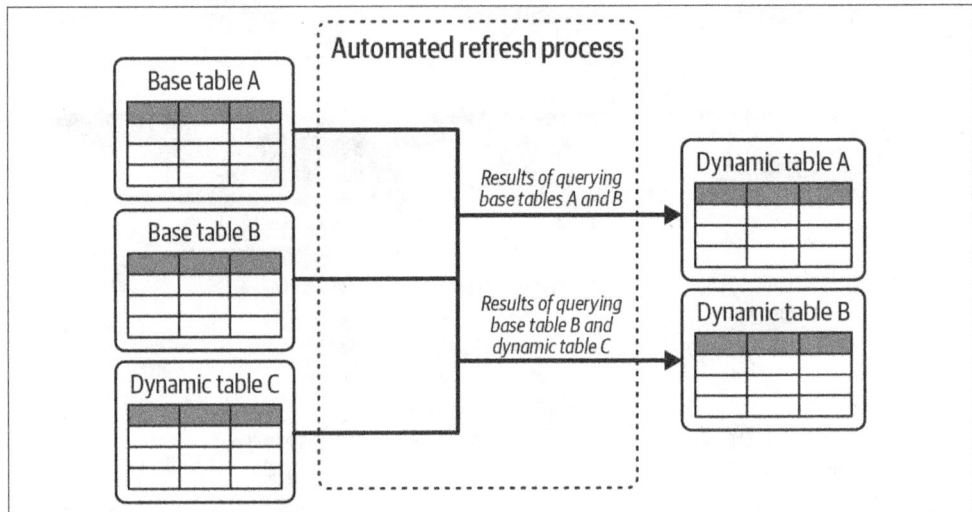

Figure 2-3. Dynamic table overview (source: Snowflake (https://oreil.ly/cQ5f7))

To create dynamic tables, you don't need any other tool apart from SQL. Here is an example of how you can create a dynamic table:

```
CREATE OR REPLACE DYNAMIC TABLE product
    TARGET_LAG = '20 minutes'
    WAREHOUSE = COMPUTE_WH
    REFRESH_MODE = AUTO
    INITIALIZE = ON_CREATE
AS
    SELECT product_id, product_name
    FROM staging_table
    ;
```

The TARGET_LAG field is important to note. This field specifies the maximum time a particular dynamic table can go without a refresh (20 minutes in this example). It can be considered a measure of freshness for the dynamic table. However, you can use the keyword DOWNSTREAM for TARGET_LAG, which would make it an "on-demand" dynamic table, i.e., it will only refresh when any downstream dynamic table that references this dynamic table is refreshed. If a scheduled refresh is not finished by the time of the next interval, the interval will be skipped.

> I recommend setting a larger warehouse for the initialization (that runs either on CREATE or the first scheduled run), then altering the dynamic table and setting the warehouse appropriate for the incremental size.

Hybrid tables/Unistore

Hybrid tables are also a new table type in Snowflake. These are optimized tables for both your transactional and operational workloads. Snowflake mentions in its documentation that they are optimized for workloads that require low latency and high throughput on small random-point reads and writes.

Since hybrid tables support both online analytical processing (OLAP) and online transaction processing (OLTP), Snowflake has added some additional features to them.

Table 2-4 summarizes the differences between hybrid tables and Snowflake standard tables.

Table 2-4. Differences between hybrid tables and standard Snowflake tables

Feature	Hybrid tables	Standard tables
Primary data layout	Row-oriented, with secondary columnar storage	Columnar micro-partitions (*https://oreil.ly/Jeaav*)
Locking	Row-level	Partition or table

Feature	Hybrid tables	Standard tables
PRIMARY KEY constraints	Required, enforced	Optional, not enforced
FOREIGN KEY constraints	Optional, enforced (referential integrity)	Optional, not enforced
UNIQUE constraints	Optional (except for PRIMARY KEY), enforced	Optional, not enforced
NOT NULL constraints	Optional (except for PRIMARY KEY), enforced	Optional, enforced
Indexes	Supported for performance; updated synchronously on writes	The search optimization service indexes columns for better point-lookup performance; batch updated/maintained asynchronously

In summary, hybrid tables excel in situations where individual records need to be retrieved by ID, such as in customer lookups. They are also well-suited for managing high-volume data modifications, including inserts, updates, and merges. Essentially, if your application frequently interacts with and retrieves small subsets of data at high speeds, hybrid tables are the ideal choice.

Iceberg tables

Iceberg tables are an Apache Iceberg (*https://iceberg.apache.org*) abstraction layer provided on top of the files stored in an external storage system that allows for features such as the following:

- ACID[1] transactions
- Schema evolution
- Hidden partitions
- Table snapshots

Iceberg tables in Snowflake offer a powerful way to manage large, evolving datasets with enhanced performance and flexibility. Apache Iceberg itself is a high-performance open-table format designed for huge analytical tables, bringing SQL-like table capabilities to data in cloud storage providers like Amazon Simple Storage Service (S3), Google Cloud Storage (GCS), and Azure Blob Storage. Since it's an open-table format, the data lives outside of Snowflake; hence, the user is responsible for managing the external cloud storage. The main advantages of using Iceberg tables in Snowflake include improved query performance through optimized data organization, reliable schema evolution that allows changes without disrupting queries, and

---

1 ACID stands for atomicity, consistency, isolation, durability

the flexibility to use various compute engines while maintaining a consistent table format.

Views

A view is a piece of a SQL query that generates results that can be accessed just like a table. It does not store any data permanently, and everything is processed on the fly when the view is accessed.

Secure views

Secure views are a special type of view that is created when it's important to keep security in mind. With secure views, users can still access the data the same way, but the view definition or the SQL code used to generate the results is hidden away. Only authorized users can see the definition of a secure view.

Materialized views

Materialized views are only available for Snowflake Enterprise customers. As the name suggests, materialized views materialize the data underneath and save it. This significantly improves the performance of the views as everything is pre-calculated and only the data read is performed on querying the materialized view. However, they do have a cost impact, not just when it comes to storage; they are updated automatically as soon as the base table updates. The cloud services layer automatically updates the data materialized if the data it queries has changed. Thus, it is only recommended to use the materialized views when the query results from the view don't change often.

User-Defined Functions

User-defined functions (UDFs) are pieces of code that can help you move repeated and complex logic behind a function call that is not available by default. You can write UDFs in any of the following languages: Java, JavaScript, Python, Scala, and SQL.

Scalar functions

A scalar UDF is a function that returns only one value for a given row.

A good example of this is when you have the birth dates of your employees in a table and you want to calculate their age. It is not always straightforward to use the DATE DIFF function, and you may want to write a UDF that can take the date of birth and return the age in years. Now, each row has one date of birth, and your function will only return one value per row, which is the age of the person that row belongs to.

Table functions

User-defined table functions (UDTFs) are functions that can return a tabular value for each given row.

UDTFs do not support Scala yet.

A good example of UDFTs would be when you want to create some dummy data in a language of your choice. You can create a UDTF that produces 10 sentences in the language you input. Then, depending on what you want to test, you can simply call that function and give that language as a parameter.

User-defined aggregate functions

User-defined aggregate functions (UDAFs) let you create custom aggregations that go beyond the standard SQL functions like SUM, COUNT, or AVG. Think of them as your way to define exactly how multiple rows should be collapsed into a single meaningful custom result. While built-in aggregates handle the common cases, UDAFs become essential when you need specialized calculations that don't fit the standard patterns, e.g., if there is a need to calculate a weighted median, implement a custom statistical measure, or perform complex calculations with specific business logic.

The power of UDAFs lies in their ability to process entire result sets in ways that would be cumbersome or impossible with regular SQL functions. For example, you might create a UDAF that builds a custom JSON object by aggregating related records with specific formatting rules. Unlike scalar functions, which operate on individual values, UDAFs maintain state across all the rows they process, allowing them to perform sophisticated operations such as running calculations, tracking intermediate results, or applying complex algorithms that require knowledge of the entire dataset before producing their final output. You can read more about them in the Snowflake documentation (*https://oreil.ly/xZEd0*).

External functions

External functions are functions that are used the same way as UDFs, but they don't contain their code definition. Instead, they call a function or a piece of code that is hosted outside of Snowflake (Figure 2-4).

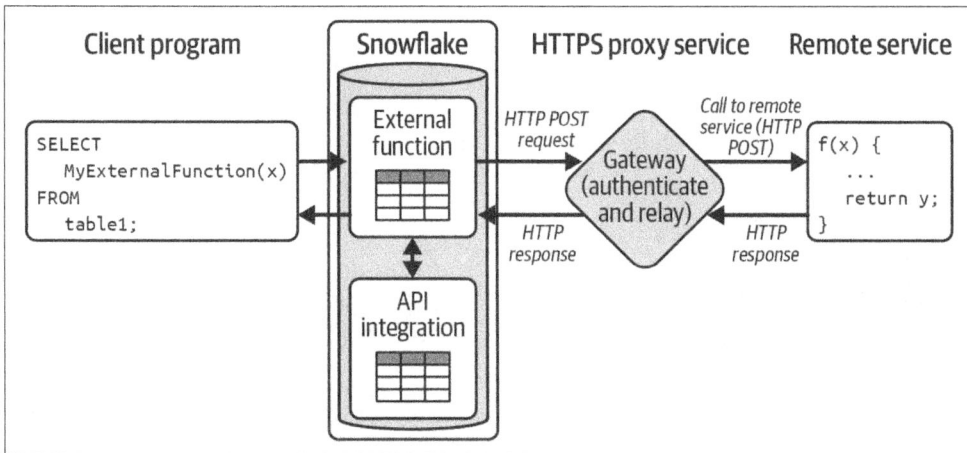

Figure 2-4. Snowflake external functions overview (source: Snowflake (https://oreil.ly/ K5Giy))

Stored Procedures

Stored procedures are pieces of code that are bound together to execute SQL statements. Typically, they are used to perform database operations.

One big advantage of Snowflake stored procedures is that you can execute the code using the rights of the owner for that stored procedure rather than your rights as a caller in the Snowflake environment. This allows for complex SQL operations that are defined within the procedure to be executed by the users without having explicit rights to perform the actions. These are called caller and owner rights on a stored procedure.

Stored procedures are supported in the following languages: Java (using the Snowpark API), JavaScript, Python (using the Snowpark API), Scala (using the Snowpark API), and Snowflake Scripting (SQL).

Shares and Secure Data Sharing

Snowflake shares or secure data sharing allows you to share the objects from your Snowflake account with other Snowflake accounts. Snowflake allows the following objects to be shared:

- Databases
- Tables
- Dynamic tables
- External tables
- Iceberg tables
- Secure views
- Secure materialized views
- Secure UDFs

In Snowflake, you can share data in a variety of ways. Listing, direct share, and Data Exchange are the most prominent:

Listing
> A listing is a type of share in which you share a data product with one or more accounts. Think of it as a classified listing that can be requested by many Snowflake accounts.

Direct share
> A direct share is a type of share in which you explicitly share the objects with another account in your region.

Data Exchange
> A Data Exchange is a closed group share in which you can define which accounts you want to offer your data product to.

Figure 2-5 gives an excellent overview of different sharing options and how they can all simultaneously work together to truly unlock the power of data.

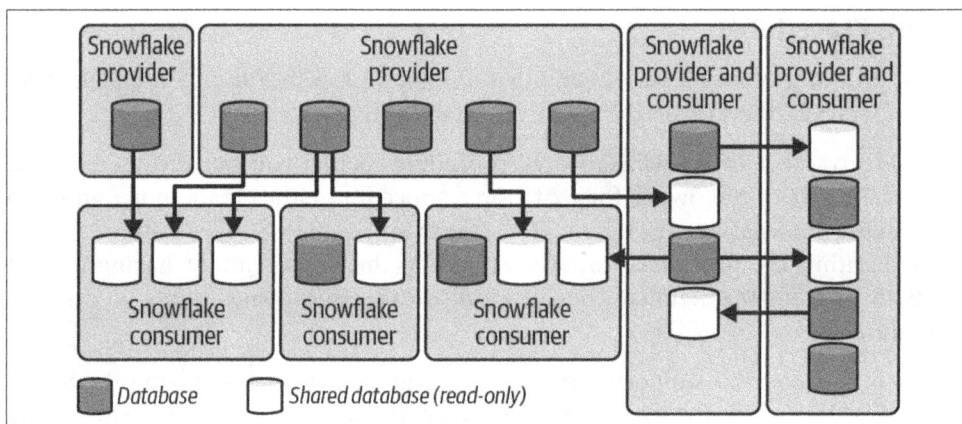

Figure 2-5. Overview of Snowflake Secure Data Sharing

Streams

Streams in Snowflake are what enable change data capture. When they are created, they store the table state and then record all the changes that occur on the table using DML operations. A stream does not store the table data but rather only the changes that happen to the data.

I won't go into the details of streams in this book. If you are interested in reading further, please refer to the Snowflake documentation for streams (*https://oreil.ly/wlPTO*).

Tasks

A task is a Snowflake object that can run SQL code and orchestrate your data jobs. A task can execute a single SQL statement, it can call a stored procedure, or it can run some procedural scripted logic.

I won't go into the details of tasks in this book. If you are interested in reading further, check out the Snowflake documentation for tasks (*https://oreil.ly/Dlwi8*).

Stages

A stage is a Snowflake object that points to a certain storage location. Snowflake offers two types of stages:

Internal stage
> An internal stage is a stage that points to a storage location within your Snowflake account. Table and user stages are two automatically managed internal stages provided by Snowflake. The third type is called the named stage, which refers to manually created stages.

External stage
> An external stage, like the name suggests, is a storage location outside of your Snowflake account. It can be any storage bucket, like an Amazon S3 bucket or a Google Cloud Storage bucket.

Pipe

A pipe is a Snowflake object containing a `COPY` command to ingest your data into Snowflake. It can be used to define how you want to read, process, and store the data in your table:

```
CREATE PIPE mypipe
    AS
    COPY INTO mytable
    FROM @mystage
    FILE_FORMAT = (TYPE = 'JSON');
```

Snowpipe is a serverless service provided by Snowflake that uses a reference pipe to automatically ingest data into Snowflake tables. This allows you to do microbatches or streaming ingestion of your data in Snowflake without using any external tools.

Application

Snowflake Native Applications are covered in detail in Chapter 5.

Summary

In this chapter, I gave an overview of the core Snowflake architecture. You now know about Snowflake's three-layered architecture and its cloud-agnostic nature. You also got a detailed explanation of all three layers and their features, followed by different Snowflake objects. I tried covering all core Snowflake objects objects, from tables and views to Snowflake streams, tasks, stages and pipes.

> Since this is an advanced book, I did not cover all the details of each object, but rather gave you an overview that can be useful to remember whenever you need them.

With that said, let's now jump into Chapter 3 about Snowflake SQL.

Snowflake SQL

In this chapter, I will go through some of the more advanced Snowflake SQL functions. Let's start by looking at Snowflake's order of execution, then move to the different window functions and see where you can use them. Following that, you'll learn about Snowflake's geospatial functions.

Order of Execution

Snowflake follows a very logical order of execution of SQL clauses. However, with the introduction of a QUALIFY clause, things got a little interesting. A lot of Snowflake users using window functions and QUALIFY were confused about what would be executed when, and how that affects the result of their queries. In essence, the QUALIFY clause is very similar to the WHERE clause because it filters the data. However, when it does so in the order of execution, the QUALIFY clause differs, and thus, confusion arises. Snowflake executes the SQL clauses in the following order:

1. FROM
2. WHERE
3. GROUP BY
4. HAVING
5. WINDOW
6. QUALIFY
7. DISTINCT
8. ORDER BY
9. LIMIT

Let's walk through this and see what happens when you execute the following query:

```
SELECT *
FROM legends
WHERE first_name = 'Cristiano'
    AND last_name = 'Ronaldo';
```

This is a simple query, extracting details with a very simple WHERE clause. In this case, Snowflake will execute the FROM clause first, which tells Snowflake which table to read the data from. Then comes the WHERE clause, which tells Snowflake what data to filter, or in other words, which micro-partitions to read and which ones to skip.

Let's move on to GROUP BY and HAVING clauses. GROUP BY runs after the WHERE clause on the filtered data and is used to aggregate the data. The HAVING clause helps filter the results of the GROUP BY clause. Let's assume we have a table named Employees with records of thousands of employees, their departments, and their salaries, ranging from $100 up to $5,000.

Let's take a look at these two queries in Table 3-1.

Table 3-1. Order of execution (WHERE and HAVING)

Query 1	Query 2

`SELECT DEPARTMENT,`
`       SUM(SALARY) AS`
`       TOTAL_SALARY`
`FROM EMPLOYEES`
`GROUP BY DEPARTMENT`
`HAVING TOTAL_SALARY < 1000`
	`SELECT DEPARTMENT,`
	`       SUM(SALARY) AS`
	`       TOTAL_SALARY`
	`FROM EMPLOYEES`
	`WHERE SALARY < 1000`
	`GROUP BY DEPARTMENT`

This query reads the table employees, groups them by departments, takes the sum of all the salaries in that department, and in the end, filters the departments where the total salary of all employees in those departments is less than 1000. This query is an answer to the request, "Give me the departments with a total salary of less than 1000."	This query reads the table employees, filters the employees with salaries less than 1000, groups them by departments, and takes the sum of all remaining salaries in that department. This query is an answer to the request, "Give me the total salaries of all employees earning less than 1000 per department." In this case, the TOTAL_SALARY column is always above 1000 since it has filtered the employees with lower salaries.

A very subtle difference in the two queries in Table 3-1 gives completely different results. Let's look at the third variant now, with WHERE and HAVING clauses:

```
SELECT DEPARTMENT, SUM(SALARY) AS TOTAL_SALARY
FROM EMPLOYEES
WHERE SALARY < 500
GROUP BY DEPARTMENT
HAVING TOTAL_SALARY < 1000
```

This variant reads the `Employees` table again, filters employees (`WHERE`) with a salary less than 500, `GROUP`s the departments, sums their salaries, and then filters (`HAVING`) the departments with total salaries less than 1000. This variant is an answer to the question, "Show me departments with a total salary of less than 1000, for people earning less than 500."

The next clause is the `WINDOW` clause. (I will go through the window functions in detail in "Window Functions" on page 46.) Window functions run on a subset of rows called windows and perform an aggregation. They are often used with a `QUALIFY` statement.

A good example of both is the deduplication of records in a table. Have a look at the following two queries. Let's assume we have a table called `EMPLOYEES_RAW` that contains all historical updates for all employees, i.e., all their previous salaries and departments, along with a timestamp (`ROW_UPDATED_AT`) signifying when they were updated:

Variant I
```
SELECT *,
    ROW_NUMBER()
        OVER (PARTITION BY EMPLOYEE_ID ORDER BY ROW_UPDATED_AT DESC) AS ROW_N
FROM EMPLOYEES_RAW
QUALIFY ROW_N = 1;
```

Variant II
```
SELECT *,
    ROW_NUMBER()
        OVER (PARTITION BY EMPLOYEE_ID ORDER BY ROW_UPDATED_AT DESC) AS ROW_N
FROM EMPLOYEES_RAW
WHERE EMPLOYEE_ID = 1
QUALIFY ROW_N = 1;
```

The Variant I query reads (`FROM`) from the `EMPLOYEES_RAW` table, runs a window function (`ROW_NUMBER()`) on it, and assigns a number from 1 to n (n = number of records for each employee in the raw table) in reverse order. The latest row is assigned 1, and then a `QUALIFY` clause is used to filter the latest records.

In Variant II, you read (`FROM`) from the `EMPLOYEES_RAW` table, filter (`WHERE`) the data for the employee with ID 1, run a window function (`ROW_NUMBER()`) on it where it assigns a number from 1 to n (n = number of records for each employee in the raw table) in reverse order, i.e., latest row is assigned 1, and then use the `QUALIFY` clause to filter the latest record. This query will only produce one row as a result.

The rest, `DISTINCT`, `ORDER BY`, and `LIMIT`, can be considered the result-level clauses. You can think of them as the clauses that run on the result set produced by the clauses mentioned earlier. These clauses do not process any data themselves:

DISTINCT
> Keeps unique rows. If duplicate rows are produced, using DISTINCT will keep only one of them.

ORDER BY
> Orders the result set according to the defined column and row order.

LIMIT
> Reduces the number of records to show in the result set.

> I won't go into details and examples of these in this book; refer to the Snowflake documentation (*https://docs.snowflake.com*) if you want to dive deeper.

Advanced Snowflake Functions

In this section, I will go through some of the more advanced Snowflake functions. These functions simplify the tasks that take several subqueries to execute.

Aggregate Functions

Aggregate functions are functions that return only one row from a given group. SUM, AVG, MAX, MIN, COUNT, etc., are all examples of aggregate functions. You will learn six very interesting aggregate functions in this book:

- ANY_VALUE
- MIN_BY
- MAX_BY

- BOOLAND_AGG
- BOOLOR_AGG
- BOOLXOR_AGG

ANY_VALUE

This aggregate function is a nondeterministic one that returns a random value from the specified column. ANY_VALUE is particularly helpful when you want to include another column with your existing aggregations that doesn't need any aggregation logic, e.g., if you want to see how many orders have a particular order status and also want to check a random order out of those. The ANY_VALUE aggregate function is defined as follows:

```
ANY_VALUE( [ DISTINCT ] expr1 )
```

DISTINCT might seem odd in this particular function, and rightly so; it does not have any effect on the output of this function:

```
SELECT
    O_ORDERSTATUS,
    COUNT(*) AS N_ORDERS,
    ANY_VALUE(O_ORDERKEY) AS RANDOM_ORDER
FROM SNOWFLAKE_SAMPLE_DATA.TPCH_SF100.ORDERS
GROUP BY O_ORDERSTATUS
;
```

As you see in Figure 3-1, there are three different order statuses in TPCH_SF100.ORDERS, and to get a random order, we just used an ANY_VALUE() function to get the order key.

	A O_ORDERSTATUS	# N_ORDERS	# RANDOM_ORDER
1	P	3841445	32449378
2	O	73086053	345215010
3	F	73072502	243965030

Figure 3-1. Results of the ANY_VALUE() sample query

This could be helpful in several scenarios. For example, if a new status starts showing up, you can quickly see the order ID and debug the issue. Similarly, if there's an incoming order with no priority assigned, you can use ANY_VALUE to quickly see how many such orders there are and get a random order ID.

MIN_BY

MIN_BY and MAX_BY are two very interesting aggregate functions. These functions address common questions like, "What is the lowest salary in the IT department, and who has it?" or "What is the maximum revenue order we have, and which customer placed it?". These functions answer the "who" and "which," in these examples.

MIN_BY has the following syntax:

```
MIN_BY(col_to_return, col_containing_mininum
       [ , maximum_number_of_values_to_return ] )
```

Let's go through the parameters of this function:

col_to_return
    Here you can specify which column to return when the minimum value of col_containing_mininum is found.

col_containing_maximum
    Here we can specify which column to find the minimum value of.

```
maximum_number_of_values_to_return
```
This is an optional parameter that takes a number as input and returns an ordered list if the number is greater than 1.

Here's a sample query calculating every customer's minimum order price and also getting the `order_id` for that order using the `MIN_BY` function:

```
SELECT
    O_CUSTKEY,
    MIN(O_TOTALPRICE) AS MIN_TOT_PRICE,
    MIN_BY(O_ORDERKEY, O_TOTALPRICE) AS MIN_TOT_PRICE_ORDER_KEY
FROM SNOWFLAKE_SAMPLE_DATA.TPCH_SF10.ORDERS
GROUP BY 1
LIMIT 10;
```

You can view the results in Figure 3-2.

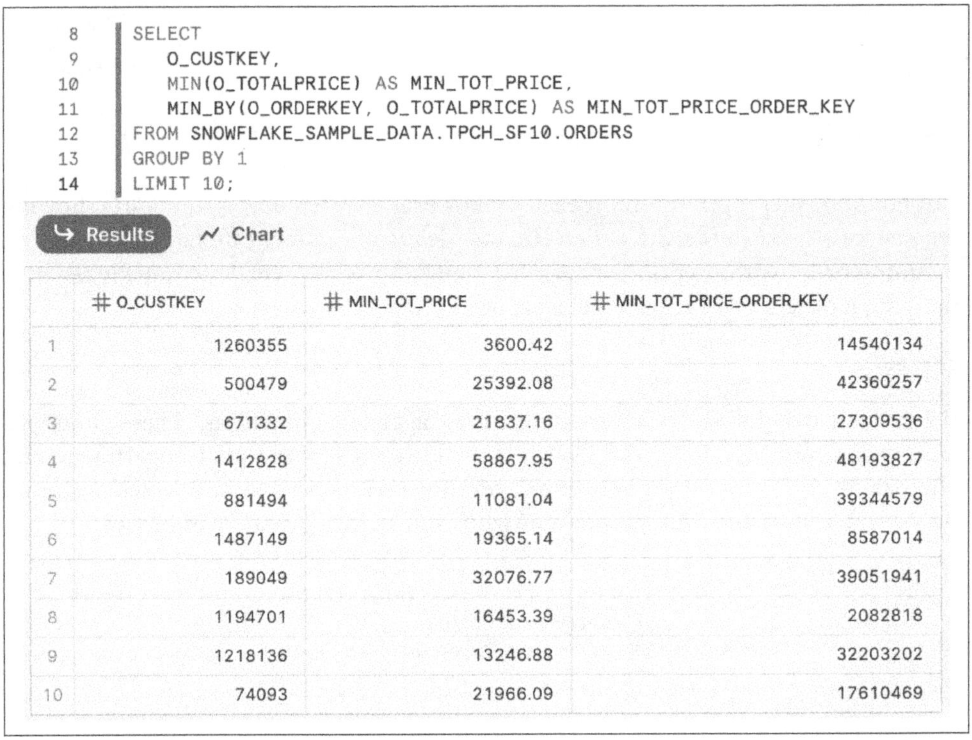

```
 8   SELECT
 9       O_CUSTKEY,
10       MIN(O_TOTALPRICE) AS MIN_TOT_PRICE,
11       MIN_BY(O_ORDERKEY, O_TOTALPRICE) AS MIN_TOT_PRICE_ORDER_KEY
12   FROM SNOWFLAKE_SAMPLE_DATA.TPCH_SF10.ORDERS
13   GROUP BY 1
14   LIMIT 10;
```

↳ Results   ∕ Chart

	# O_CUSTKEY	# MIN_TOT_PRICE	# MIN_TOT_PRICE_ORDER_KEY
1	1260355	3600.42	14540134
2	500479	25392.08	42360257
3	671332	21837.16	27309536
4	1412828	58867.95	48193827
5	881494	11081.04	39344579
6	1487149	19365.14	8587014
7	189049	32076.77	39051941
8	1194701	16453.39	2082818
9	1218136	13246.88	32203202
10	74093	21966.09	17610469

Figure 3-2. Results of the MIN_BY sample query

MAX_BY

This function is similar to MIN_BY, but MAX_BY brings the maximum value instead of a minimum one.

MAX_BY has the following syntax:

```
MAX_BY(col_to_return, col_containing_maximum
       [ , maximum_number_of_values_to_return] )
```

The parameters work exactly the same as MIN_BY, but now you specify what column to take the *maximum* from:

col_to_return

> Here, we can specify which column to return when the maximum value of col_containing_maximum is found.

col_containing_maximum

> Here we can specify which column to find the maximum value of.

maximum_number_of_values_to_return

> This is an optional parameter that takes a number as input and returns an ordered list if the number is greater than 1.

Here's a sample query calculating every customer's maximum order price and also getting the order_id for that order using the MAX_BY function:

```
SELECT
    O_CUSTKEY,
    MAX(O_TOTALPRICE) AS MAX_TOT_PRICE,
    MAX_BY(O_ORDERKEY, O_TOTALPRICE) AS MAX_TOT_PRICE_ORDER_KEY
FROM SNOWFLAKE_SAMPLE_DATA.TPCH_SF10.ORDERS
GROUP BY O_CUSTKEY
LIMIT 10;
```

You can view the results in Figure 3-3.

```
 7    SELECT
 8       O_CUSTKEY,
 9       MAX(O_TOTALPRICE) AS MAX_TOT_PRICE,
10       MAX_BY(O_ORDERKEY, O_TOTALPRICE) AS MAX_TOT_PRICE_ORDER_KEY
11    FROM SNOWFLAKE_SAMPLE_DATA.TPCH_SF10.ORDERS
12    GROUP BY O_CUSTKEY
13    LIMIT 10;
```

↳ Results   ∿ Chart

	# O_CUSTKEY	# MAX_TOT_PRICE	# MAX_TOT_PRICE_ORDER_KEY
1	1171498	342278.74	10841250
2	1327343	309316.06	9000674
3	794176	324292.87	9001511
4	1364581	322854.26	47170977
5	1323613	305872.98	48313318
6	1055278	456050.53	52270886
7	1202282	286651.35	20590854
8	73985	296925.56	29395813
9	379853	287064.36	43716551
10	1424393	369550.55	9007938

Figure 3-3. Results of the MAX_BY sample query

BOOLAND_AGG

BOOLAND_AGG is a Boolean aggregation function that ANDs all the Boolean values in the column provided as an argument. It is particularly useful when we are doing "all or nothing" aggregations in Snowflake, e.g., "Are all line items in the order shipped?", "Does a customer only order with a discount code and never otherwise?", etc.

BOOLAND_AGG uses the following syntaxes:

```
BOOLAND_AGG(expr)
BOOLAND_AGG(expr) OVER ( [ PARTITION BY partition_expr ] )
```

Here, *expr* is the name of the column, and in syntax two, the partition clause is the window function clause that I will cover in Chapter 4.

Here's a sample query to see which orders do not have all line items set to F:

```
SELECT
    L_ORDERKEY,
    BOOLAND_AGG(L_LINESTATUS = 'F') AS BOOLAND_LINESTATUS_F
FROM SNOWFLAKE_SAMPLE_DATA.TPCH_SF100.LINEITEM
GROUP BY L_ORDERKEY
LIMIT 10;
```

You can view the results in Figure 3-4.

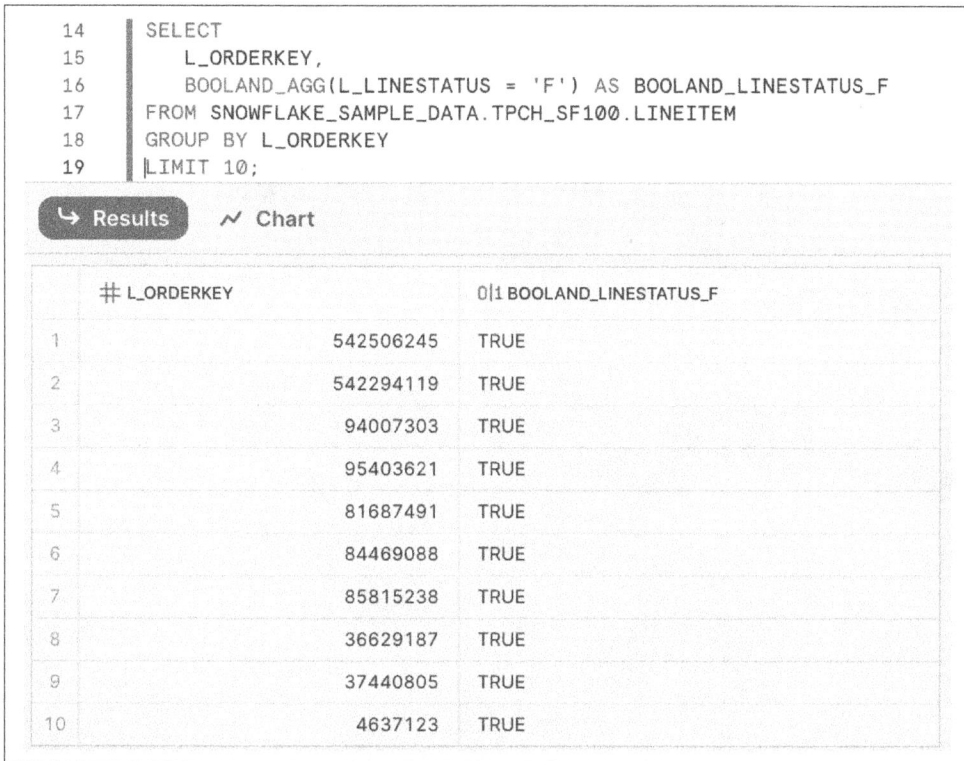

```
14   SELECT
15       L_ORDERKEY,
16       BOOLAND_AGG(L_LINESTATUS = 'F') AS BOOLAND_LINESTATUS_F
17   FROM SNOWFLAKE_SAMPLE_DATA.TPCH_SF100.LINEITEM
18   GROUP BY L_ORDERKEY
19   LIMIT 10;
```

↳ Results   ∿ Chart

# L_ORDERKEY	0|1 BOOLAND_LINESTATUS_F
1	542506245	TRUE
2	542294119	TRUE
3	94007303	TRUE
4	95403621	TRUE
5	81687491	TRUE
6	84469088	TRUE
7	85815238	TRUE
8	36629187	TRUE
9	37440805	TRUE
10	4637123	TRUE

Figure 3-4. Results of the BOOLAND_AGG sample query

BOOLOR_AGG

BOOLOR_AGG is a Boolean aggregation function that ORs all the Boolean values in the column provided as an argument. It is particularly useful when you are doing "any or nothing" aggregations in Snowflake, e.g., "Were any line items delayed in the order?", "Do we have customers that have never ordered a skincare product?", etc.

BOOLOR_AGG uses the following syntaxes:

```
BOOLOR_AGG(expr)
BOOLOR_AGG(expr)  OVER ( [ PARTITION BY partition_expr ] )
```

Here also, *expr* is the name of the column, and in syntax two, the partition clause is the window function clause that we will cover in the next chapter. Here's a sample query to see which orders have a LINEITEM with a RETURNFLAG set to R:

```
SELECT
    L_ORDERKEY,
    BOOLOR_AGG(L_RETURNFLAG = 'R') AS BOOLOR_RETURNFLAG_R
FROM SNOWFLAKE_SAMPLE_DATA.TPCH_SF10.LINEITEM
GROUP BY L_ORDERKEY
LIMIT 10;
```

You can view the results in Figure 3-5.

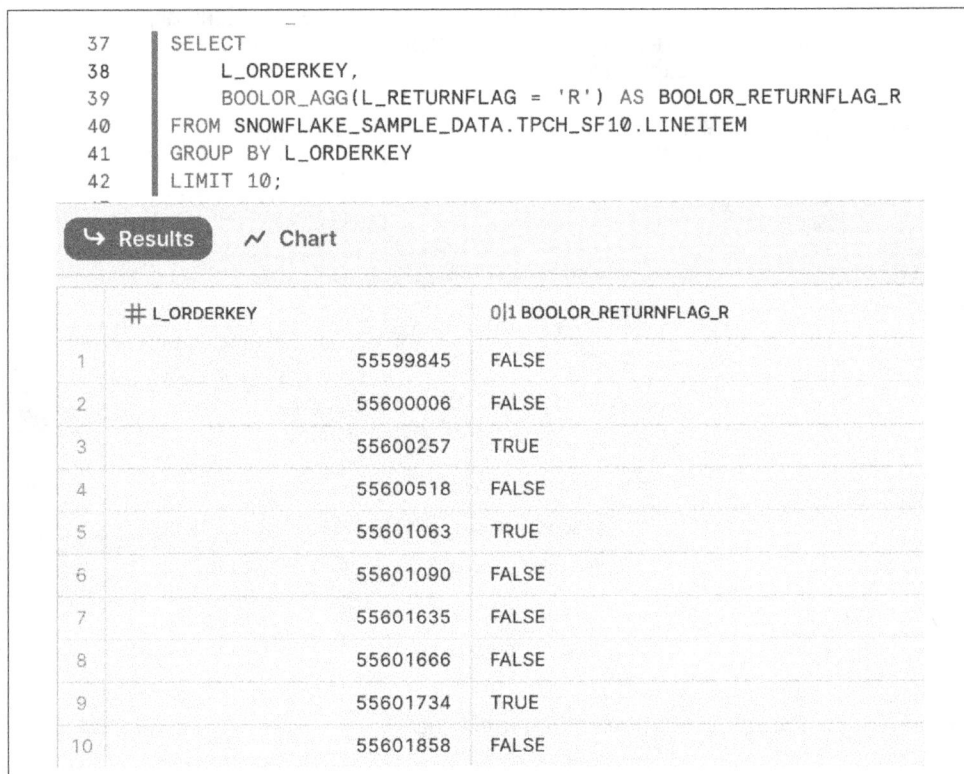

Figure 3-5. Results of the BOOLOR_AGG sample query

BOOLXOR_AGG

Similar to BOOLAND_AGG and BOOLOR_AGG, BOOLXOR_AGG takes the XOR of all the Boolean values in the provided column. XOR is an exclusive OR operator that evaluates to true when two values differ, as you'll see in Table 3-2.

Table 3-2. XOR truth table

A	B	XOR(A, B)
F	F	F
F	T	T
T	F	T
T	T	F

Table 3-2 shows the truth table of the XOR operation, and Snowflake, using the same logic, aggregates multiple values under the BOOLXOR_AGG function. This means it will return TRUE if exactly one value in the Boolean column is TRUE.

BOOLXOR_AGG uses the following syntaxes:

```
BOOLXOR_AGG(expr)
BOOLXOR_AGG(expr) OVER ( [ PARTITION BY partition_expr ] )
```

Here also, *expr* is the name of the column, and in syntax two, the partition clause is the window function clause that I will cover in the next chapter. Let's look at the sample query to see which orders have exactly one LINEITEM with a RETURNFLAG set to R:

```
SELECT
    L_ORDERKEY,
    BOOLXOR_AGG(L_RETURNFLAG = 'R') AS BOOLXOR_RETURNFLAG_R
FROM SNOWFLAKE_SAMPLE_DATA.TPCH_SF10.LINEITEM
GROUP BY L_ORDERKEY
LIMIT 10;
```

You can view the results in Figure 3-6.

```
26  ∨  SELECT
27        L_ORDERKEY,
28        BOOLXOR_AGG(L_RETURNFLAG = 'R') AS BOOLXOR_RETURNFLAG_R
29     FROM SNOWFLAKE_SAMPLE_DATA.TPCH_SF10.LINEITEM
30     GROUP BY L_ORDERKEY
31     LIMIT 10;
32
```

↳ Results   ∿ Chart

# L_ORDERKEY	0|1 BOOLXOR_RETURNFLAG_R
1	54425026	FALSE
2	54425187	FALSE
3	54425319	FALSE
4	54425253	TRUE
5	54425440	FALSE
6	54425605	FALSE
7	54425792	FALSE
8	54425892	FALSE
9	54425952	FALSE
10	54426215	FALSE

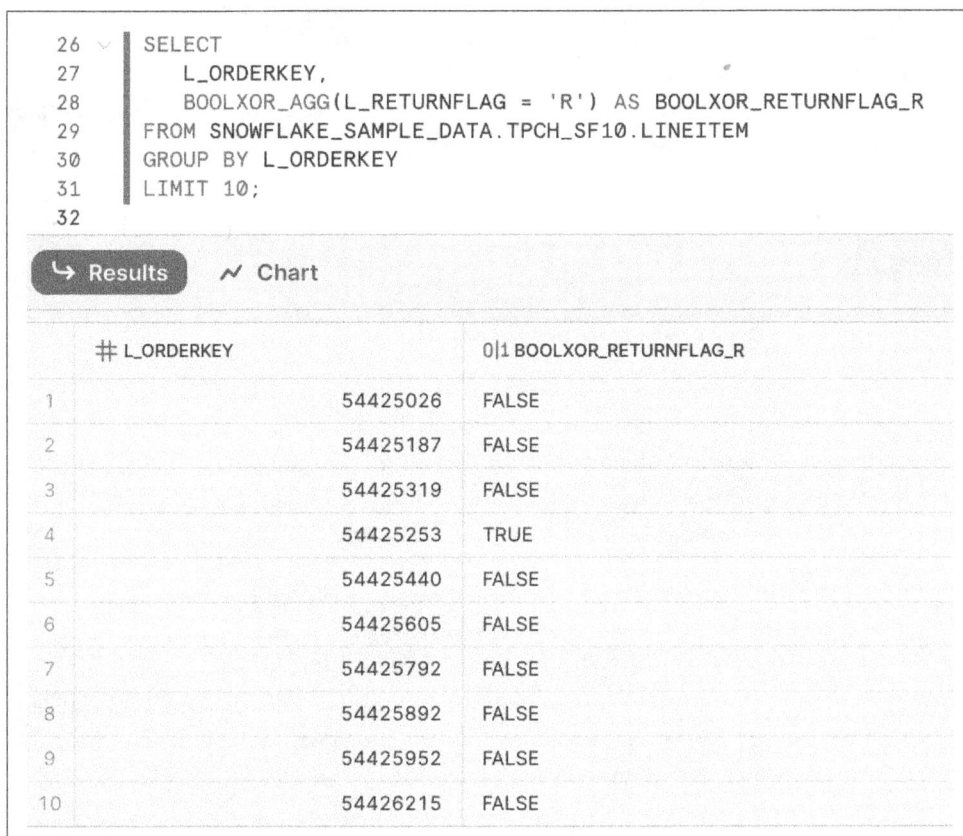

Figure 3-6. Results of BOOLXOR_AGG sample query

Window Functions

Window functions are a group of analytical functions that work on a subset of row groups within your dataset, or as the name suggests, they work on a window of your data. Snowflake's window functions can be divided into two categories:

Rank-related window functions
    These functions allow you to assign a rank/index to a row within your window.

Window frame functions
    This category of window functions allows you to perform rolling calculations.

The data landscape is continuously evolving; the more data you produce, the more there is a need to consolidate the data smartly. These functions are important tools to have in your toolkit to extract insights from your data.

Think of your dataset as having data around orders from customers. For each customer you want to have a rolling sum of order values and order numbers, and a rolling average of order values. How would you go about it? Pretty challenging, no? That is exactly where these functions come in handy. You can perform such calculations without having to write too much extra-complex code. In the following sections, let's look into how we can apply these functions.

ROW_NUMBER()

ROW_NUMBER() is one of the most commonly used window functions, defined as follows:

```
ROW_NUMBER() OVER (
 [ PARTITION BY expr1 [, expr2 ... ] ]
 ORDER BY expr3 [ , expr4 ... ] [ { ASC | DESC } ]
 )
```

Notice the different parameters of these functions:

Function name

    ROW_NUMBER()—some functions also accept optional parameters.

Partition clause

    PARTITION BY *expr*—here you specify the dimension(s) you want to use to partition your data.

Ordering clause

    ORDER BY *expr*—here you specify the column names that you want to use to order the partition by. Each partition is ordered independently.

Let's say you want to see a customer's orders ordered by date, but also with order numbers. In this case, you can use the following query:

```
SELECT
    O_ORDERKEY,
    O_CUSTKEY,
    O_TOTALPRICE,
    O_ORDERDATE,
    ROW_NUMBER() OVER (PARTITION BY O_CUSTKEY ORDER BY O_ORDERDATE ASC) AS RN
FROM SNOWFLAKE_SAMPLE_DATA.TPCH_SF10.ORDERS
WHERE O_CUSTKEY = 81910
LIMIT 100;
```

You can view the results in Figure 3-7.

```
15   SELECT
16       O_ORDERKEY,
17       O_CUSTKEY,
18       O_TOTALPRICE,
19       O_ORDERDATE,
20       ROW_NUMBER() OVER (PARTITION BY O_CUSTKEY ORDER BY O_ORDERDATE ASC) AS RN
21   FROM SNOWFLAKE_SAMPLE_DATA.TPCH_SF10.ORDERS
22   WHERE O_CUSTKEY = 81910
23   LIMIT 100;
```

↳ Results   ∿ Chart

	# O_ORDERKEY	# O_CUSTKEY	# O_TOTALPRICE	⏱ O_ORDERDATE	# RN
1	52557121	81910	33311.62	1992-03-09	1
2	56356513	81910	170445.68	1992-06-28	2
3	21171232	81910	154050.77	1992-10-12	3
4	25867911	81910	151096.55	1992-10-23	4
5	43171584	81910	22507.65	1993-02-21	5
6	12067623	81910	31347.23	1993-08-03	6
7	29028897	81910	70493.43	1994-02-01	7
8	5048835	81910	148729.58	1994-03-25	8
9	23276870	81910	176945.73	1994-04-29	9
10	40383137	81910	238291.07	1994-06-09	10
11	747331	81910	297126.37	1995-01-03	11

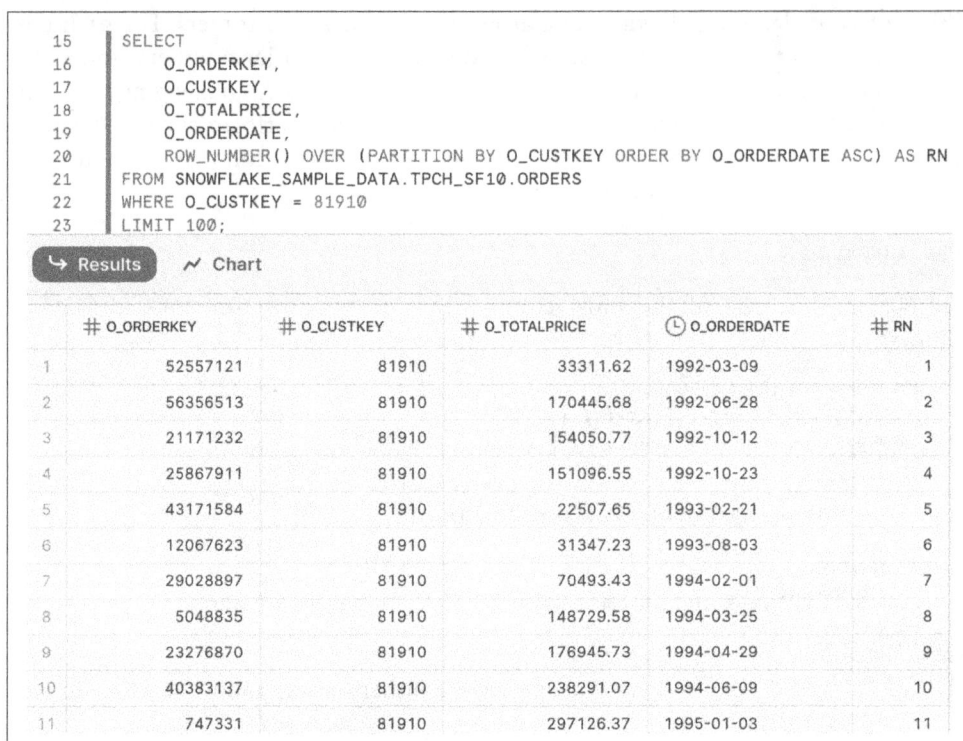

Figure 3-7. Results of the ROW_NUMBER() sample query

Let us now dissect the different parts of the window function (ROW_NUMBER() OVER PARTITION BY O_CUSTKEY ORDER BY O_ORDERDATE ASC) and see how they come into play:

1. We partition by a customer key; this will tell Snowflake to only calculate the ROW_NUMBER() on the set of rows separated by the customer key.

2. We specify an ordering clause. This will tell Snowflake how to order the partitioned rows.

Here's an analogy: think of window functions as a bag of candies with different sizes (small, medium, large) and different colors (white, blue, gold). If you separate them by color; that's equivalent to "partition by color" in a window function. Then, in each of those three groups, you sort them by size and put the smallest one first and the largest one last; this is equivalent to "order by size." This has now given you the ordered group sets to perform any action on. Maybe you just want to count them, or maybe you want to see their cumulative weight—the possibilities become endless.

RANK() / DENSE_RANK()

These two functions, RANK() and DENSE_RANK(), as their names suggest, rank your data rows. They work very similarly to ROW_NUMBER(), but there is a slight difference in how the rank is calculated. Here is what their syntax looks like:

```
RANK() OVER ( [ PARTITION BY expr1 ]
        ORDER BY expr2 [ { ASC | DESC } ] [ window_frame ] )

DENSE_RANK() OVER ( [ PARTITION BY expr1 ]
        ORDER BY expr2 [ { ASC | DESC } ] [ window_frame ] )
```

Notice that there is an extra parameter option here called window_frame. This is used to define the number of rows in the partition to scan after they have been ordered. The Snowflake docs define it as follows:

```
windowframeclause ::=
{
    { rows | range } unbounded preceding
  | { rows | range } <n> preceding
  | { rows | range } current row
  | { rows | range } between unbounded preceding and current row
  | { rows | range } between current row and unbounded following
  | { rows | range } between unbounded preceding and unbounded following
  | { rows | range } between <n> { preceding | following }
        and <n> { preceding | following }
  | { rows | range } between unbounded preceding
        and <n> { preceding | following }
  | { rows | range } between <n> { preceding | following } and unbounded following
}
```

Let's return to the RANK() and DENSE_RANK() functions. We'll skip the sample dataset and create a new table to understand this. You can create a temporary table named SAVINGS and add four people with different savings amounts in their accounts:

```
USE DATABASE OREILLY_DB;
USE SCHEMA OREILLY_SCHEMA;
CREATE OR REPLACE TEMPORARY TABLE TBL_SAVINGS (
    ID INTEGER,
    SAVINGS_USD INTEGER
);

INSERT INTO TBL_SAVINGS (ID, SAVINGS_USD) VALUES
    (1, 100),
    (2, 500),
    (3, 500),
    (4, 1200);

SELECT *
FROM TBL_SAVINGS;
```

You can view the results in Figure 3-8.

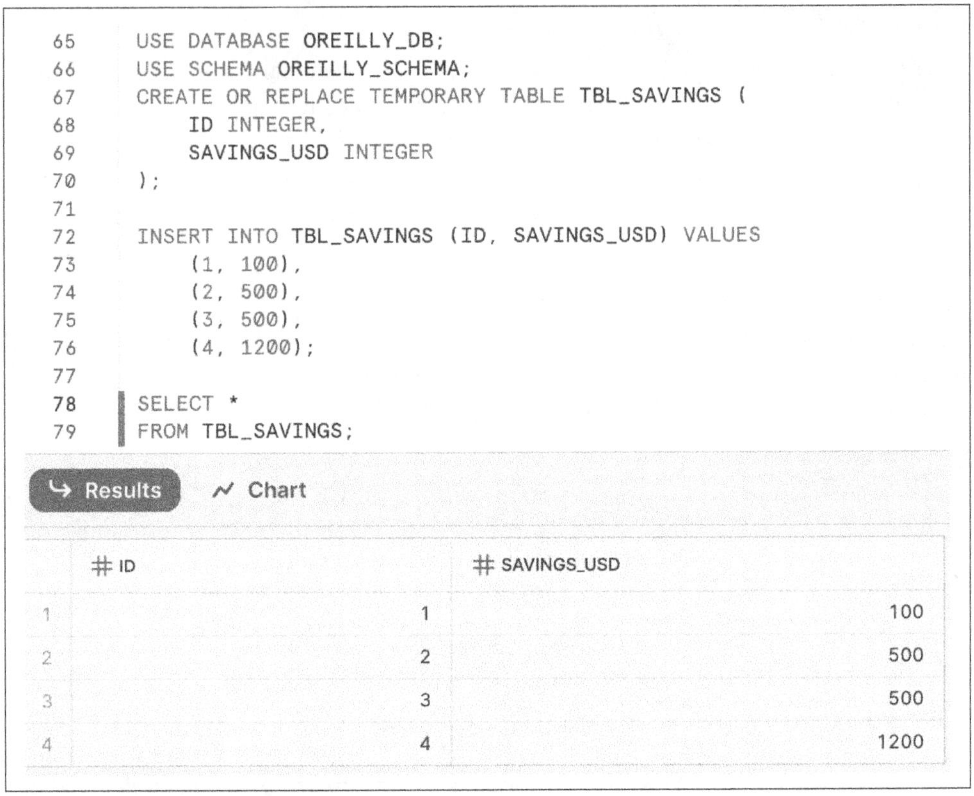

```
65    USE DATABASE OREILLY_DB;
66    USE SCHEMA OREILLY_SCHEMA;
67    CREATE OR REPLACE TEMPORARY TABLE TBL_SAVINGS (
68          ID INTEGER,
69          SAVINGS_USD INTEGER
70    );
71
72    INSERT INTO TBL_SAVINGS (ID, SAVINGS_USD) VALUES
73          (1, 100),
74          (2, 500),
75          (3, 500),
76          (4, 1200);
77
78    SELECT *
79    FROM TBL_SAVINGS;
```

↳ Results   ∿ Chart

# ID	# SAVINGS_USD
1	100
2	500
3	500
4	1200

Figure 3-8. Creating and adding data to the table SAVINGS

Now let's use the rank functions to rank the savings. You will use the following query, and the result is shown in Figure 3-9:

```
SELECT *,
    RANK() OVER (ORDER BY SAVINGS_USD) AS RANK,
    DENSE_RANK() OVER (ORDER BY SAVINGS_USD) AS DENSE_RANK
FROM TBL_SAVINGS;
```

Review the results in Figure 3-9 closely. The difference comes after the rows with the same rank (ID: 2 and ID: 3). The RANK() function would skip the subsequent ranks, whereas DENSE_RANK() would not skip it and would continue from the next rank.

```
81    SELECT *,
82        RANK() OVER (ORDER BY SAVINGS_USD) AS RANK,
83        DENSE_RANK() OVER (ORDER BY SAVINGS_USD) AS DENSE_RANK
84    FROM TBL_SAVINGS;
```

↳ Results   ∿ Chart

# ID	# SAVINGS_USD	# RANK	# DENSE_RANK
1	1	100	1	1
2	2	500	2	2
3	3	500	2	2
4	4	1200	4	3

Figure 3-9. Results of the sample query for RANK( ) and DENSE_RANK( )

FIRST_VALUE() / LAST_VALUE()

FIRST_VALUE() and LAST_VALUE() are two very helpful functions, especially when you're dealing with sequential data and want to check what the first data value was that occurred for this partition. For example, imagine you are monitoring temperature values in a factory, and you want to check the first logged value per hour per machine, and the last logged value.

The syntax of both functions is as follows:

```
FIRST_VALUE( expr ) [ { IGNORE | RESPECT } NULLS ] OVER ( [ PARTITION BY expr1 ]
    ORDER BY expr2 [ { ASC | DESC } ] [ window_frame ] )

LAST_VALUE( expr ) [ { IGNORE | RESPECT } NULLS ]  OVER ( [ PARTITION BY expr1 ]
    ORDER BY expr2 [ { ASC | DESC } ] [ window_frame ] )
```

Let's see the sample query (in this case, similar results can be achieved with the MIN, MAX window functions):

```
SELECT *,
    FIRST_VALUE(SAVINGS_USD) OVER (ORDER BY SAVINGS_USD) AS FIRST_VALUE,
    LAST_VALUE(SAVINGS_USD) OVER (ORDER BY SAVINGS_USD) AS LAST_VALUE
FROM TBL_SAVINGS
;
```

View the results in Figure 3-10.

```
87   SELECT *,
88       FIRST_VALUE(SAVINGS_USD) OVER (ORDER BY SAVINGS_USD) AS FIRST_VALUE,
89       LAST_VALUE(SAVINGS_USD) OVER (ORDER BY SAVINGS_USD) AS LAST_VALUE
90   FROM TBL_SAVINGS
91   ;
```

↳ Results   ～ Chart

# ID	# SAVINGS_USD	# FIRST_VALUE	# LAST_VALUE
1	1	100	100	1200
2	2	500	100	1200
3	3	500	100	1200
4	4	1200	100	1200

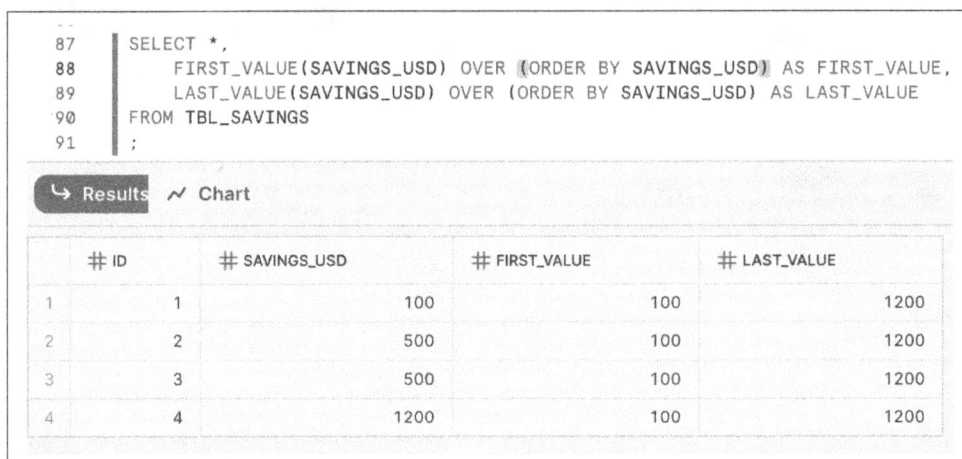

Figure 3-10. Results of FIRST_VALUE() and LAST_VALUE() sample queries

LAG()/LEAD()

LAG() and LEAD() are two functions that are particularly useful when dealing with time series data. They are used to get the previous/next value of a given field. For example, you might have a use case where you're sampling time series data at fixed intervals, and you want to check the previous or the next value of a sensor. They both have very similar syntax:

```
LAG ( expr [ , offset, default ] ) [ { IGNORE | RESPECT } NULLS ]
    OVER ( [ PARTITION BY expr1 ] ORDER BY expr2 [ { ASC | DESC } ] )

LEAD (expr [ ,offset, default ] ) [ { IGNORE | RESPECT } NULLS ]
    OVER ( [ PARTITION BY expr1 ] ORDER BY expr2 [ { ASC | DESC } ] )
```

Here you see two new optional parameters, OFFSET and DEFAULT.OFFSET means how many rows to look back (in the case of LAG()) or look forward (in the case of LEAD()). A negative offset will invert the functions, i.e., if you use a negative offset in the LAG() function, it will become a LEAD() function, and vice versa. DEFAULT is the default fallback in case the indexes go out of bounds, i.e., if you just have one row and you use LEAD() or LAG() with offset 1, the default value of NULL will appear unless you have specified a value in this parameter.

Let's look at a sample query for these functions on the SAVINGS table:

```
SELECT *,
    LAG(SAVINGS_USD) OVER (ORDER BY SAVINGS_USD) AS LAG,
    LEAD(SAVINGS_USD) OVER (ORDER BY SAVINGS_USD) AS LEAD
FROM TBL_SAVINGS;
```

In Figure 3-11, you can see the values are ordered by the SAVINGS_USD column, and the LAG function reads the previous value. In the first row, you can see that the value is NULL (as we didn't specify the DEFAULT parameter, and there's no previous row). Similarly, LEAD() is reading the next value of the SAVINGS_USD column, and if you notice, in the last row it defaults to NULL since there's no next row to look forward to.

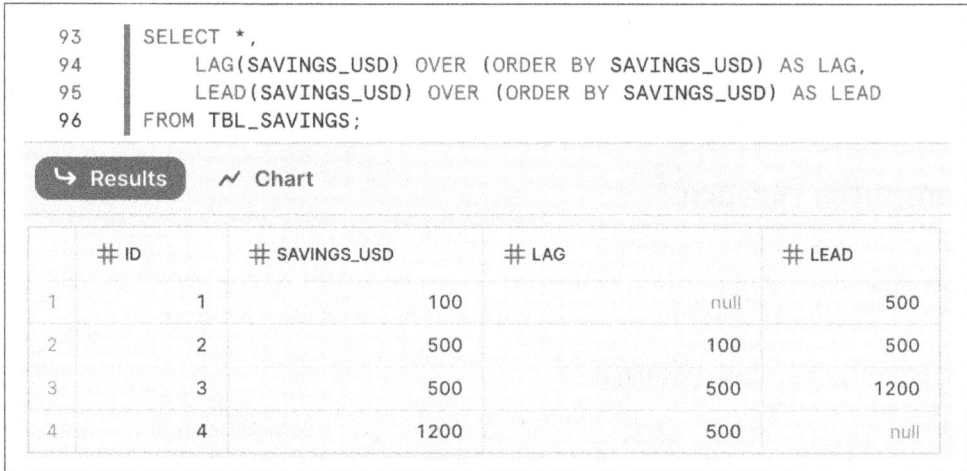

```
93    SELECT *,
94        LAG(SAVINGS_USD) OVER (ORDER BY SAVINGS_USD) AS LAG,
95        LEAD(SAVINGS_USD) OVER (ORDER BY SAVINGS_USD) AS LEAD
96    FROM TBL_SAVINGS;
```

↳ Results   〜 Chart

# ID	# SAVINGS_USD	# LAG	# LEAD
1	1	100	null	500
2	2	500	100	500
3	3	500	500	1200
4	4	1200	500	null

Figure 3-11. Results of LAG() and LEAD() sample query

Snowflake Geospatial

Snowflake Geospatial has been a big step forward by Snowflake in making Snowflake the single best solution for all your analytical needs. Geospatial analytics refers to a branch of analytics where you can use geographies and geometries to perform spatial calculations and aggregations. Snowflake now natively supports the handling of geospatial data and functions.

Geospatial Data Types

Snowflake Geospatial natively supports two main data types:

- GEOGRAPHY models Earth as if it were a perfect sphere.
- GEOMETRY models a planar coordinate system (Euclidean, Cartesian).

While GEOGRAPHY and GEOMETRY are the two main data types, they can encapsulate numerous types of objects. Just like numeric data types can hold integers and floats, GEOGRAPHY and GEOMETRY can hold Point, MultiPoint, LineString, MultiLine String, Polygon, MultiPolygon, and GeometryCollection.

I won't go into details, features, and limitations of each of the preceding object types in this book. For more technical details on these data types, see the Snowflake docs (*https://oreil.ly/5nFow*).

Snowflake Geospatial Functions

Snowflake geospatial functions provide support for both GEOGRAPHY and GEOMETRY data types. Some functions are exclusive to particular data types, but most of the functions provided by Snowflake support both. ST_GEOGRAPHYFROMWKT (*https://oreil.ly/MPeq7*) works only with the GEOGRAPHY data type, while an equivalent function for the GEOMETRY data type would be ST_GEOMETRYFROMWKT (*https://oreil.ly/TKHFr*). Now, let's have a look at some of the geospatial constructor functions.

Constructor Functions

Constructor functions are functions that take a certain input and construct a certain data type. For example, given two points, create a GEOMETRY data type. Let's look at some of the constructor functions that are a part of Snowflake Geospatial.

ST_MAKEGEOMPOINT/ST_GEOMPOINT

This function is used to create a GEOMETRY object from given longitude and latitude values. These functions are aliases for one another; you can use either one of them to get the same results. They have the following syntax:

```
ST_MAKEGEOMPOINT(longitude, latitude)
ST_GEOMPOINT(longitude, latitude)
```

You can try it yourself by simply running the following query:

```
SELECT ST_MAKEGEOMPOINT(90, 90) AS GEOM_PT;
```

ST_MAKEPOINT/ST_POINT

ST_ MAKEPOINT and ST_POINT are similar to ST_MAKEGEOMPOINT and ST_GEOMPOINT. They only differ in their return data type. While the prior functions return the GEOMETRY data type, these two return the GEOGRAPHY data type. They have the following syntax:

```
ST_MAKEPOINT(longitude, latitude)
ST_POINT(longitude, latitude)
```

You can run the following query to try them out:

```
SELECT ST_MAKEPOINT(90, 90) AS GEOG_PT;
```

ST_MAKELINE

ST_MAKELINE is a function that can be used to connect two GEOGRAPHY or GEOMETRY objects. The objects must be one of the following: Point, MultiPoint, or LineString. It has the following syntax:

```
ST_MAKELINE(geography_expression_1, geography_expression_2)
ST_MAKELINE(geometry_expression_1, geometry_expression_2)
```

Let's create a line using the `MAKELINE` function using two `POINT`s:

```
SELECT ST_MAKELINE(
    ST_POINT(15, 60),
    ST_POINT(0, 45)
) AS LINE;
```

The preceding query will create a line from point (15,60) in France to Sweden, point (0, 45) (see Figure 3-12). You can copy the result and visualize it using a tool like *https://geojson.io*. You can see how it looks on the map in Figure 3-13.

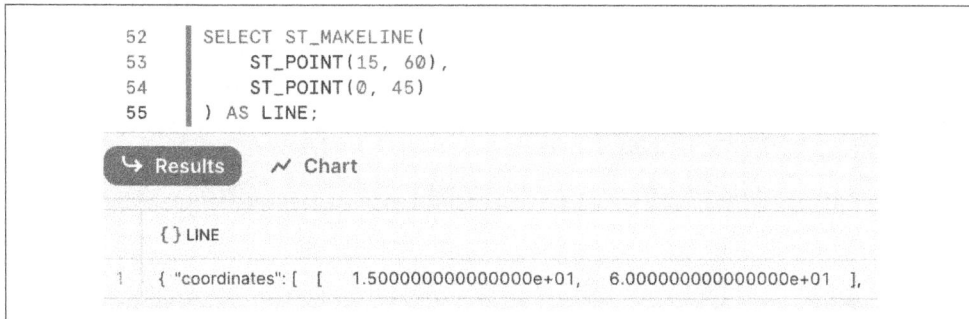

Figure 3-12. Results of ST_MAKELINE sample query

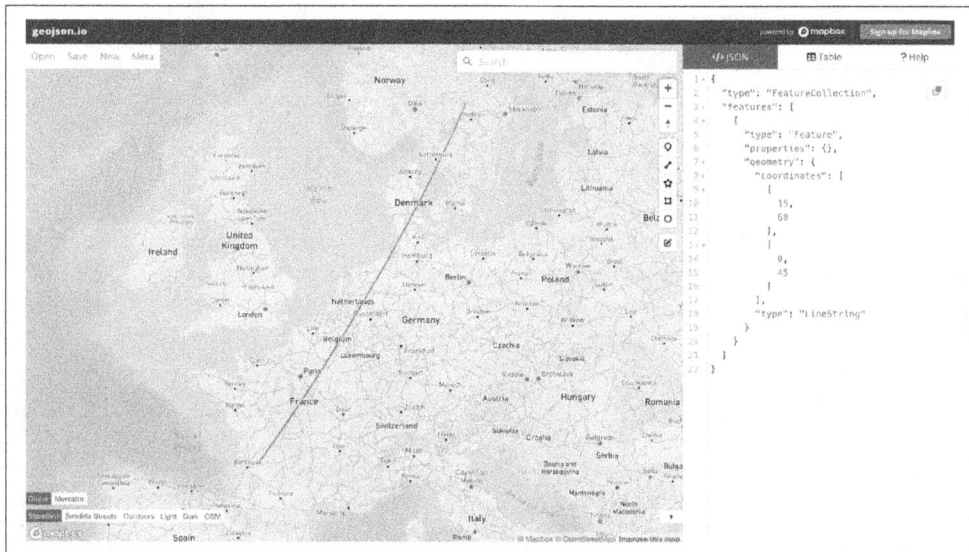

Figure 3-13. Visual of ST_MAKELINE sample query using https://geojson.io

Let's create a second line when the objects underneath are already `LineStrings` (Figure 3-14):

```
SELECT ST_MAKELINE(
    ST_MAKELINE(
        ST_POINT(15, 60),
        ST_POINT(0, 45)
    ),
    ST_MAKELINE(
        ST_POINT(25, 40),
        ST_POINT(45, 40)
    )
) AS LINE;
```

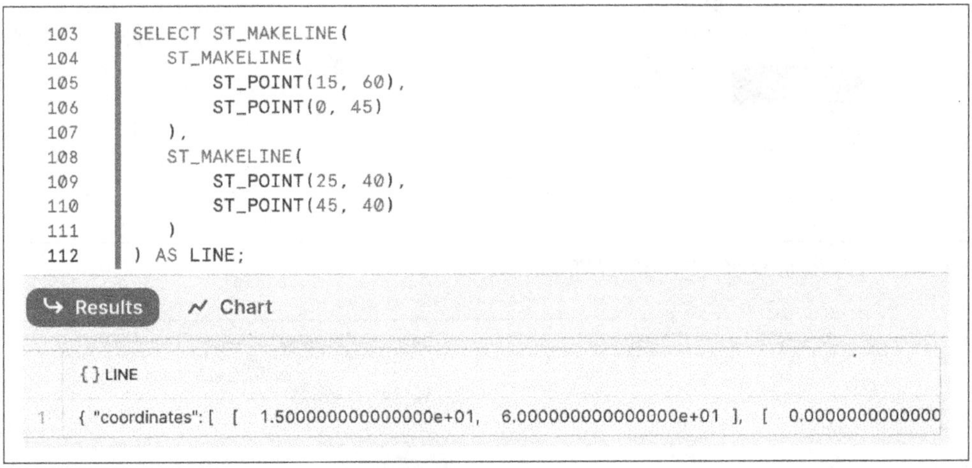

Figure 3-14. Results of ST_MAKELINE sample query with two lines

You may notice in Figure 3-15 that the pasted result on the right-hand side of the screen isn't exactly the same as what we saw in Snowflake, and that is because *https:// geojson.io* normalizes the results automatically.

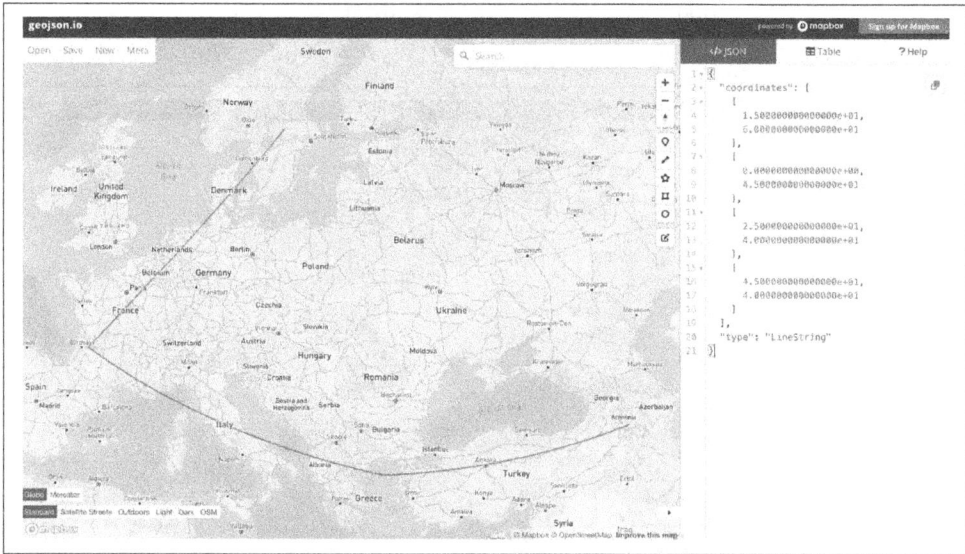

Figure 3-15. Visual of ST_MAKELINE sample query with two lines

ST_MAKEPOLYGON/ST_POLYGON

ST_MAKEPOLYGON is an extension of ST_MAKELINE. It basically loops around the point and makes a closed shape without holes. The syntax is quite simple:

```
ST_MAKEPOLYGON(geography_or_geometry_expression)
```

It will take a LineString in which the first and last points are the same (to complete the loop) and create a closed shape. Let's take the same line that you created in the last example and create a Polygon from it:

```
SELECT ST_MAKEPOLYGON(
    TRY_TO_GEOGRAPHY('LINESTRING(15 60, 0 45, 15 45, 15 60)')
) AS POLYGON;
```

View the results in Figure 3-16.

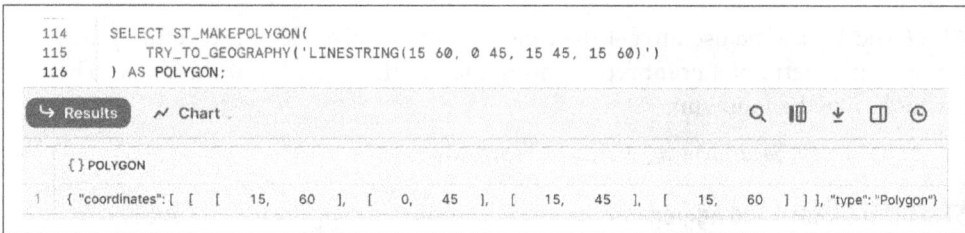

Figure 3-16. Results of ST_MAKEPOLYGON sample query

Notice in Figure 3-17 that you used a different method to generate a `LineString` this time, using a text format known as *well-known text* (WKT) (*https://oreil.ly/4vWuC*).

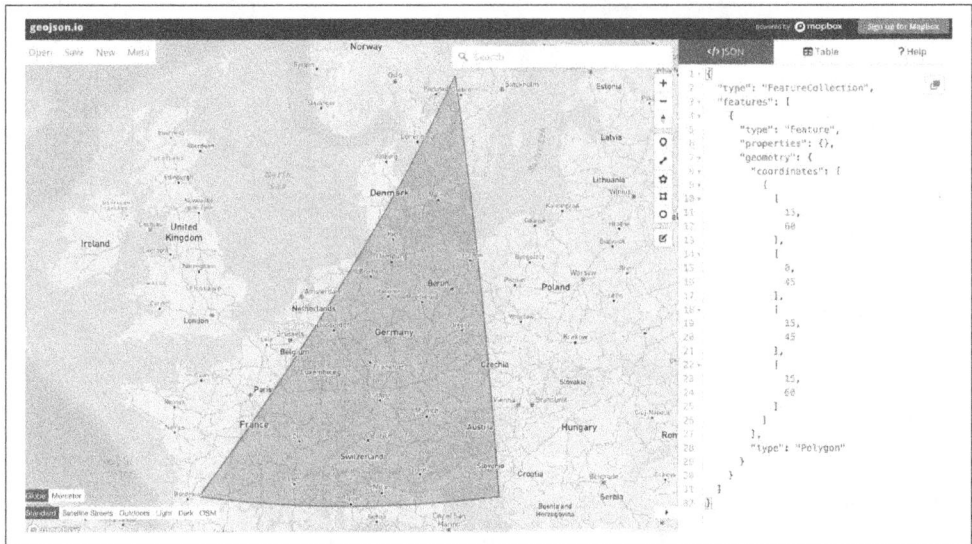

Figure 3-17. Visual of ST_MAKEPOLYGON sample query

> The preceding list of geospatial functions is not exhaustive and only includes some of the most relevant functions. For a complete list, visit Snowflake's geospatial functions page. (*https://oreil.ly/DFUJT*)

Transformer Functions

Transformer functions are functions that are used to transform given inputs. Let's have a look at some of the transformer functions that Snowflake Geospatial supports.

ST_CENTROID

`ST_CENTROID` can be used to get the center point of a given shape. It returns the geography or geometry of a point representing the geometric center of the shape. The syntax looks like the following:

```
ST_CENTROID(geography_or_geometry_expression)
```

ST_COLLECT (Scalar and Aggregate)

`ST_COLLECT`, as the name suggests, is used to collect or combine multiple geographies into one. It has two variants:

- `Scalar` takes two inputs and combines them into one geography.

- `Aggregate` takes a column and combines the whole column into one geography.

The syntax is as follows:

```
Scalar: ST_COLLECT(geography_expression_1, geography_expression_2)
Aggregate: ST_COLLECT(geography_expression_1)
```

ST_INTERSECTION

`ST_INTERSECTION` is a very interesting geospatial function that returns the overlapping parts of the two geographies. A good example of `ST_INTERSECTION` could be to see the coverage of cellular towers. For example, if you have two towers covering an area and you want to see what area is covered by both towers, you can simply take their coverage polygons and find the intersection. The returned polygon will be the area that is covered by both towers.

It has the following syntax:

```
ST_INTERSECTION(geography_expression_1, geography_expression_2)
```

ST_UNION

`ST_UNION` is the opposite of `ST_INTERSECTION` but very similar to `ST_COLLECT`. It can also be used to combine two geographies into one. The main difference between `ST_UNION` and `ST_COLLECT` is the speed, as `ST_COLLECT` does not try to dissolve boundaries or validate that a constructed `MultiPolygon` doesn't have overlapping regions.[1] It has the following syntax:

```
ST_UNION(geography_expression_1, geography_expression_2)
```

> The preceding list of transformer functions is not exhaustive and only includes some of the most relevant functions. For a complete list, visit the Snowflake documentation (*https://oreil.ly/8PcCH*).

Measurement and Relationship Functions

Measurement and relationship functions are functions that are used to measure something or find relationships from the given inputs. The following are some of the measurement and relationship functions that Snowflake Geospatial supports.

---

1 For details, check out the PostGIS docs (*https://oreil.ly/mJLcY*).

ST_AREA

ST_AREA is used to find the area of a given geospatial object. It uses the following syntax:

```
ST_AREA(geography_or_geometry_expression)
```

If the input is a GEOGRAPHY object, the output is a numeric value in square meters.

If the input is a GEOMETRY object, the output is a numeric value in the same unit as the GEOMETRY object.

Let's have a look at how it will differ if the same polygon is created as a GEOMETRY object and a GEOGRAPHY object. You will use the same polygon as before as our input. The query you will use is as follows:

```
SELECT
    ST_AREA(
        ST_MAKEPOLYGON(
            TRY_TO_GEOGRAPHY('LINESTRING(15 60, 0 45, 15 45, 15 60)')
        )
    ) AS AREA_OF_GEOG_POLYGON,
    ST_AREA(
        ST_MAKEPOLYGON(
            TRY_TO_GEOMETRY('LINESTRING(15 60, 0 45, 15 45, 15 60)')
        )
    ) AS AREA_OF_GEOM_POLYGON,
;
```

As you can see in Figure 3-18, the area differs quite significantly between the types. The geographical polygon returns square meters, but the geometrical polygon returns the Euclidean area.

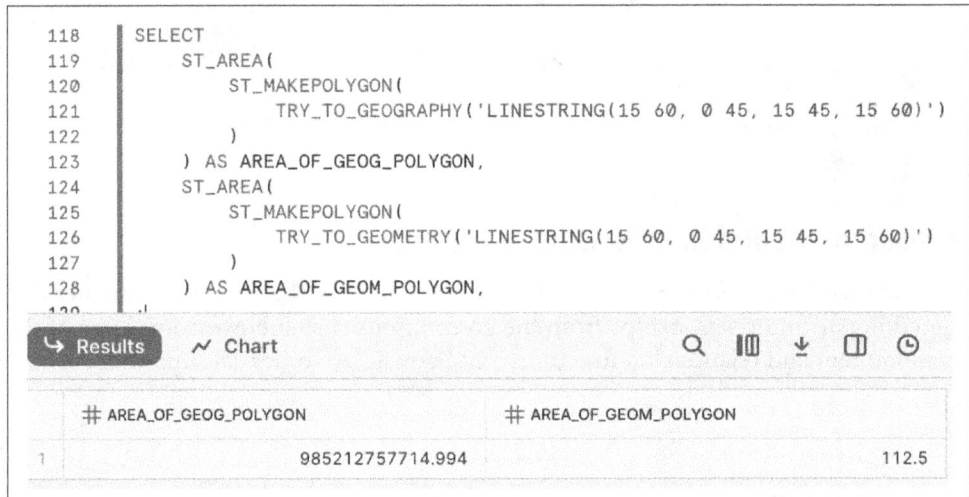

Figure 3-18. Results of the ST_AREA sample query

ST_CONTAINS

ST_CONTAINS is a Boolean function that returns true if a GEOMETRY or a GEOGRAPHY object is completely inside the other object of the same type. It has the following syntax:

```
ST_CONTAINS(geography_expression_1 , geography_expression_2)
ST_CONTAINS(geometry_expression_1 , geometry_expression_2)
```

I won't provide examples and sample queries for this function in this book. To see examples, visit the Snowflake documentation (*https://oreil.ly/-9rEF*).

ST_DISTANCE

ST_DISTANCE is a function that is used to measure the smallest difference between two objects. Similar to ST_AREA, the returned output value is in square meters if the inputs are geographies, and it will be in the same unit as the input if the inputs are geometries. It has the following syntax:

```
ST_DISTANCE(
        geography_or_geometry_expression_1,
        geography_or_geometry_expression_2
)
```

I won't provide examples and sample queries for this function in this book. Visit the Snowflake documentation (*https://oreil.ly/NtKrj*) for examples.

ST_DWITHIN

ST_DWITHIN is a function that returns true if the geodesic distance between geographical objects is within the specified range. It is particularly useful when you have to see objects within a certain proximity, e.g., what percentage of connected devices are within a 100-meter radius of the tower. It has the following syntax:

```
ST_DWITHIN(geography_expression_1, geography_expression_2, distance_in_meters)
```

I won't provide examples and sample queries for this function in this book. For examples, see the Snowflake documentation (*https://oreil.ly/1hUmt*).

ST_INTERSECTS

ST_INTERSECTS is also a Boolean function. It returns true if any parts of the two GEOGRAPHY objects or GEOMETRY objects intersect. It has the following syntax:

```
ST_INTERSECTS(geography_expression_1, geography_expression_2)
ST_INTERSECTS(geometry_expression_1, geometry_expression_2)
```

I won't provide examples and sample queries for this function in this book. Check out the Snowflake documentation (*https://oreil.ly/9Eizs*) for examples.

> The preceding list of measurement and relationship geospatial functions is not exhaustive and only lists some of the most relevant functions. For a complete list, see the Snowflake documentation (*https://oreil.ly/JTnZC*). You can find the examples for all the functions that we missed in their respective function pages.

Snowflake and H3

H3 is Uber's open source hierarchical hexagonal geospatial indexing system. It divides the world into hexagonal cells of different sizes, making it efficient for location data analysis, spatial indexing, and mapping. The hexagonal grid system provides more uniform neighboring distances than rectangular grids, making it particularly useful for geospatial analytics and visualization. Snowflake now natively supports H3 functions.

I will go through two basic functions to pique your interest in exploring it, but for a complete list of functions, you can visit the Snowflake documentation (*https://oreil.ly/SWIH3*).

H3_POINT_TO_CELL/H3_POINT_TO_CELL_STRING

H3 uses unique indexes for every hexbin. Given a point and resolution (zoom level), it generates a unique ID for a cell.[2] The H3_POINT_TO_CELL function does exactly that. It returns a unique ID for a cell as a numeric value. You can also get a similar identifier as a hexadecimal number if you use the function H3_POINT_TO_CELL_STRING. It has the following syntax:

```
H3_POINT_TO_CELL(geography_point, target_resolution)
H3_POINT_TO_CELL_STRING(geography_point, target_resolution)
```

You can use the following query to generate both indexes on resolution 5 on a point (15, 60):

```
SELECT
    H3_POINT_TO_CELL(
        TRY_TO_GEOGRAPHY('POINT(15 60)'),
        5
    ) AS H3_CELL,
    H3_POINT_TO_CELL_STRING(
        TRY_TO_GEOGRAPHY('POINT(15 60)'),
        5
    ) AS H3_CELL_STRING;
```

View the results in Figure 3-19.

---

2 See the "Tables of Cell Statistics Across Resolutions" (*https://oreil.ly/F2KFy*).

```
132   SELECT
133       H3_POINT_TO_CELL( TRY_TO_GEOGRAPHY('POINT(15 60)'), 5) AS H3_CELL,
134       H3_POINT_TO_CELL_STRING( TRY_TO_GEOGRAPHY('POINT(15 60)'), 5) AS H3_CELL_STRING
135   |;
```

# H3_CELL	A H3_CELL_STRING
599130647327408127	8508a263fffffff

Figure 3-19. Results of H3_POINT_TO_CELL sample query

H3_CELL_TO_BOUNDARY

Now that you have converted a point into a cell, it's time to map it as a hexagon and get the boundary of that hexagon. The H3_CELL_TO_BOUNDARY function does exactly that. It takes an H3 index (numeric or hexadecimal) and returns a polygon boundary of the hexagon. Its syntax looks like this:

```
H3_CELL_TO_BOUNDARY(cell_id)
```

The cell ID here is the H3 index. Now let's take the same indexes and create a boundary using the following query:

```
SELECT
    H3_CELL_TO_BOUNDARY(H3_POINT_TO_CELL(
        TRY_TO_GEOGRAPHY('POINT(15 60)'), 5)
    ) AS H3_BOUNDARY_FROM_CELL,
    H3_CELL_TO_BOUNDARY(H3_POINT_TO_CELL_STRING(
        TRY_TO_GEOGRAPHY('POINT(15 60)'), 5)
    ) AS H3_BOUNDARY_FROM_CELL_STRING
;
```

You may notice that in Figure 3-20, the resulting polygon is exactly the same.

```
58   SELECT
59       H3_CELL_TO_BOUNDARY(H3_POINT_TO_CELL(
60           TRY_TO_GEOGRAPHY('POINT(15 60)'), 5)
61       ) AS H3_BOUNDARY_FROM_CELL,
62       H3_CELL_TO_BOUNDARY(H3_POINT_TO_CELL_STRING(
63           TRY_TO_GEOGRAPHY('POINT(15 60)'), 5)
64       ) AS H3_BOUNDARY_FROM_CELL_STRING
65   ;|
```

{ } H3_BOUNDARY_FROM_CELL	{ } H3_BOUNDARY_FROM_CELL_STRING
{ "coordinates": [[[1.484149242975966e+01, 6	{ "coordinates": [[[1.484149242975966e+01, 6.000751

Figure 3-20. Results from H3_CELL_TO_BOUNDARY sample query

As you can see in Figure 3-21, it generated a valid hexagon, and you can also validate visually that you got the same result using both the numeric ID and the hexadecimal string.

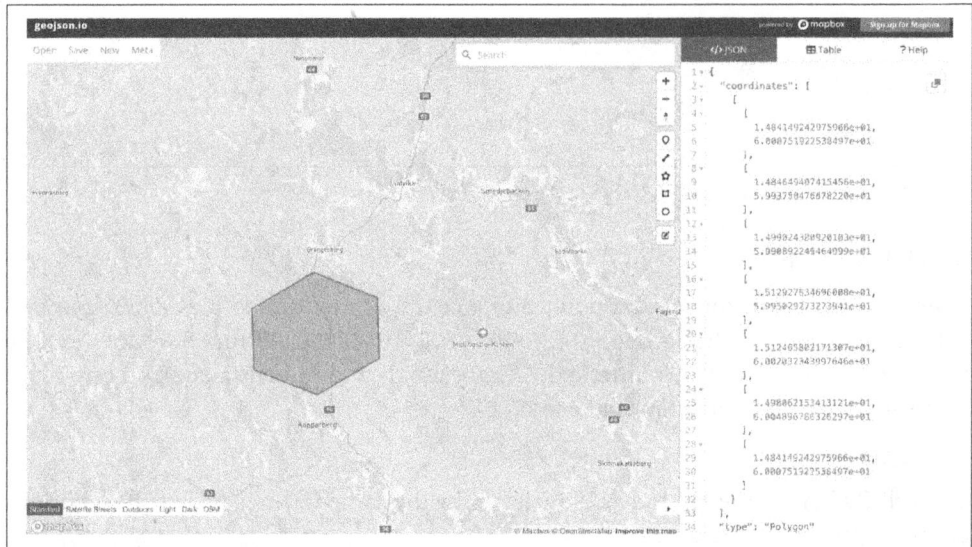

Figure 3-21. Visual of H3_CELL_TO_BOUNDARY *sample query*

Summary

In this chapter, you looked at Snowflake SQL. The most important takeaway is the order of execution of Snowflake queries. You looked at how different SQL clauses take precedence over others and studied some SQL examples. Following that, we dived into advanced Snowflake functions and looked at everything from some uncommon aggregate functions to window functions, which are a very important skill to have under your belt as an analyst. Lastly, we looked at Snowflake Geospatial and how Snowflake can work with different geographical objects to unlock another analytical dimension for you.

Following SQL, the natural next step is to explore how similar things can be done in different programming languages, and that's exactly what we will do in Chapter 4.

Snowpark

Snowpark is a powerful tool within the Snowflake ecosystem, offering developers a flexible and efficient way to interact with Snowflake. Consider Sarah, a data scientist who was spending hours extracting data from Snowflake, processing it in Python locally, training fraud detection models, and then struggling to get results back into production. With Snowpark, she rewrote her entire pipeline to run directly inside Snowflake using familiar pandas-like syntax, processing millions of transactions, training models, and deploying them for real-time scoring without ever moving data outside the platform. What once took hours of coordination between systems now happens in minutes. This is the power of Snowpark: bringing your existing Python skills directly to where your data lives, eliminating the friction that has traditionally made advanced analytics a complex orchestration challenge.

In this chapter, I will go through Snowpark, its key concepts, and some of Snowflake's machine learning (ML) capabilities. I will start by explaining what Snowpark is and will then take a look at Snowpark's DataFrame API and inline UDFs. Following that, I will introduce Snowflake ML, and lastly, in this chapter, I will go through some hands-on examples of using Snowpark.

Why Snowpark?

Using Snowpark, you can build scalable applications that can query or process data within Snowflake, eliminating the need to move the data out of Snowflake, and fully utilize the infinite scale of the cloud. Snowpark is a vectorized engine that operates near where data is located without having to return to higher processing mechanisms such as memory, so it is extremely fast. Snowpark provides a unified programming interface to work with vectorized data or datasets in standard Snowflake tables across three programming languages: Java, Scala, and Python. All in all, it's one complete package designed to remove barriers to entry to Snowflake and allow more technical users who might not want to write SQL scripts to be able to write code in their preferred interface and achieve the same results that an SQL user would. It will achieve the following things:

Enhance productivity
Technical users/developers can write code in their environment without having to learn a new interface.

Allow apps to scale
Developers can use the infinite scale of the cloud to write and build scalable apps without having to worry about resources.

Reduce data movement
Developers will no longer need to move data outside of Snowflake to be able to process it, reducing data movement over the network.

Now let's look at what Snowpark provides on the client and server sides.

Client Side Versus Server Side

Snowpark can be seen as both a client- and server-side solution.

The client-side solution of Snowpark consists of Snowpark API libraries in three different languages (Java, Scala, and Python), including the DataFrame API, which I'll explain in the following section, and Snowpark machine learning support (now often referred to as Snowflake ML). In Figure 4-1, you'll see Snowflake ML's overview and different parts of the ML workflow that it supports.

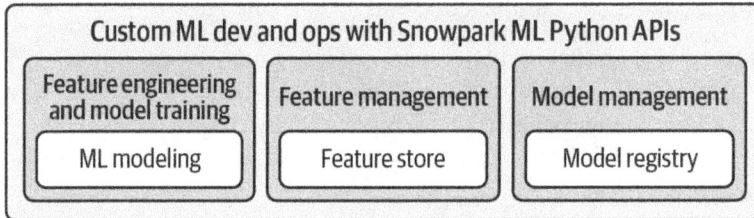

Figure 4-1. Snowflake ML workflow overview

The server-side solution of Snowpark is wrapped as UDFs and stored procedures in Snowflake, where users can write them in any of the three languages supported by Snowpark. It now also includes the Snowpark Container Services, a fully managed container offering for application development within Snowflake. More on this in the following sections. First, let's explore some key concepts of Snowpark.

Snowpark Key Features

In this section, I'll go through the following key features of the Snowpark API: Data-Frame API, reduced data transfer, and inline UDFs.

What makes these features particularly powerful is how they work together to create a seamless development experience. The DataFrame API gives you the familiar pandas-like interface you're already comfortable with, while reduced data transfer ensures your operations run efficiently at scale without the typical bottlenecks of moving data between systems. Inline UDFs then allow you to extend this capability with custom logic that executes directly within Snowflake's compute environment. Together, these features eliminate the traditional trade-offs between ease of use, performance, and flexibility. You can write intuitive Python code that leverages Snowflake's massive parallel processing power while keeping your data secure and governance-compliant within the platform.

DataFrame API

Snowflake developed a native DataFrame API in Snowpark. It is a standard, highly performant approach to interacting with your data within Snowflake using the familiar Python syntax. Note that this is not to be confused with the Snowpark pandas API that brings the Python pandas familiarity into Snowflake. Snowflake acquired Ponder (*https://oreil.ly/hFZAp*) in 2023 to get a robust pandas API to Snowpark. Both options are available in Snowpark, and, depending on the developer's preference, the user can use any of the options.

Snowflake's native DataFrames (Snowpark DataFrames) are based on PySpark (*https://oreil.ly/XiDZF*) (a Python API for Apache Spark), which provides a distributed solution to manage and process data at scale. On the other hand, the Snowpark pandas is an extension of Snowpark DataFrames, which provides a familiar interface to the developers coming from a pandas background. This also means that Snowpark DataFrames operate directly on the original data source, giving you the most recent snapshot of data and not maintaining a fixed order of operations. In contrast, Snowflake pandas is designed to mimic the behavior of pandas, which does not maintain the most recent snapshot of data but preserves the order of operations and supports positional indexing of your datasets.

Snowflake provides a good overview of when you should use Snowpark pandas and when you should use Snowpark DataFrames. The overview is shown in Table 4-1.

Table 4-1. An overview of Snowpark pandas versus DataFrames

Use Snowpark pandas if you ...	Use Snowpark DataFrames if you ...
Prefer working with or have existing code written in pandas	Prefer working with or have existing code written in SPARK
Have workflow that involves interactive analysis and iterative exploration	Have a workflow that involves batch processing and limited iterative development
Are familiar with working with DataFrame operations that get executed immediately	Are familiar with working with DataFrame operations that are lazily evaluated
Prefer data being consistent and ordered during the operations	Are OK with data not being ordered
Are OK with slightly slower performance compared to Snowpark DataFrames in favor of an easier-to-use API	Want to prioritize performance over ease of use

You can read more about this in the Snowflake docs (*https://oreil.ly/OXIFL*).

Reduced Data Transfer

In the previous section, I explained that Snowpark DataFrames are based on PySpark and do not preserve the order of operations. This is simply because they are lazy. Well, not lazy like humans (luckily). What I mean by lazy here is that no data is retrieved while you are writing code and doing your transformations, and the server will try to delay the fetching of data as much as possible. It will then try to batch the maximum operations performed on a DataFrame together and retrieve the data, thus not saving the order of operations and reducing the data transfer by optimizing the data retrieval at the source.

In simple terms, no data is retrieved when the DataFrame is created, and operations like filtering, aggregations, and sorting are not applied by the code, but rather when the results are requested, an optimized SQL code is run against the Snowflake engine to retrieve the results you want.

Let's have a look at the code block:

```
# Query the lineitem table in TPCH_SF10 schema from Snowflake Sample Data
# Select a few columns from the lineitem table
# Filter the results only for L_ORDERKEY = 199

df = session.table("tpch_sf10_lineitem").select(
    col("L_ORDERKEY"),
    col("L_PARTKEY"),
    col("L_LINENUMBER"),
    col("L_QUANTITY"),
    col("L_EXTENDEDPRICE"),
    col("L_DISCOUNT"),
    col("L_LINESTATUS")
)

# Apply filter
```

```
df_filtered = df.filter(col("L_ORDERKEY") == 199)

# collect() method will trigger the execution of the query
# against Snowflake engine
results = df_filtered.collect()
```

Here, the first line reads the table and the selected columns. The second line filters on the L_ORDERKEY column, and the third line gathers the results. Because I used Snowpark DataFrames in the preceding example, the Snowflake engine is only queried when the collect() method is run. Let's quickly hop over to Snowsight and see what was actually executed in Snowflake. If you navigate to Query History under the Monitoring tab, you will see the query coming from Client Driver: PythonSnowpark. Figure 4-2 shows how it looks for me.

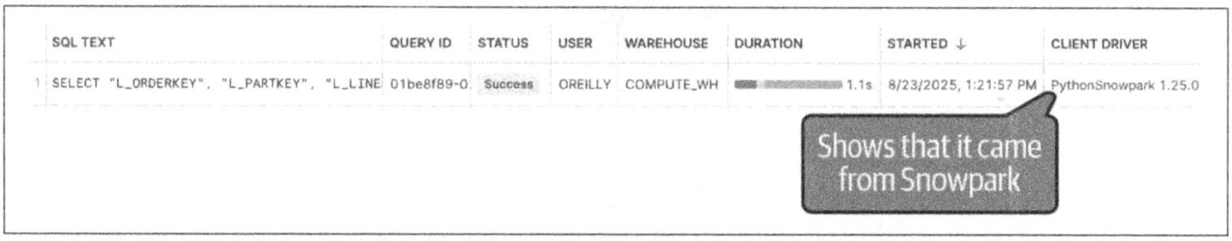

Figure 4-2. Query coming from Snowpark in Query History

If you click on it, you will see the query details. In Query Details, you can find the exact SQL that ran and other things like results, query tag, driver version, warehouse size, query profile, etc. Figure 4-3 shows the details, including the query from the details page.

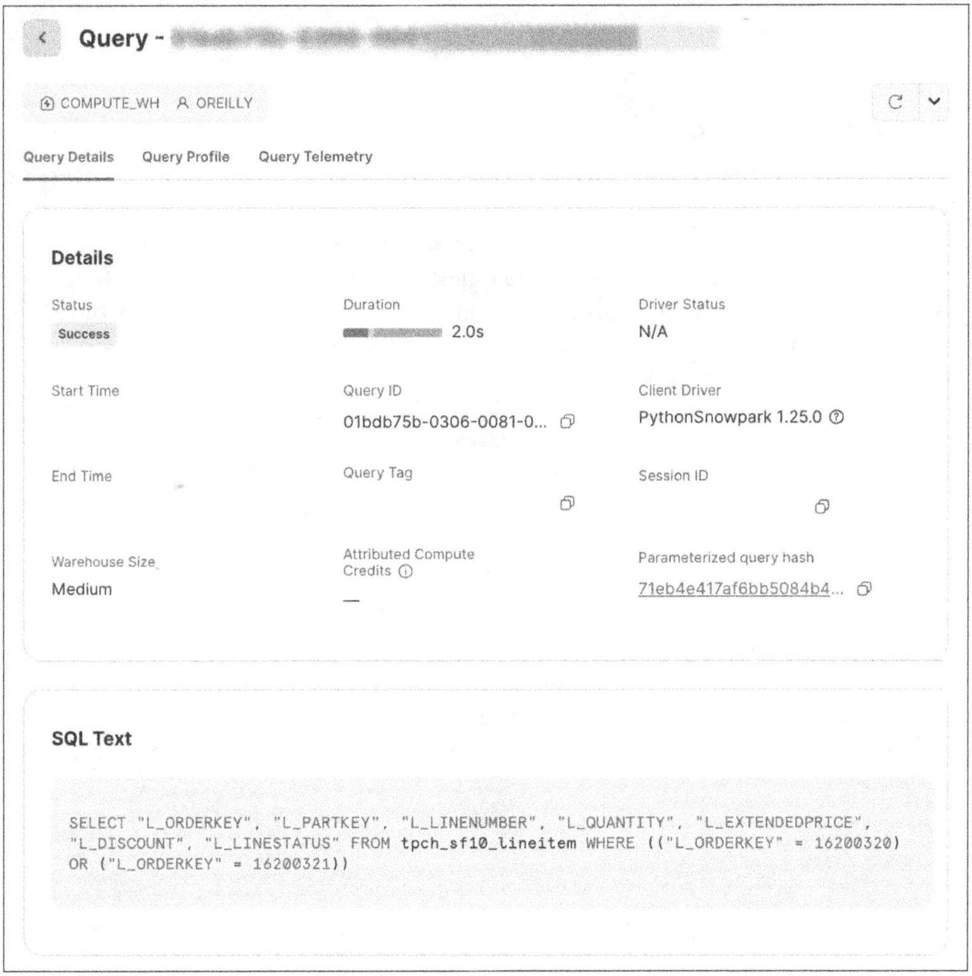

Figure 4-3. Query Details page for the code from Snowpark

Inline UDFs

Snowpark also provides the capability of writing UDFs just like one would write a lambda function in Python. This is what is known as the inline UDF. You define your lambda function, and save it as a UDF from your programming interface.

You simply write inline code and Snowpark will seamlessly push it to Snowflake. This allows Snowflake to process the data and apply the UDF at scale, making it a perfect tool for work that requires looping or batch processing. The biggest gain from this feature is code parallelization. Snowflake's engine understands the code and can distribute your code across multiple nodes to ensure efficient and scalable performance. Snowpark is responsible for shipping your inline UDF code to the Snowflake server whenever the execution happens. This allows for complex transformations that previously required you to move your data outside of Snowflake's ecosystem to perform them within Snowflake. It not only ensures the efficient execution of your code but also maintains the integrity and performance of your data processing tasks.

Let's look at an example. Here, I created a UDF that takes a number and squares it by multiplying the number by itself and returns the value. You'll see the results in Figure 4-4:

```
from snowflake.snowpark.functions import col, udf
from snowflake.snowpark.types import IntegerType

square_number = udf(
    lambda x: x*x,
    return_type=IntegerType(),
    input_types=[IntegerType()],
    name="square_udf",
    replace=True
)
session.sql('select square_udf(5)').collect()[0]
```

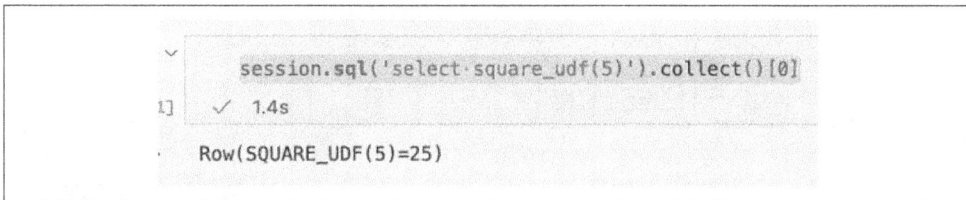

Figure 4-4. Results of calling an inline UDF

Snowflake ML

Snowflake ML (formerly known as Snowpark ML) is an integrated suite of tools to bring you an advanced toolkit within Snowflake for machine learning. It's like having a single platform with governed data where you can also perform end-to-end machine learning tasks without additional complexity.

For out-of-the-box machine learning use cases, Snowflake has built ready-to-use machine learning functions that are available in SQL. These ML functions are game-changers and provide a very low barrier to start with forecasting or anomaly detection use cases without having to write any code. The core purpose of these functions is to reduce the development time and make machine learning accessible for all.

But what if you need something more tailored? It is often the case that within machine learning workflows, ML engineers need to build a custom solution tailored to their needs, and for that, Snowflake offers custom ML workflows. A Python-based approach is used to perform machine learning tasks using the snowflake-ml-python library. It allows developers to build scalable and secure machine learning applications without moving any data around, reducing the overhead and silos. Isn't it exciting to be able to build a complete machine learning application in one place and enjoy all of the underlying Snowflake features like scalability, governance, and security?

The complete suite that Snowflake offers for ML goes beyond the snowflake-ml-python library. The Snowflake ML modeling API provides a wrapper around your favorite machine learning libraries from Python within Snowpark. You can load large datasets efficiently, do feature engineering, and train models using distributed workloads on CPUs or GPUs (graphics processing units). To move your ML model from the sandbox environment to production, Snowflake provides a Feature Store and a Model Registry, organized and accessible ways to develop machine learning applications. Snowflake ML is accessible to you through Snowsight UI, Snowflake Notebooks, or your favorite IDE.

To summarize, let's take a look at Figure 4-5, which shows Snowflake's ML ecosystem and where it comes into play.

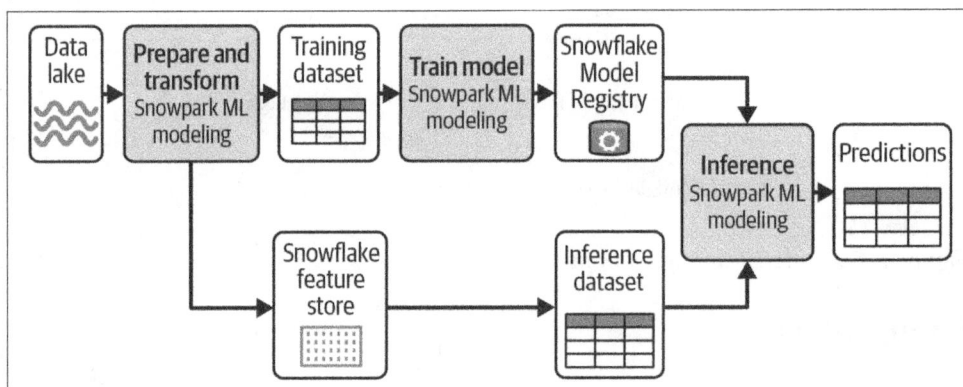

Figure 4-5. Snowflake ML components

In the following sections, I'll explain the components in a bit more detail.

Snowflake + Anaconda

Anaconda is an open source distribution of Python that is very famous among the data community. It takes away the pain of managing packages, software dependencies, and environments, which can become a nightmare quickly if you're working on several projects with shared dependencies. Anaconda comes with conda, a package manager that gives you the tools to install and maintain a curated set of packages and their dependencies.

Snowflake offers a selection of popular Python packages out of the box with Snowflake virtual warehouses without any additional cost. You have access to their packages in Snowsight, Snowflake Notebooks, and native applications. The complete list of packages provided by Anaconda in Snowflake can be found here (*https://oreil.ly/R0Oaq*). To be able to use the Anaconda packages within your Snowflake environment, your organization admin must enable them and accept the terms and conditions. In Figure 4-6, you can see the steps for how to find and enable it on your account.

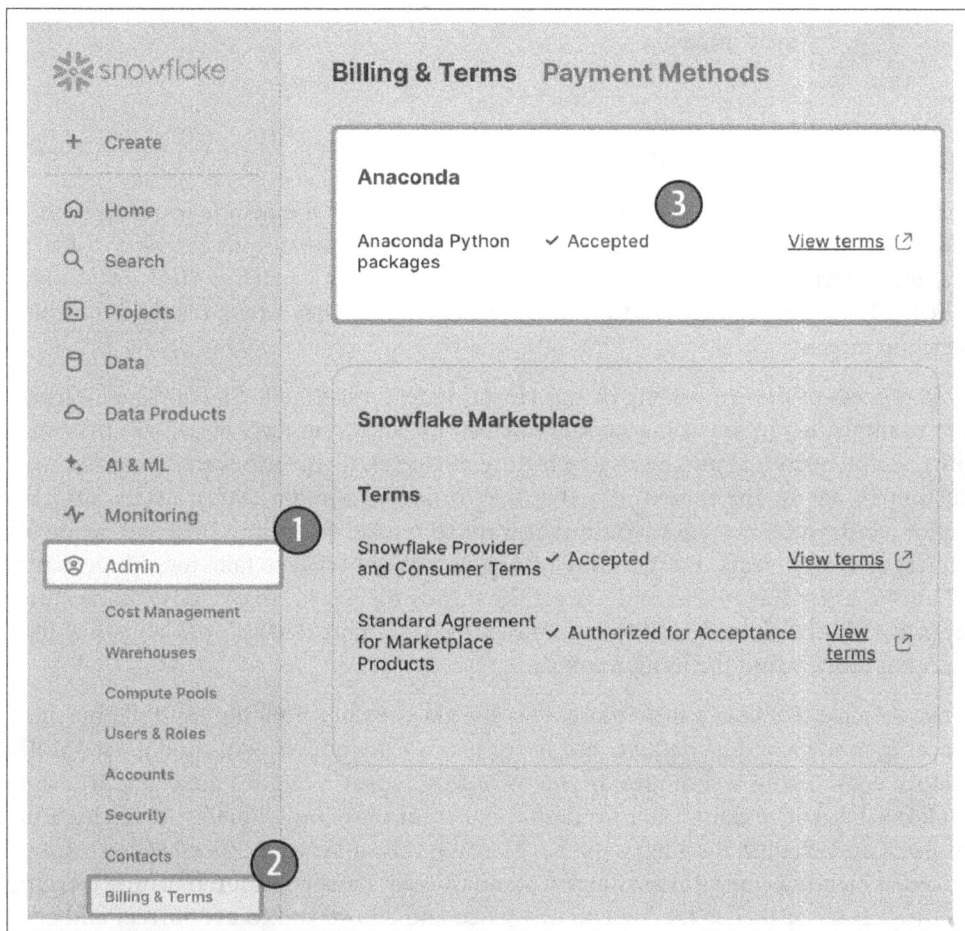

Figure 4-6. How to enable Anaconda packages

Here are the steps (see the Snowflake documentation (*https://oreil.ly/q4FEX*)):

1. Sign in to Snowsight.
2. Go to Admin → Billing & Terms.
3. In the Anaconda section, select Enable.

4. In the Anaconda Packages dialogue box, click the link to review the External Offerings Terms page (*https://oreil.ly/b-hdv*).

5. If you agree to the terms, select Acknowledge & Continue.

> Remember that if you want to use Python packages in a container for Snowflake Container Services, you will have to manually install them using pip.

Snowflake Feature Store

Machine learning features are simply the inputs given to a machine learning model. All the dataset columns that add value or contribute to the output can be considered features. Some features or inputs are given directly to a machine learning model, while others are preprocessed or transformed before they are given to a machine learning model.

This process of pre-processing or transforming features is called *feature engineering*. For example, if you are doing sales prediction for an ecommerce store, you may simply take the historical purchases as a feature; however, if you also want to consider the customer's age or the time of day that they order, you might want to transform the inputs. For customers' ages, you might want to bucket them into different segments of, let's say, 5–10 years. For the time of day, you might want to take the timestamp of when the order was placed and extract the day of the week, time of day, etc., features from it. All of this adds additional context to the input dataset and helps machine learning models find the hidden trends.

Now, to scale this idea a little more, you should consider building multiple machine learning models on one dataset, and in some of those models, you should use similar feature engineering techniques. If you were to discover a bug in one of the transformations that you're doing, you would have to enter those individual machine learning projects and change the buggy code. To solve this, a Feature Store has been introduced, which is a central repository of standardized, most common machine learning features. It encapsulates the logic in one place and allows you to use correct and consistent logic across your ecosystem, reducing bugs while maintaining the single source of truth (like a Git repo, but for ML features). The Snowflake Feature Store was designed while keeping these technicalities in mind. It helps create, store, and manage features for data science and machine learning workloads more efficiently, and since it's hosted natively within Snowflake, it enjoys all the perks of Snowflake's security, governance, scalability, etc.

A Snowflake Feature Store is simply a Snowflake schema containing *feature views*. A feature view is a logical collection of features (encapsulated code written in Python or SQL) containing all the transformations that are supposed to refresh on the same schedule. When you create a Feature Store in Snowflake, you dedicate a schema to it. Feature views within that schema are either managed by Snowflake or externally managed. I won't go through an externally managed Feature Store in this book.

The first concept of a Feature Store is an *entity*. An entity is a logical separation of everything within your Feature Store. Think of it as a bucket, so if you are an ecommerce store, there will be a bucket (entity) for customers, orders, products, etc. Entities also hold information on key columns you will use to join the data later on. Snowflake provides the following syntax for creating entities:

```python
from snowflake.ml.feature_store import Entity

entity = Entity(
    name="MY_ENTITY",
    join_keys=["UNIQUE_ID"],
    desc="my entity"
)

fs.register_entity(entity)
```

Let's walk through the parameters of an `Entity()`:

Name
:   This is the name of the entity (a unique identifier).

Join_key
:   This is the column that will be used to join the data.

Desc
:   This is a plain-text description of the entity for anyone using it.

Once entities are created, you can create feature views and assign them an entity.

Snowflake provides the following syntax for creating feature views:

```python
from snowflake.ml.feature_store import FeatureView

managed_fv = FeatureView(
    name="MY_MANAGED_FV",
    entities=[entity],
    feature_df=my_df,
    timestamp_col="ts",
    refresh_freq="5 minutes",
    desc="my managed feature view"
)
```

Now let's walk through the parameters of a `FeatureView()`:

Name
> This is the name of the feature view (a unique identifier).

Entity
> This is the name of the entity this feature view will go to (for logical separation only).

Feature_df
> This is a Snowpark DataFrame containing the transformations. (It can be a SQL query defined as a Snowpark DataFrame.)

Timestamp_col
> This is an optional parameter, but holds info if there is a timestamp column in the DataFrame.

Refresh_freq
> This is a `time delta` or `cron` expression that dictates how often this feature view should refresh.

Desc
> This is a plain text description of the feature view for anyone using it.

Once a feature view is created, you can register it within your Feature Store using the `register_feature_view` function. The syntax of the function is as follows:

```
from snowflake.ml.feature_store import FeatureStore

registered_fv: FeatureView = FeatureStore.register_feature_view(
    feature_view=managed_fv,
    version="1",
    block=True,
    overwrite=False,
)
```

The parameters of the functions are as follows:

feature_view
> This is the name of the feature view that is being registered.

version
> This is a version number to keep version control.

block
> This is a Boolean that dictates whether to block any calls to this feature view before it is first run.

`overwrite`
>
> This is a Boolean that decides whether to accept overwrites of this feature view in the Feature Store or not.

Now that we have the Feature Store ready, let's generate the dataset from it and perform machine learning tasks, which brings us to the next section, Snowflake datasets.

Snowflake Datasets

Snowflake datasets are specifically designed by Snowflake to support machine learning workflows. A Snowflake dataset is a version-controlled snapshot of your data with guaranteed immutability and an interface to famous machine learning frameworks like PyTorch or TensorFlow.

According to the Snowflake docs (*https://oreil.ly/ISsN9*), you should use Snowflake datasets in the following situations:

- You need to manage and version large datasets for reproducible machine learning model training and testing.
- You want to leverage Snowflake's scalable and secure data storage and processing capabilities.
- You need fine-grained file-level access and/or data shuffling for distributed training or data streaming.
- You need to integrate with external machine learning frameworks and tools.

The `generate_dataset()` function has the following syntax:

```
from snowflake.ml.feature_store import FeatureStore

ds = FeatureStore.generate_dataset(
    name="name",
    spine_df=spine_df,
    features=[f1, f2],
    version="1",
    spine_timestamp_col="timestamp_col",
    spine_label_cols=["label1", "label2"],
    desc="desc",
)
```

The parameters of the function are as follows:

`name`
>
> The name of the dataset to be generated. Datasets are uniquely identified within a schema by their name and version.

`spine_df`
>
> The Snowpark DataFrame to join features into.

features
:   A list of feature views that contain features to be joined.

version
:   The version of the dataset to be generated.

spine_timestamp_col
:   Identifier for the timestamp column in the DataFrame.

spine_label_cols
:   List of the names of the columns with labels.

desc
:   A description of this dataset.

Now that we have a dataset, let's look at how to register the models and what the Snowflake Model Registry is.

Snowflake Model Registry

After you've generated the Feature Store, created datasets, and trained machine learning models, you need a place to register the models, from which you can perform inferences. That is where the Snowflake Model Registry (sometimes called the Snowpark Model Registry) comes in.

The Snowflake Model Registry is a model management tool where you can securely store and manage your machine learning models. Using the Model Registry, you can also run inference in a distributed fashion, track model performance, and delegate role-based access.

I'll talk about machine learning inference in the following sections. A machine learning inference is simply the process of giving unseen data to the trained model and getting predictions or results from it. For example, imagine you have trained the machine learning model to detect whether there's a cat in an image, and you give it a new random image that it has not seen before and get the results from it.

The first step to working with the Snowflake Model Registry is to have the right privileges. You must be a schema owner to be able to create a new model in it. After you have the right privileges on a schema, you have to open up a new registry before you can register a new model in it. To open a new registry, use the following code:

```
from snowflake.ml.registry import Registry

reg = Registry(
    session=session,
    database_name="OREILLY_DB",
    schema_name="REGISTRY"
)
```

The parameters of the `Registry()` constructor are as follows:

`session`
> The active Snowpark session

`database_name`
> The name of the database where you want to open the new registry

`schema_name`
> The name of the schema where you want to open the new registry

Once you run this, you have created a registry in your desired database and schema. Now, the next step is to register a model within this registry. Here, assume that there's a machine learning model that exists; the following code will show how to register that within the registry.

> The following code uses the same `reg` variable from the preceding code. This is because we want to explicitly use the reference of the registry in Python to register the model within that registry. We do this by using the `log_model()` method, and logging is the same as registering a model. Snowflake provides the code in the docs (*https://oreil.ly/yoRkP*).

Let's have a look at the code:

```
from snowflake.ml.model import type_hints

mv = reg.log_model(
    model=clf,
    model_name="my_model",
    version_name="v1",
    conda_dependencies=["scikit-learn"],
    comment="My awesome ML model",
    metrics={"score": 96},
    sample_input_data=train_features,
    task=type_hints.Task.TABULAR_BINARY_CLASSIFICATION
)
```

The parameters of the `log_model()` method are as follows:

`model`
> A Python model object of any supported model type (scikit-learn, XGBoost, PyTorch, TensorFlow, etc.)

`model_name`
> A unique immutable identifier for the model

version_name
: Used with `model_name` to determine the version of the model

conda_dependencies
: A list of dependencies that the model depends upon

comment
: A description or an insightful comment about the model

metrics
: A dictionary having metrics for the model

sample_input_data
: A DataFrame containing some sample data that allows the model to infer features and their data types

task
: Takes an enum that defines what problem the model is tackling

Now that the model is registered, you can simply call the `get_model()` method to get the model and perform inference tasks. We will see that in action in a hands-on example in Chapter 6.

Hands-on Example 1: Connecting to a Snowpark Session

Let's start with our first hands-on example. In this example, I'll connect to Snowflake using a Snowpark session and query a table. Let's walk through this tutorial in a notebook, using Microsoft Visual Studio Code to create and manage it.

First, activate the conda session:

```
conda activate oreilly
```

Next, create a new Jupyter notebook to execute your code. The first step is to load the dependencies you will be using in this notebook:

```
from dotenv import load_dotenv
import os

from snowflake.snowpark import Session
```

Here, you load a `Session` from `snowflake.snowpark`, which will help to create a session and connect and interact with Snowflake. To connect to Snowflake, you need to provide the credentials, Snowflake warehouse, and context to Snowflake. To manage them securely, use an *.env* file to keep the credentials and `dotenv` and `os` packages to load them as environment variables. The contents of the *.env* file should look something like this:

```
# Snowflake credentials
SNOWFLAKE_USERNAME="USERNAME"
SNOWFLAKE_PASSWORD="PASSWORD"
SNOWFLAKE_ACCOUNT="ACCOUNT IDENTIFIER"
SNOWFLAKE_WAREHOUSE="WAREHOUSE"
SNOWFLAKE_DATABASE="DATABASE"
SNOWFLAKE_SCHEMA="SCHEMA"
SNOWFLAKE_ROLE="ROLE"
```

Always remember to list your *.env* file in *.gitignore* to avoid publishing sensitive credentials to your Git repository.

Now, to load these credentials and read environment variables in the notebook, you can use the following block of code:

```
load_dotenv()

SNOWFLAKE_USERNAME  = os.getenv("SNOWFLAKE_USERNAME")
SNOWFLAKE_PASSWORD  = os.getenv("SNOWFLAKE_PASSWORD")
SNOWFLAKE_ACCOUNT   = os.getenv("SNOWFLAKE_ACCOUNT")
SNOWFLAKE_WAREHOUSE = os.getenv("SNOWFLAKE_WAREHOUSE")
SNOWFLAKE_DATABASE  = os.getenv("SNOWFLAKE_DATABASE")
SNOWFLAKE_SCHEMA    = os.getenv("SNOWFLAKE_SCHEMA")
SNOWFLAKE_ROLE      = os.getenv("SNOWFLAKE_ROLE")

connection_parameters = {
    "user": SNOWFLAKE_USERNAME,
    "password": SNOWFLAKE_PASSWORD,
    "account": SNOWFLAKE_ACCOUNT,
    "warehouse": SNOWFLAKE_WAREHOUSE,
    "database": SNOWFLAKE_DATABASE,
    "schema": SNOWFLAKE_SCHEMA,
    "role": SNOWFLAKE_ROLE,
}
```

The first function, load_dotenv(), reads your *.env* file, and in the next steps, you load the environment variables in Python variables. Then, in the last step, you create a connection parameters dictionary that can be used for connecting with a Snowpark session. Now you have all the building blocks in place to create a new Snowpark session.

Run the following line to create a session:

```
session = Session.builder.configs(connection_parameters).create()
```

If you want to see the session variable details, you can simply print them, and the values should match what you have defined in your *.env* file:

```
print(session)

<snowflake.snowpark.session.Session: account="*****", role="OREILLY_ROLE",
database="OREILLY_DB", schema="OREILLY_SCHEMA", warehouse="COMPUTE_WH">
```

Use the `session.table(table_name)` function to read a table from Snowflake directly in Snowpark:

```
df = session.table("tpch_sf10_lineitem")
```

Is the data loaded in DataFrame at this point?

No. Remember that in the previous section, I explained that Snowpark is lazy and does not load or move any data unless there's a need to. You can define your code and transformations, and Snowpark will auto-optimize the data loading. We won't load all the columns and rows to reduce the data-loading overhead for the scope of this tutorial.

```
from snowflake.snowpark.functions import col

df = session.table("tpch_sf10_lineitem").select(
col("L_ORDERKEY"),
col("L_PARTKEY"),
col("L_LINENUMBER"),
col("L_QUANTITY"),
col("L_EXTENDEDPRICE"),
col("L_DISCOUNT"),
col("L_LINESTATUS")
)

# Apply filter
df_filtered = df.filter(
    (col("L_ORDERKEY") == 16200320) |
    (col("L_ORDERKEY") == 16200321)
)

# collect() method will trigger the execution of the query against
# Snowflake engine
results = df_filtered.collect()
```

The first section selects the table and the columns from the table. As you'll notice, we have imported the `col` function from the `snowflake.snowpark.functions` module and used it to select the columns. The section part applies the filter and selects two orders from the table. However, this line won't trigger the table run. To fetch the data, the `collect()` function can be used. In the last line, we will trigger the query execution. Let's now look at the results in Figure 4-7.

It's always good to clean up and close the session before leaving the notebook, which you can do by simply calling the `close()` function on the session variable:

```
session.close()
```

Now, if you run the following code again, you should see an error:

```
print(session)
```

```
SnowparkSessionException: (1404): Cannot perform this operation
because the session has been closed.
```

```
   results
 ✓ 0.0s

[Row(L_ORDERKEY=16200320, L_PARTKEY=1894542, L_LINENUMBER=1, L_QUANTITY=Decimal('14.00'),
 Row(L_ORDERKEY=16200320, L_PARTKEY=1557865, L_LINENUMBER=2, L_QUANTITY=Decimal('31.00'),
 Row(L_ORDERKEY=16200321, L_PARTKEY=1985456, L_LINENUMBER=1, L_QUANTITY=Decimal('11.00'),
 Row(L_ORDERKEY=16200321, L_PARTKEY=1552967, L_LINENUMBER=2, L_QUANTITY=Decimal('23.00'),
 Row(L_ORDERKEY=16200321, L_PARTKEY=715753, L_LINENUMBER=3, L_QUANTITY=Decimal('38.00'),
```

Figure 4-7. Results from Snowpark table read and filter

And that's it for the first tutorial. You will find the notebook with complete code in the book's GitHub repo (*https://oreil.ly/advanced-snowflake-repoch41*).

Hands-on Example 2: Creating UDFs Using Snowpark

Let's look into our second hands-on example now. In this example, I will connect to Snowflake using a Snowpark session, create some UDFs using Python, and then use them on my data. I will walk through this tutorial in a notebook, using Microsoft Visual Studio Code to create and manage them. You can easily follow this example using Snowflake notebooks.

The first steps are the same: activating your conda virtual environment, importing required packages, loading your *.env* file, and connecting to a Snowpark session.

In your terminal, activate the conda virtual environment:

```
conda activate oreilly
```

In a new Jupyter notebook, load the dependencies we will use in this notebook:

```
from dotenv import load_dotenv
import os

from snowflake.snowpark import Session
from snowflake.snowpark.functions import col
```

Load your *.env* file, create `connection_parameters`, and connect to a Snowpark session:

```
load_dotenv()

SNOWFLAKE_USERNAME  = os.getenv("SNOWFLAKE_USERNAME")
SNOWFLAKE_PASSWORD  = os.getenv("SNOWFLAKE_PASSWORD")
SNOWFLAKE_ACCOUNT   = os.getenv("SNOWFLAKE_ACCOUNT")
SNOWFLAKE_WAREHOUSE = os.getenv("SNOWFLAKE_WAREHOUSE")
SNOWFLAKE_DATABASE  = os.getenv("SNOWFLAKE_DATABASE")
SNOWFLAKE_SCHEMA    = os.getenv("SNOWFLAKE_SCHEMA")
```

```
SNOWFLAKE_ROLE        = os.getenv("SNOWFLAKE_ROLE")

connection_parameters = {
    "user": SNOWFLAKE_USERNAME,
    "password": SNOWFLAKE_PASSWORD,
    "account": SNOWFLAKE_ACCOUNT,
    "warehouse": SNOWFLAKE_WAREHOUSE,
    "database": SNOWFLAKE_DATABASE,
    "schema": SNOWFLAKE_SCHEMA,
    "role": SNOWFLAKE_ROLE,
}
session = Session.builder.configs(connection_parameters).create()
print(session)

<snowflake.snowpark.session.Session:
account="*****", role="OREILLY_ROLE",
database="OREILLY_DB",
schema="OREILLY_SCHEMA",
warehouse="COMPUTE_WH">

# Query the lineitem table in TPCH_SF10 schema from Snowflake Sample Data
# Select a few columns from the lineitem table
# Filter the results only for L_ORDERKEY = 199

df = session.table("tpch_sf10_lineitem").select(
col("L_ORDERKEY"),
col("L_PARTKEY"),
col("L_LINENUMBER"),
col("L_QUANTITY"),
col("L_EXTENDEDPRICE"),
col("L_DISCOUNT"),
col("L_LINESTATUS")
)

# Apply filter
df_filtered = df.filter(
(col("L_ORDERKEY") == 16200320) |
(col("L_ORDERKEY") == 16200321)
)

# The collect() method will trigger the execution of the query against
# Snowflake engine
results = df_filtered
```

Now that you have successfully connected to a Snowpark session and loaded the data, let's see your options for UDFs. Note the important difference in the last line: I didn't use the collect() method because I didn't want to process any data at this point. I can be lazy!

There are three primary UDFs you can define in Snowpark: anonymous UDFs, named temporary UDFs, and named permanent UDFs.

Anonymous UDFs

Let's have a look at anonymous UDFs first. Anonymous UDFs, as the name suggests, are anonymous functions that can be assigned to a variable. Such UDFs are available while your variable is in scope. In the following code, you can see how to define an anonymous UDF and how to call it. In this example, we will create a UDF that takes the quantity and price as inputs and returns the total price (quantity * price) as an output.

The first step is to fix our imports. The first import, udf, will help create UDFs, and the second one will help define input and output variables:

```
from snowflake.snowpark.functions import udf
from snowflake.snowpark.types import IntegerType, DecimalType
```

Now, let's define the anonymous UDF and assign it to a variable:

```
def total_price(qty:int, price:float) -> float:
    return qty * price

total_price_var = udf(
    func=total_price,
    return_type=DecimalType(),
    input_types=[IntegerType(), FloatType()]
)
```

Great—as you see, we have defined a function named total_price, which takes a quantity as an integer and price as a float and returns a float by multiplying both values. Later, we call the UDF() constructor and give it the function return_types and input_types. Note that we don't have any name for this UDF (because it is anonymous!). Let's see how we can use it now:

```
results.select(
    col("L_ORDERKEY"),
    col("L_LINENUMBER"),
    col("L_QUANTITY"),
    col("L_EXTENDEDPRICE"),
    call_udf("total_price_temp_udf",
            [col("L_QUANTITY"), col("L_EXTENDEDPRICE")]
        ).alias("TOTAL_PRICE")
).show()
```

That's it. The last line in the select function calls the UDF() and gives it the input variables, and renames the output to TOTAL_PRICE. Figure 4-8 shows the results of the code.

```
--------------------------------------------------------------------------------------
|"L_ORDERKEY"  |"L_LINENUMBER"  |"L_QUANTITY"  |"L_EXTENDEDPRICE"  |"TOTAL_PRICE"  |
--------------------------------------------------------------------------------------
|16200320      |1               |14.00         |21510.30           |301140         |
|16200320      |2               |31.00         |59606.49           |1847786        |
|16200321      |1               |11.00         |16954.96           |186505         |
|16200321      |2               |23.00         |46457.47           |1068511        |
|16200321      |3               |38.00         |67211.36           |2554018        |
--------------------------------------------------------------------------------------
```

Figure 4-8. Result of calling the anonymous UDF from Python

The last column, TOTAL_PRICE, is a multiplication done by the UDF of the L_QUAN
TITY and L_EXTENDEDPRICE columns.

> Think float. The solution is shared in "Anonymous UDF Solution"
> on page 92 at the end of this hands-on example, but I really want
> you to give it a try before taking a peek there.
>
> The decimals are truncated. Why do you think that is? This is a
> good point to stop and think about what's going on in the back-
> ground to cause TOTAL_PRICE to be without decimal points, and try
> fixing it.

Named Temporary UDFs

Let's have a look at named temporary UDFs now. They're different from anonymous
UDFs, as you can create them as functions using the decorator @udf. Now that they
have a name, they can also be called from the call_udf() function in the functions
module of Snowpark.

Let's see how they work. In the following example, I will create the same UDF as we
created in the anonymous UDF example, but now it is named:

```
total_price_temp_udf_var = udf(
    lambda x, y: x*y,
    return_type=DecimalType(),
    input_types=[IntegerType(), DecimalType()],
    name="total_price_temp_udf",
)
```

I have defined the UDF simply as a Python lambda function, and similar to the
anonymous UDF, I have added return_type and input_types. However, this time,
there's a new field, name, which defines the unique name of the UDF. You can also add
replace=True at the end; if you add replace=True then it will overwrite the existing
UDF. If you try creating a UDF in the same Snowflake context with the same name, it
will give you an error, which holds for a Snowpark session as well. Let's see how to
call it using the call_udf() function:

```
# Import the call_udf function from Snowpark functions module
from snowflake.snowpark.functions import call_udf

results.select(
    col("L_ORDERKEY"),
    col("L_LINENUMBER"),
    col("L_QUANTITY"),
    col("L_EXTENDEDPRICE"),
    call_udf("total_price_temp_udf",
        [col("L_QUANTITY"), col("L_EXTENDEDPRICE")]).alias("TOTAL_PRICE")
).show()
```

Note how I used `call_udf()` in the last line this time instead of the variable. The following block shows the result of the preceding statement, and Figure 4-10 shows that Snowflake did not create any object in the database, as the temporary UDF is session-scoped. If there were an object, we would see a new section called Functions in Figure 4-9.

```
-----------------------------------------------------------------------------------------------
|"L_ORDERKEY"   |"L_LINENUMBER"   |"L_QUANTITY"   |"L_EXTENDEDPRICE"   |"TOTAL_PRICE"   |
-----------------------------------------------------------------------------------------------
|16200320       |1                |14.00          |21510.30            |301140          |
|16200320       |2                |31.00          |59606.49            |1847786         |
|16200321       |1                |11.00          |16954.96            |186505          |
|16200321       |2                |23.00          |46457.47            |1068511         |
|16200321       |3                |38.00          |67211.36            |2554018         |
-----------------------------------------------------------------------------------------------
```

Figure 4-9. Result of running the Named Temporary UDF in Python

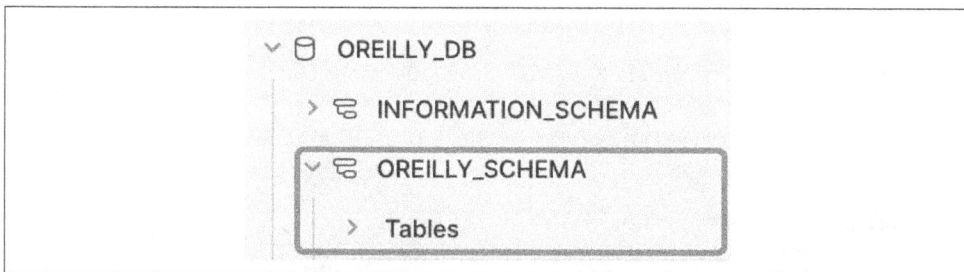

Figure 4-10. No permanent UDF object in the database

Named Permanent UDFs

This brings us to the last type of UDF, a named permanent UDF. It is defined in the same way as the temporary named UDF, but with two differences:

- We have to explicitly state that it is permanent.
- We have to define a location (stage) to host the UDF.

Now, the logical next step is to create a stage in Snowflake. Let's do that first:

```
# Create a stage if it doesn't already exist
session.sql("create stage if not exists oreilly_stage").show()
```

The stage should be created now. Hop over to your Snowflake instance and have a look at it. Figure 4-11 shows what it will look like in your Snowflake instance.

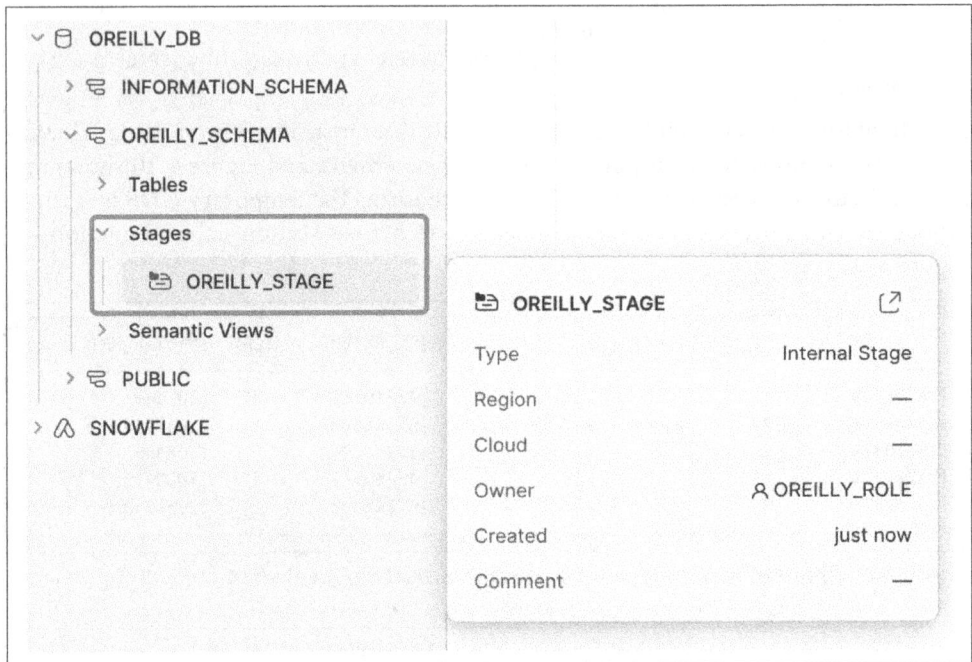

Figure 4-11. Creating the `OREILLY_STAGE` in the Snowflake UI

Now that the stage is created, we can create our UDF and save it. Let's see how to do it:

```
total_price_permanent_udf_var = udf(
    lambda x, y: x*y,
    return_type=DecimalType(),
    input_types=[IntegerType(), DecimalType()],
    name="total_price_permanent_udf",
    replace=True,
    is_permanent=True,
    stage_location="@oreilly_stage",
)
```

We added three new lines: replace=True, is_permanent=True, and stage_location. is_permanent tells the UDF function that it is a permanent UDF and to save it in the defined stage_location. If you run it as you ran the temporary named UDF, you will see results similar to Figure 4-12:

```
results.select(
    col("L_ORDERKEY"),
    col("L_LINENUMBER"),
    col("L_QUANTITY"),
    col("L_EXTENDEDPRICE"),
    call_udf("total_price_permanent_udf",
        [col("L_QUANTITY"), col("L_EXTENDEDPRICE")]
    ).alias("TOTAL_PRICE_NAMED_UDF") ).show()
```

```
---------------------------------------------------------------------------------------------
|"L_ORDERKEY"  |"L_LINENUMBER"|"L_QUANTITY"|"L_EXTENDEDPRICE"|"TOTAL_PRICE_NAMED_UDF"|
---------------------------------------------------------------------------------------------
|16200320      |1             |14.00       |21510.30         |301140                 |
|16200320      |2             |31.00       |59606.49         |1847786                |
|16200321      |1             |11.00       |16954.96         |186505                 |
|16200321      |2             |23.00       |46457.47         |1068511                |
|16200321      |3             |38.00       |67211.36         |2554018                |
---------------------------------------------------------------------------------------------
```

Figure 4-12. Result of running the Named Permanent UDF in Python

You will also see this pop up in your Snowflake instance. Figure 4-13 shows how your Snowflake UI will show it.

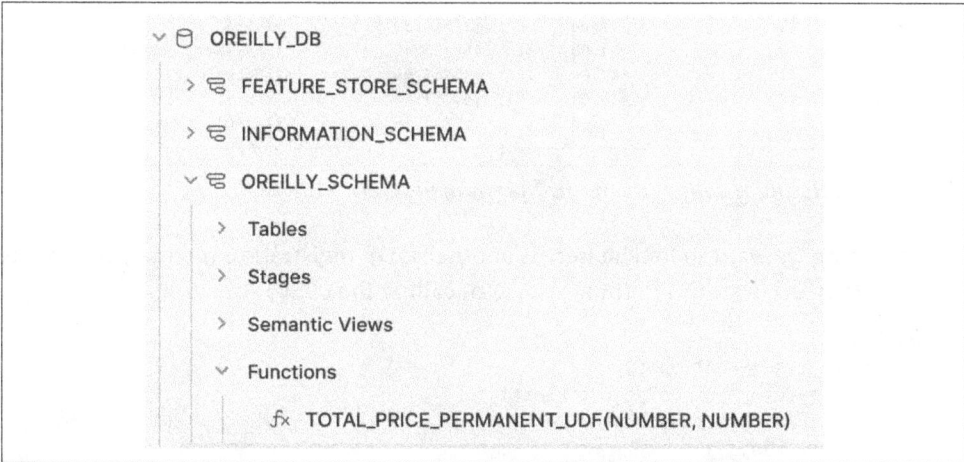

Figure 4-13. Snowflake UI showing a UDF created through Snowpark

You can also call this function in SQL and get the same results (shown in Figure 4-14):

```
session.sql("""
    SELECT
        L_ORDERKEY,
        L_LINENUMBER,
        L_QUANTITY,
        L_EXTENDEDPRICE,
```

```
        TOTAL_PRICE_PERMANENT_UDF(
            L_QUANTITY,
            L_EXTENDEDPRICE
        ) AS TOTAL_PRICE_NAMED_UDF
    FROM TPCH_SF10_LINEITEM
    WHERE
        L_ORDERKEY = 16200320
        OR L_ORDERKEY = 16200321
""").show()
```

```
    session.sql("""
        SELECT
            L_ORDERKEY,
            L_LINENUMBER,
            L_QUANTITY,
            L_EXTENDEDPRICE,
            TOTAL_PRICE_PERMANENT_UDF(L_QUANTITY, L_EXTENDEDPRICE) AS TOTAL_PRICE_NAMED_UDF
        FROM TPCH_SF10_LINEITEM
        WHERE L_ORDERKEY = 16200320 OR L_ORDERKEY = 16200321
    """).show()
```
✓ 1.3s   Python

```
|"L_ORDERKEY"  |"L_LINENUMBER"  |"L_QUANTITY"  |"L_EXTENDEDPRICE"  |"TOTAL_PRICE_NAMED_UDF"  |
-----------------------------------------------------------------------------------------------
|16200320      |1               |14.00         |21510.30           |301140                   |
|16200320      |2               |31.00         |59606.49           |1847786                  |
|16200321      |1               |11.00         |16954.96           |186505                   |
|16200321      |2               |23.00         |46457.47           |1068511                  |
|16200321      |3               |38.00         |67211.36           |2554018                  |
-----------------------------------------------------------------------------------------------
```

Figure 4-14. Result of calling the named permanent UDF from SQL

The last thing we want to look at here is another UDF registration method, and that is using an @udf decorator in Python instead of calling the UDF() function:

```
@udf(
    return_type=FloatType(),
    input_types=[IntegerType(), FloatType()],
    name="total_price_decorator_udf",
    replace=True,
    is_permanent=True,
    stage_location="@oreilly_stage")
def total_price_decorator(qty:int, price:float) -> float:
    return qty * price
```

The preceding code defines the UDF like we defined it before, but in a decorator @udf, and it is followed by a Python function, total_price_decorator, that will trigger when this UDF is called. A new function should appear in your Snowflake UI now, as shown in Figure 4-15.

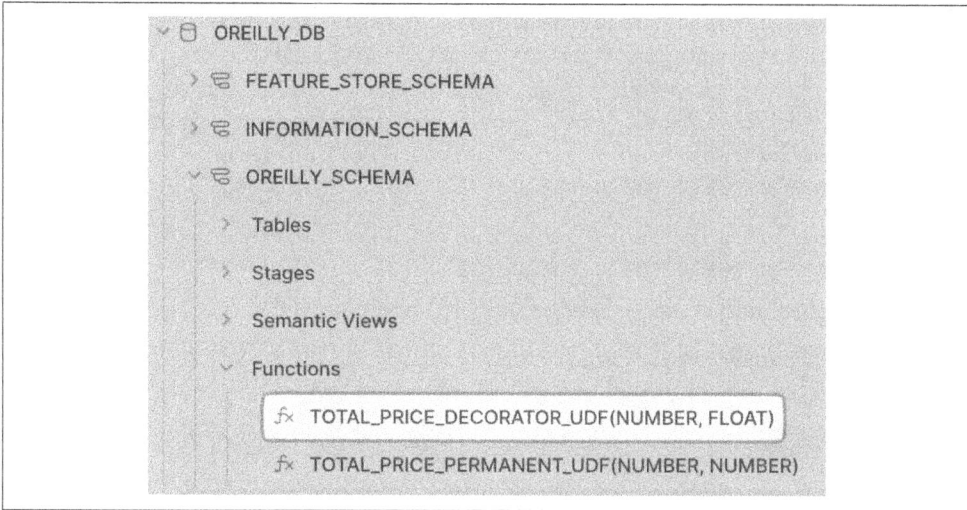

Figure 4-15. UDF created using a decorator in the Snowflake UI

You can call it in the same way as you did for the named permanent UDF, and the results should be the same (as shown in Figure 4-16):

```
results.select(
    col("L_ORDERKEY"),
    col("L_LINENUMBER"),
    col("L_QUANTITY"),
    col("L_EXTENDEDPRICE"),
    call_udf("total_price_decorator_udf",
                [col("L_QUANTITY"), col("L_EXTENDEDPRICE")]
            ).alias("TOTAL_PRICE_NAMED_UDF")
).show()
```

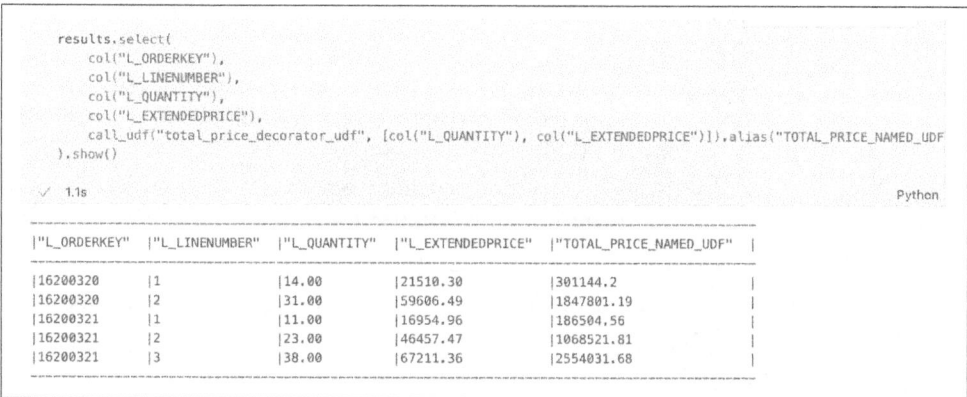

Figure 4-16. Result of calling the named permanent UDF created using the decorator

If you want to go even further, Snowflake now supports creating UDFs using Python source files, and also using third-party packages. I will not be covering those two topics in this book, but if you want to read more, head over to the Snowflake documentation (*https://oreil.ly/OsY83*), which provides a good overview of the latest and greatest info in the realm of Snowpark UDFs. You will find the notebook with complete code in the book's GitHub repo (*https://oreil.ly/advanced-snowflake-repo*).

Anonymous UDF Solution

Here is the solution to the little riddle from "Anonymous UDFs" on page 85:

```
from snowflake.snowpark.functions import udf
from snowflake.snowpark.types import IntegerType, FloatType

def total_price(qty:int, price:float) -> float:
    return qty * price

total_price_var = udf(
    func=total_price,
    return_type=FloatType(),
    input_types=[IntegerType(), FloatType()]
)

results.select(
    col("L_ORDERKEY"),
    col("L_LINENUMBER"),
    col("L_QUANTITY"),
    col("L_EXTENDEDPRICE"),
    total_price_var(col("L_QUANTITY"), col("L_EXTENDEDPRICE")).alias("TOTAL_PRICE")
).show()
```

Summary

In this chapter, I walked you through Snowpark—a different way to interact with your data in Snowflake. You learned what Snowpark is, what its advantages are, how it can be used, and its key components. Following that, you looked at Snowflake ML and how you can use the whole ML offering from Snowflake to make your ML workloads more efficient. Lastly, you looked at two hands-on examples and saw how to practically use Snowpark to create reusable functions written in Python and deploy them to Snowflake.

Next, I will show you the tools Snowflake provides to package it all up and build an app. Let's move on to Chapter 5.

Snowflake Developer Ecosystem and Native Application Framework

Snowflake started as a cloud data warehouse but has steadily evolved into a comprehensive data cloud platform. This evolution includes robust support for developers seeking to take the platform's capabilities to the next level. The Snowflake developer ecosystem provides support for exactly that. It encompasses various tools, interfaces, and frameworks designed to enable developers to build sophisticated data applications and services.

At the heart of the Snowflake developer ecosystem is the recognition that data applications work best when they operate close to the data they process. The traditional approach of extracting data from storage environments to process it in separate application servers introduced latency, security risks, and operational complexity. The Snowflake developer ecosystem aims to eliminate these issues by providing mechanisms for running application code directly within the Snowflake environment.

This chapter explores the Snowflake developer ecosystem and Snowflake Native Application Framework from multiple perspectives—from understanding the broader developer ecosystem and the technical aspects of application development to the processes of publishing and consuming these applications. You will also see how Streamlit integration enhances the framework by enabling interactive data applications with minimal coding effort, and I provide practical guidance on deploying Streamlit applications within the Snowflake environment.

Core Components of the Developer Ecosystem

The Snowflake developer ecosystem consists of several components that, at their core, are developed to simplify different aspects of building with Snowflake. Whether it's the applications you're building or internal tooling, it provides you with the toolset you need to take your Snowflake game to the next level.

Snowpark

As I covered in Chapter 4, Snowpark is a developer framework that brings data processing closer to the data through DataFrame-style programming in languages like Java, Scala, and Python. Snowpark enables developers to write code in their preferred languages while executing operations within Snowflake's processing engine.

User-Defined Functions

As I covered in Chapter 4, UDFs extend Snowflake's built-in functionality with custom code written in SQL, JavaScript, Java, Python, and other supported languages. UDFs can be used to implement specialized business logic, complex calculations, or integration with external services.

Stored Procedures

Stored procedures help developers to package and execute procedural code within Snowflake, supporting transaction control, error handling, and complex multistep operations.

External Functions

External functions provide a mechanism for calling functions that are hosted outside of Snowflake securely from within Snowflake queries, enabling integration with external services and systems.

Native Application Framework

The Native Application Framework builds upon these foundational components to enable full-fledged applications that run entirely within the Snowflake environment, complete with user interfaces, persistent storage, and lifecycle management.

Developer Tools

Snowflake complements its core components by providing several developer tools to make its offering more holistic.

Snowflake CLI

Snowflake CLI is an open source command-line tool designed for developer workflows and SQL operations, offering flexibility to support modern development practices across various Snowflake technologies. It enables developers to create, manage, and monitor apps running on Snowflake across multiple workloads while supporting features like user-defined functions, stored procedures, and SQL execution.

Figure 5-1 shows the official Snowflake CLI GitHub repository (*https://oreil.ly/uceus*).

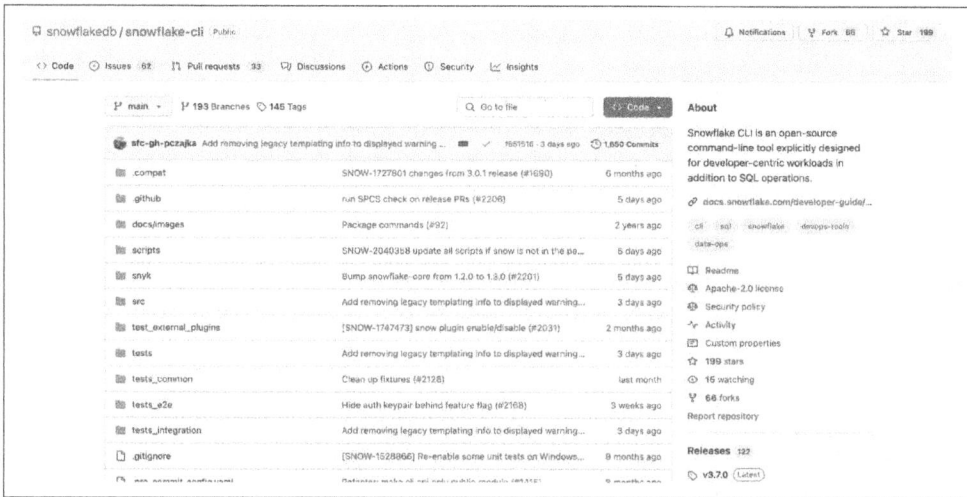

Figure 5-1. Official GitHub repository page for Snowflake CLI

VS Code extension

The VS Code extension for Snowflake allows you to create and run Snowflake SQL queries directly within Visual Studio Code. Additionally, it works with Snowpark Python to deliver features like debugging, syntax highlighting, and autocomplete functionality for SQL embedded in Python code.

Figure 5-2 shows the welcome page of the VS Code extension.

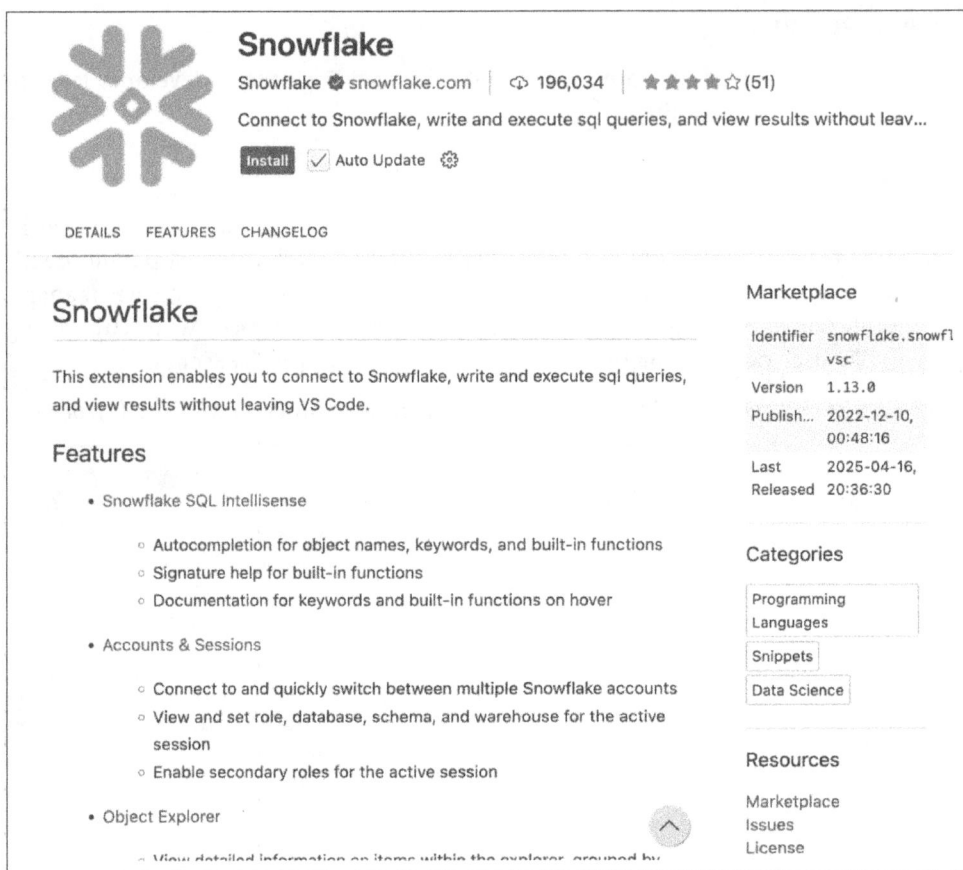

Figure 5-2. Welcome page of the Snowflake VS Code extension

Snowflake web interface (Snowsight)

As you saw in Chapter 1, Snowsight is a browser-based development environment for SQL development, data visualization, and application management, making it easier for everyone to visually track all their Snowflake data products in one place.

Snowflake Marketplace

The Snowflake Marketplace is a managed marketplace platform for exploring, accessing, and discovering third-party data and services. Additionally, it allows Snowflake developers to market their data products throughout the Snowflake Data Cloud.

This rich ecosystem forms the foundation upon which the Snowflake developer ecosystem is built, providing developers with the tools, resources, and community support needed to create innovative data applications. Let's now dive deeper into the Snowflake Native Application Framework.

Snowflake Native Application Framework

The Snowflake Native Application Framework represents a paradigm shift in how data applications are built, distributed, and consumed. This framework eliminates the traditional separation between data storage and application logic by enabling developers to create applications that run entirely within the Snowflake Data Cloud. Instead of extracting data from Snowflake to process it elsewhere, Native Apps bring computation directly to where the data resides, preserving security boundaries and dramatically simplifying deployment. This opens up new possibilities for leveraging Snowflake's capabilities: from building applications to deploying them and sharing them with others using Snowflake Marketplace, all without managing complex integrations, architecture, and data movement. Developers gain a powerful medium to showcase their work directly to Snowflake's growing customer base, with built-in mechanisms for deployment, security, and monetization.

Developing applications for the Snowflake Native Application Framework requires understanding its unique architecture. Unlike traditional applications that run on separate infrastructure and access data through APIs or connectors, Native Apps run entirely within Snowflake's environment, directly accessing data through Snowflake's security and governance mechanisms.

The core building block of a Snowflake application is an *application package*. An application package is a container for all the components that make up a Native App, including code, configuration, and dependencies. The core components for the application package are as follows:

Manifest file
> This is a YAML file that defines the configuration and setup properties required by the application, including the location of the setup script, versions, etc.

Setup script
> This is a collection of SQL statements that are run when a consumer installs or upgrades the application. The path to the setup script is defined in the *manifest.yml* file.

Project definition file
> The Snowflake CLI relies on a configuration file called *snowflake.yml* that defines deployable Snowflake objects. This mandatory file determines the application package name and object specifications, and identifies which files should be uploaded to the project stage.

For details on how to create the manifest file and setup script, please refer to the Snowflake documentation (*https://oreil.ly/L01aC*).

Snowpark Container Services

Snowpark Container Services (SPCS) represents Snowflake's strategic approach to solving the data gravity problem that has long plagued enterprise data architectures. Rather than forcing organizations to choose between the flexibility of containerized applications and data proximity, this fully managed service enables containerized workloads to execute directly within the Snowflake ecosystem, eliminating the architectural complexity and performance penalties associated with cross-platform data movement. At this point, you might have realized that everything Snowflake is building is to keep all the bits and pieces around the data in one place, so you don't have to manage the complex architectures or operational overhead to bring your data apps to life. Snowpark Container Services does just that.

Fundamentals of Snowpark Container Services

The fundamental design principle behind Snowpark Container Services centers on eliminating the traditional boundaries between data storage and compute execution. Unlike conventional container orchestration platforms such as Docker (Swarm) or Kubernetes that operate as separate infrastructure layers, Snowpark Container Services provides an Open Container Initiative (OCI)-compliant runtime environment that is natively integrated with Snowflake's data platform. This integration extends beyond simple connectivity, i.e., containerized applications gain direct access to Snowflake's elastic scale and governance, can execute SQL queries, and can seamlessly access data files stored in Snowflake stages. Traditional hybrid architectures, where containers running on external platforms access Snowflake data, introduced additional security boundaries and compliance complexities. By executing containers within Snowflake's governance perimeter, organizations can maintain consistent access control policies and data protection mechanisms without the need for complex cross-platform security configurations. This extends to Snowflake's role-based access control (RBAC) system, ensuring that containerized applications inherit the same data access permissions as the user or service account under which they execute. The result is a unified security model that reduces the surface area for potential vulnerabilities while simplifying compliance reporting and audit procedures.

SPCS doesn't reinvent the wheel of how containerized applications work, but instead provides a familiar environment to the developers. The teams can continue using familiar tools like Docker for image creation and management, but benefit from Snowflake's managed infrastructure for runtime execution. This approach preserves the flexibility that makes containers attractive while eliminating the need for specialized platform engineering expertise. Congratulations to the readers with a DevOps background—you now have one less thing to worry about from your data teams.

Executing Containers on Snowpark Container Services

Running containerized applications in Snowpark Container Services introduces several new object types that extend Snowflake's traditional database and warehouse model. Understanding how these components work together is essential for effectively deploying and managing containerized workloads within the Snowflake ecosystem.

At the foundation of container deployment lies Snowflake's *image registry*, which provides an OCI-compliant service for storing container images directly within your Snowflake account. This approach eliminates the need for external container registries, ensuring that your application images remain within Snowflake's governance boundary. The registry supports standard OCI clients, meaning development teams can continue using familiar tools like Docker CLI or SnowSQL to manage their container images without needing to learn new tooling or workflows. The integration with existing Docker workflows enables the use of the same build processes and CI/CD (continuous integration and continuous delivery) pipelines that create container images for other platforms to populate Snowflake repositories.

Once container images are available in the registry, they can be executed through two distinct runtime models that serve different operational patterns. The *service model* provides long-running execution similar to traditional web services. These services continue running indefinitely until explicitly stopped, and Snowflake takes care of restarting any containers that exit unexpectedly. This model enables real-time data applications to use SPCS where availability is of utmost importance. The second one is the *job service model*, which, as the name suggests, follows a batch processing pattern—think of stored procedures or scheduled tasks. Tasks are executed for a limited time duration, and they will automatically terminate when their work is complete. This pattern enables use cases like machine learning model training, data transformation jobs, or any computational task with a clearly defined trigger or start and end. The choice between service and job service models depends on your use case, whether you need availability, or if your task is one-off.

Now that you have the container registered and have made your choice of how to run it, it's time to throw some compute at it, and we do that using *compute pools*. SPCS is executed within compute pools. Compute pools represent a collection of virtual machine (VM) nodes allocated for container execution. These compute pools are configurable, and you can select a specific machine type depending on the compute power you need and whether you need a GPU or not. The pool configuration includes both minimum and maximum node counts, enabling automatic scaling based on workload demands, all while maintaining cost control through defined upper bounds. You can choose to run multiple containers within the same compute pools. Still, the real beauty when running business-critical containers is to separate their compute pool so those resources are reserved for those applications.

Now that everything is set, i.e., the registry, the choice of how to serve the container, and the compute pool, you have everything you need to succeed with your containers. You can now write applications that have access to your Snowflake data or applications that have external API access and get data from other sources. It's an empty canvas for you to bring your magic to life.

> I highly recommend that you keep an eye on the Snowflake documentation (*https://oreil.ly/QbmCW*) to see what's the latest and greatest on SPCS. Also, Snowpark Container Services are not available for trial accounts except for running notebooks, so don't sweat it if you can't access it with your trial account. To get started with the SPCS, Snowflake has one of the best guides (*https://oreil.ly/aLYCl*), which provides the standard setup you need.

Figure 5-3 shows a summary of Snowpark Container Services.

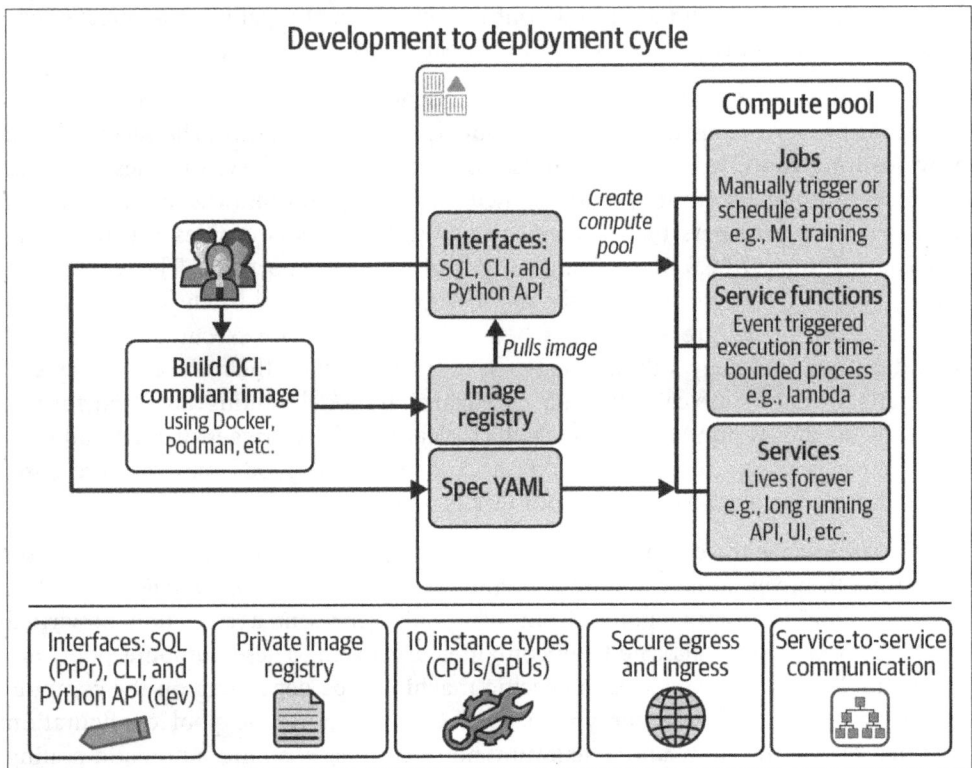

Figure 5-3. Summarizing Snowpark Container Services

Streamlit in Snowflake

Streamlit has revolutionized how data scientists and analysts share their work by turning Python scripts into interactive web applications with just a few lines of code. No more HTML, CSS, or JavaScript required. What once required a full-stack development team to build a dashboard for executives or a demo for stakeholders can now be accomplished by a single data professional. In 2022, Snowflake acquired Streamlit. Streamlit's integration in Snowflake represents one of the most powerful features of the Snowflake Native Application Framework, enabling developers to create interactive data applications with minimal coding effort. This section explores how Streamlit enhances the Native Application experience.

Streamlit in Snowflake is a powerful integration that brings Streamlit's intuitive application development framework directly into the Snowflake Data Cloud environment. This allows data professionals to build interactive, data-driven applications entirely within Snowflake, eliminating the need for external hosting or complex infrastructure management. Talk about truly doing it all in one place. This integration allows developers to write Streamlit applications in Python and deploy them directly within Snowflake. Now, your data apps sit closer to your data, in the same environment and security context, without the extra overhead of external connections.

> As long as the Streamlit app is running, even if it is idle, up to the timeout, it is associated with a background query and incurs compute costs.

When Snowflake announced integration with Streamlit, it created waves in the data community, and rightly so. There are several advantages of having it all in one place:

Simplified development workflow
Developers can create interactive dashboards and applications using familiar Python syntax. Streamlit allows for rapid application development with immediate visual feedback.

Zero data movement
Traditional analytics workflows required extracting data from Snowflake to external systems for visualization and sharing. Streamlit in Snowflake eliminates this data movement by running applications directly where the data resides, improving security and performance.

Native Snowflake integration
Applications have direct access to Snowflake data through the Snowpark Python API, inheriting all the features from Snowflake, including the security model, governance controls, and scalability. This means applications automatically

respect existing data access controls and can scale infinitely with the powerful Snowflake engine underneath.

Simplified deployment and sharing
Streamlit applications can be deployed and shared with a few simple commands, without configuring servers, containers, or any other cloud infrastructure. Once deployed, applications can be easily shared with anyone who has appropriate Snowflake access.

Rapid prototyping
Data teams can prototype their ideas quickly and transform those analyses into interactive applications that business users can explore independently, bridging the gap between data and business stakeholders.

Let's have a quick look at how you can create a Streamlit app from the existing Snowflake data. First things first: like everything in Snowflake, you need to have proper permissions, and we will be creating a new schema for this exercise. In your main Snowflake account, where you have access to the ACCOUNTADMIN or SECURITYADMIN role, run the following code. The code is also present in the GitHub repo (*https://oreil.ly/advanced-snowflake-repoch51*):

```
USE ROLE OREILLY_ROLE;
CREATE SCHEMA IF NOT EXISTS OREILLY_DB.OREILLY_STREAMLIT_SCHEMA;

USE ROLE ACCOUNTADMIN;
GRANT CREATE STREAMLIT
        ON SCHEMA OREILLY_DB.OREILLY_STREAMLIT_SCHEMA TO ROLE OREILLY_ROLE;
GRANT CREATE STAGE
        ON SCHEMA OREILLY_DB.OREILLY_STREAMLIT_SCHEMA TO ROLE OREILLY_ROLE;
```

We need a CREATE STREAMLIT grant to allow our OREILLY_ROLE to create a STREAMLIT object in the chosen schema. Once this is done, you can navigate to the Projects section in the sidebar on Snowsight and choose Streamlit using your OREILLY user account. Click on the "+ Streamlit App" button on the top right, and it will open the pop-up shown in Figure 5-4.

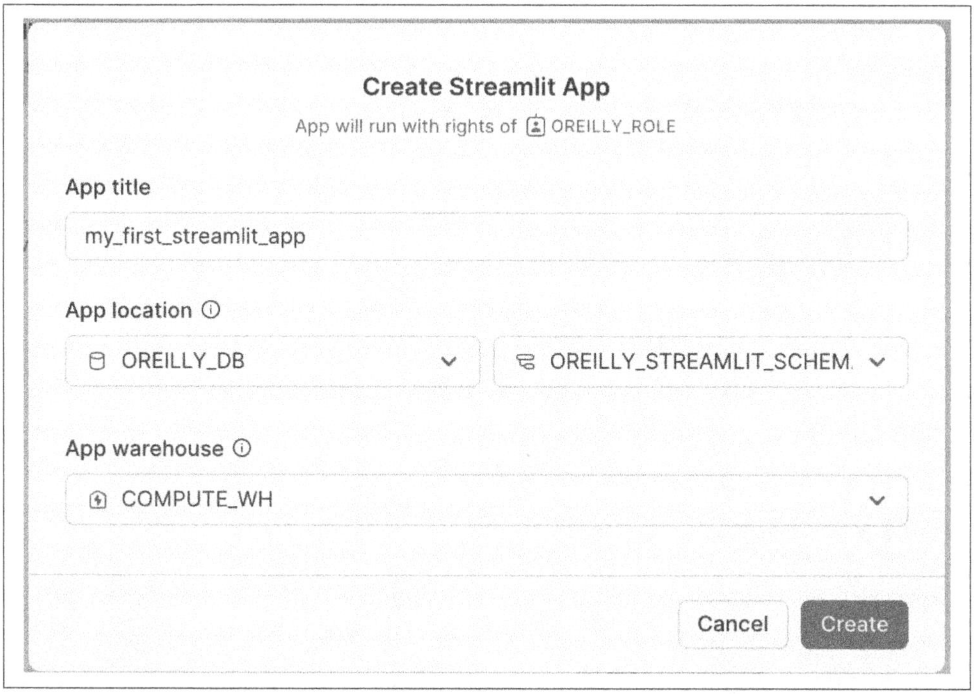

Create Streamlit App

App will run with rights of 🔲 OREILLY_ROLE

App title

my_first_streamlit_app

App location ⓘ

🗄 OREILLY_DB   ⌄   🗟 OREILLY_STREAMLIT_SCHEM. ⌄

App warehouse ⓘ

⬆ COMPUTE_WH   ⌄

Cancel   Create

Figure 5-4. Pop-up to create a new Streamlit app

Fill in the name for your Streamlit app, choose a location and a warehouse, and click Create. It will then create a Streamlit app for you with pre-filled template code that can help you get started. Note the "App location" in Figure 5-4; we have added our new schema (it should automatically appear in the drop-down menu).

Once it's done, you need to add the packages we need to use in our app from the Packages tab, but in our case, the default packages should suffice. Figure 5-5 shows the packages I have pre-installed along with the Python version I will use.

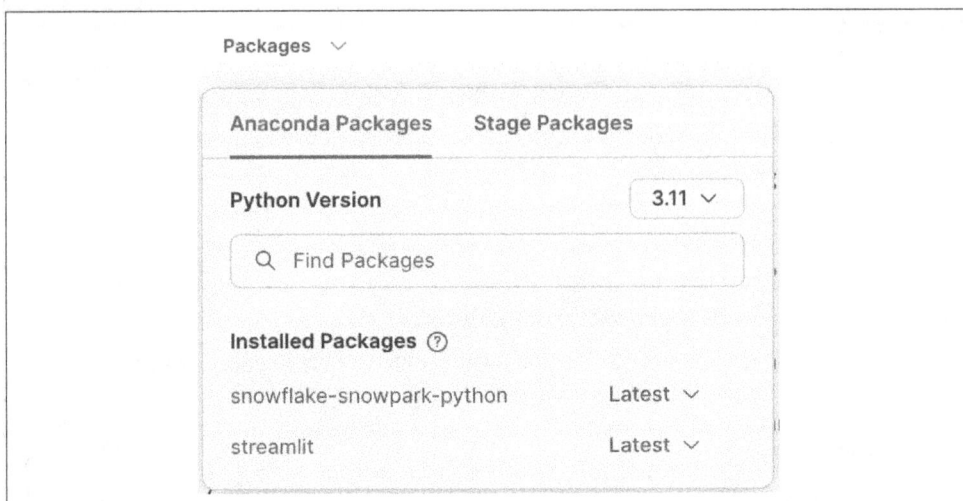

Figure 5-5. Packages in our Streamlit app

After this, I will add the code for the Streamlit app. Let's go through the code step by step.

First, let's import the packages and the functions we need:

```
# Import Python packages
import streamlit as st
from snowflake.snowpark.context import get_active_session
from snowflake.snowpark.functions import col, sum
```

Next, let's set the page configuration, and add the title and subtitle to the app:

```
# Set page configuration
st.set_page_config(
    page_title="O'Reilly - Streamlit in Snowflake",
    layout="wide"
)

# Add a title
st.title("O'Reilly - Streamlit in Snowflake")
st.write("Revenue by Ship Mode - Bar Chart from TPCH Lineitem Dataset")
```

The third step is to get the active session that will be used to run all the queries against the Snowflake engine:

```
# Get Snowflake session
session = get_active_session()
```

Now, I will create a function that loads the data from the `tpch_sf10_lineitem` table in our `OREILLY_DB` and `OREILLY_SCHEMA`. It will only read the shipping mode (`L_SHIP MODE`) and calculate the revenue per line item by taking the price and subtracting the discount percentage from it. It then returns the Snowpark DataFrame:

```
# Load data
def load_data():
    # Query the TPCH lineitem table
    # Calculate revenue as extended price * (1 - discount)
    lineitem_df = session.table("oreilly_db.oreilly_schema.tpch_sf10_lineitem") \
        .select(
            col("L_SHIPMODE"),
            (col("L_EXTENDEDPRICE") * (1 - col("L_DISCOUNT"))).alias("REVENUE")
        )
    return lineitem_df
```

Let's load the data, and while it loads, show a spinner on the screen:

```
# Load the data
with st.spinner("Loading data from Snowflake..."):
    lineitem_df = load_data()
```

Now it's time to aggregate the revenue by shipping mode and save the data in a new DataFrame (ship_mode_revenue). To be able to display the DataFrame in the Streamlit app, I need to convert it in pandas; I will use the to_pandas() function to do so:

```
# Create revenue by ship mode aggregation
ship_mode_revenue = lineitem_df \
    .group_by("L_SHIPMODE") \
    .agg(sum("REVENUE").alias("TOTAL_REVENUE")) \
    .sort("TOTAL_REVENUE", ascending=False)

# Convert to pandas for visualization
ship_mode_df = ship_mode_revenue.to_pandas()
```

Now that the data is prepared, let's display it. The first thing I'll do is create a sub-header for the chart and show the total number of shipping modes, and then display the bar chart:

```
# Display a summary of the data
st.subheader("Revenue by Ship Mode")
st.write(f"Total number of shipping modes: {len(ship_mode_df)}")

# Show the bar chart
st.bar_chart(ship_mode_df.set_index("L_SHIPMODE"))
```

Finally, we will add a footer to give the dashboard a nice ending:

```
# Add a footer
st.markdown("---")
st.caption("Created with Streamlit in Snowflake for O'Reilly")
```

Figure 5-6 shows the rendered version of the dashboard. You can find the complete code for the dashboard in the book's GitHub repo (*https://oreil.ly/advanced-snowflake-repoch52*).

Now that you have seen how Streamlit works in Snowflake, it's time to create an end-to-end Snowflake Native App. The following tutorial will walk you through that.

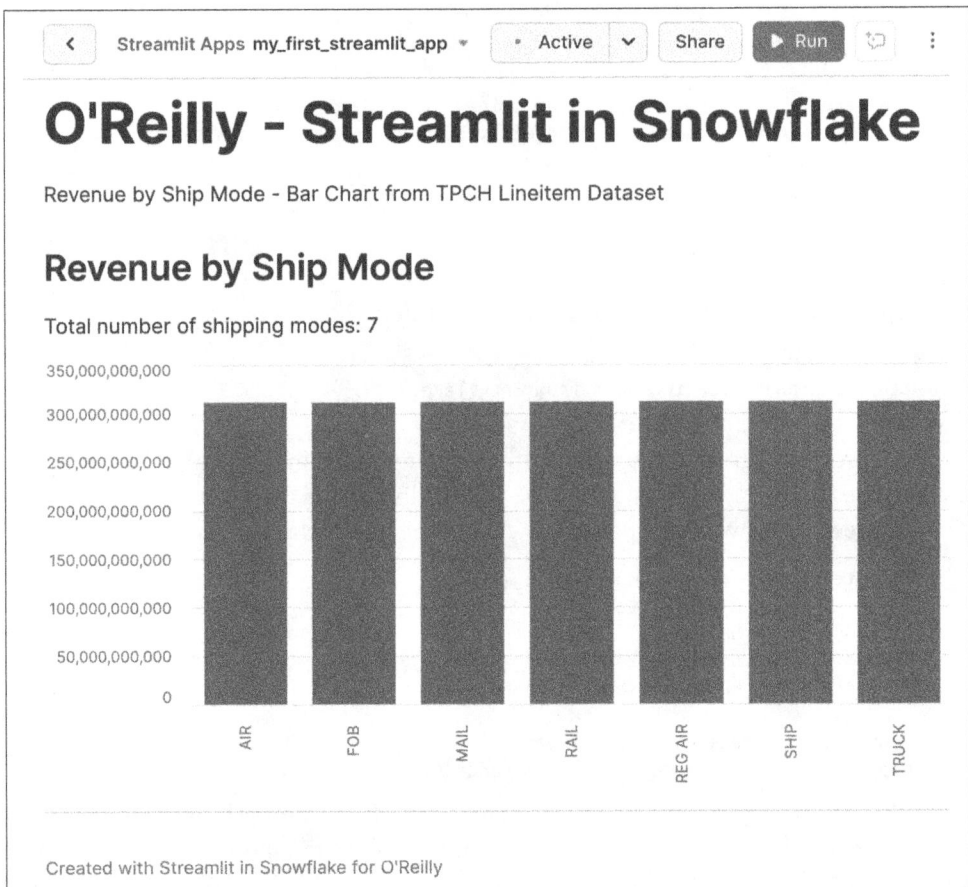

Figure 5-6. Rendered Streamlit dashboard

Hands-on Example: Build and Deploy a Snowflake Native App with Streamlit to Snowflake

Now that you have learned about different components of Snowflake's developer ecosystem, let's create a simple Snowflake Native App. We will start with adding a simple stored procedure to test our environment, then add a UDF and a Streamlit app calling the UDF, and finally deploy our application on Snowflake.

A good start is to first create a new role that has access to a virtual warehouse and to create an application package and application on your account. Here's how you can do it from our main Snowflake account from the ACCOUNTADMIN role. The following code is also available in the GitHub repo (*https://oreil.ly/advanced-snowflake-repoch53*):

```
USE ROLE ACCOUNTADMIN;
CREATE ROLE OREILLY_APP_ROLE;
GRANT ROLE OREILLY_APP_ROLE TO USER OREILLY;

GRANT ALL PRIVILEGES ON WAREHOUSE COMPUTE_WH TO ROLE OREILLY_APP_ROLE;
GRANT CREATE APPLICATION PACKAGE ON ACCOUNT TO ROLE OREILLY_APP_ROLE;
GRANT CREATE APPLICATION ON ACCOUNT TO ROLE OREILLY_APP_ROLE;
GRANT CREATE LISTING ON ACCOUNT TO ROLE OREILLY_APP_ROLE;
```

Now, to be able to run Snowflake CLI commands, you need to download and install Snowflake CLI (*https://oreil.ly/IkCXU*) on your local machine. You can follow this link and follow the steps for your machine.

Once it's done, upon running the command **snow --help**, you should see something similar to Figure 5-7 in your terminal window.

```
Usage: -c [OPTIONS] COMMAND [ARGS]...

Snowflake CLI tool for developers [v3.7.0]

─ Options ─
  --help                    -h          Show this message and exit.
  --version                             Shows version of the Snowflake CLI
  --info                                Shows information about the Snowflake CLI
  --config-file             FILE        Specifies Snowflake CLI configuration file that should be used [default: None]
  --install-completion                  Install completion for the current shell.
  --show-completion                     Show completion for the current shell, to copy it or customize the installation.

─ Commands ─
  app          Manages a Snowflake Native App
  connection   Manages connections to Snowflake.
  cortex       Provides access to Snowflake Cortex.
  git          Manages git repositories in Snowflake.
  helpers      Helper commands.
  init         Creates project directory from template.
  logs         Retrieves logs for a given object.
  notebook     Manages notebooks in Snowflake.
  object       Manages Snowflake objects like warehouses and stages
  snowpark     Manages procedures and functions.
  spcs         Manages Snowpark Container Services compute pools, services, image registries, and image repositories.
  sql          Executes Snowflake query.
  stage        Manages stages.
  streamlit    Manages a Streamlit app in Snowflake.
```

Figure 5-7. Testing Snowflake CLI installation

Now run **snow connection add** to add a new connection to your Snowflake instance where you will be building and running the app. This will ask you about Snowflake parameters needed to connect (account, user, password, role, warehouse, etc.), very similar to what we added in the *.env* file during the tutorials from Chapter 4. Once it's done, you can test your connection by running the following: **snow connection test -c your_connection_name**. You should see Status: OK as a result of this command, as you see here:

```
+------------------------------------------------------------------+
| key             | value                                          |
| Connection name | native_app_connection                          |
| Status          | OK                                             |
| Host            | xxx.snowflakecomputing.com                     |
| Account         | xxx                                            |
| User            | OREILLY                                         |
```

```
| Role       | OREILLY_ROLE |              |
| Database   | OREILLY_DB   |              |
| Warehouse  | COMPUTE_WH   |              |
+-----------------------------------------------------------+
```

Now that everything is set up, let us create an app. To create an app from CLI, you can use Snowflake's CLI project templates (*https://oreil.ly/bzA1B*). Using these will provide you with basic templates for your app. Running the following command, **snow init --template app_basic oreilly_app_tutorial**, will enable you to use a template called app_basic and create an app for you. I will name it oreilly_app_tuto rial, and once it asks for an identifier, I will provide the same name.

See Figure 5-8 on how it is set up.

```
~/p/advanced-snowflake-book/ch5-dev-ecosystem  main ?7   snow init —template app_basic oreilly_app_tutorial
Project identifier [my_native_app_project]: oreilly_app_tutorial
Initialized the new project in oreilly_app_tutorial



~/p/advanced-snowflake-book/ch5-dev-ecosystem  main ?7   cd oreilly_app_tutorial

~/p/advanced-snowflake-book/ch5/oreilly_app_tutorial  main ?7   ls
app           README.md      snowflake.yml
```

Figure 5-8. Initializing an app from a template

Note how it creates a new folder in your working directory with the same name provided before. Let's now explore the contents of the folder and look at Figure 5-9.

```
∨ 📂 ch5-dev-ecosystem
  ∨ 📂 oreilly_app_tutorial
    ∨ 📂 app
        🗋 manifest.yml
        ❶ README.md
        🗡 setup_script.sql
      🔶 .gitignore
      ❶ README.md
      🗋 snowflake.yml
```

Figure 5-9. Contents of the app template folder

As you see in Figure 5-9, we have created all the default files required for an app. Now, let's add some code to the files and bring our app to life. The first thing we do is create a new schema and a new application role to isolate our app within our working environment. The application role is just like a regular Snowflake role, but it is only valid in the context of an application. You can add the following lines at the end of our *setup_script.sql* file:

```
CREATE APPLICATION ROLE IF NOT EXISTS OREILLY_APPLICATION_ROLE
;
CREATE SCHEMA IF NOT EXISTS OREILLY_APP;
GRANT USAGE ON SCHEMA OREILLY_APP
TO APPLICATION ROLE OREILLY_APPLICATION_ROLE
;
```

The schema will hold all the Snowflake objects, like stored procedures, needed in the app. Let's now create a simple stored procedure and grant usage on the procedure to the application role we just created:

```
CREATE OR REPLACE PROCEDURE oreilly_app.say_hello()
    RETURNS STRING
    LANGUAGE SQL
    EXECUTE AS OWNER
    AS
    BEGIN
        RETURN 'Hello from Stored Procedure!';
    END;

GRANT USAGE ON PROCEDURE oreilly_app.say_hello()
TO APPLICATION ROLE OREILLY_APPLICATION_ROLE
;
```

The first part of the preceding code creates a simple stored procedure that echoes "Hello from Stored Procedure!", and the second part grants the role usage permission on the stored procedure. Once this is done, your app is ready to be tested. In your local terminal, navigate to the folder where you initialized the app before, and, from the app folder, run the following command:

`snow app run -c native_app_connection`

This command will run the app present at the given directory using the connection parameters specified in the `oreilly_app_tutorial` from the CLI setup before.

Figure 5-10 shows the results from the terminal after executing this command.

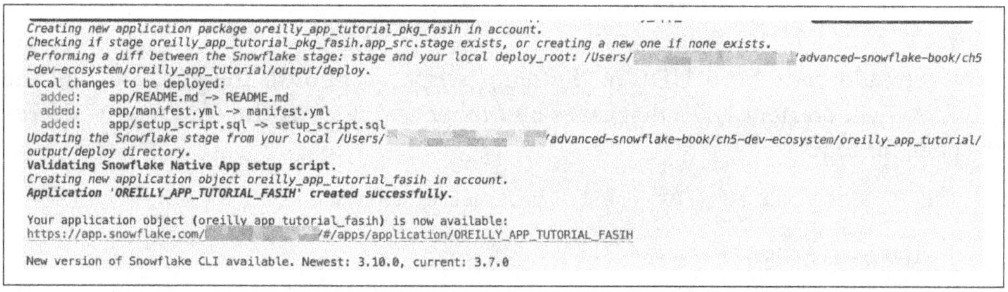

Figure 5-10. Running the app in CLI

The steps are laid out as follows in Figure 5-10: first, it created an application package, and then it checked if the stage already existed in the account and created one since there wasn't one. Then it deployed the *README.md*, *manifest.yml*, and *setup_script.sql* to the stage and created a new application, `OREILLY_APP_TUTO RIAL_FASIH`, in the account. If you now navigate to the apps section in Snowsight, you should see the deployed app, as shown in Figure 5-11.

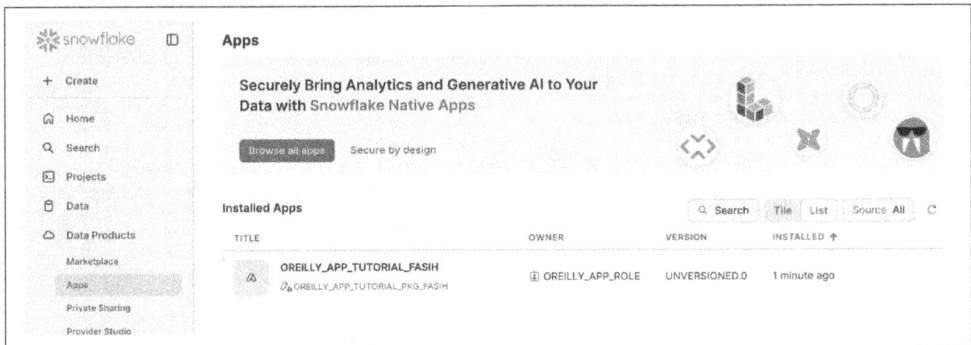

Figure 5-11. Snowsight UI showing the recently added app (see this screengrab in full size) (https://oreil.ly/adsf_0511png)

Now, to test whether the app does what we asked it to do, say hello, let's write another command in the terminal:

```
snow sql -q "call oreilly_app_tutorial.oreilly_app.say_hello()"
-c native_app_connection
```

This should call the stored procedure at the given path, i.e., *your app.schema.name of the stored procedure*. This next block shows the result of running the command in the terminal:

```
call OREILLY_APP_TUTORIAL_FASIH.OREILLY_APP.SAY_HELLO()
+-----------------------------+
| SAY_HELL0                   |
|-----------------------------|
| Hello from Stored Procedure! |
+-----------------------------+
```

Now, let's add code for a UDF in the *setup_script.sql*, publish the app, and call the UDF. We will create a UDF that takes a number and returns the square of it. Here's the code for that:

```
CREATE OR REPLACE FUNCTION oreilly_app.square_num(i INT)
    RETURNS INT
    LANGUAGE PYTHON
    RUNTIME_VERSION = '3.11'
    HANDLER = 'square_py'
AS $$
def square_py(i):
    return i*i
$$;
```

Similar to what we did for the stored procedure, we need to add appropriate permissions for UDF too. Here's the code for that:

```
GRANT USAGE ON FUNCTION oreilly_app.square_num(int)
TO APPLICATION ROLE OREILLY_APPLICATION_ROLE
;
```

Once these are added, you can simply update the app using the same code as before:

```
snow app run -c oreilly_app_tutorial
```

Notice the output this time; it will say "Upgrading existing application object oreilly_app_tutorial. Application successfully upgraded." Once it's done, you can call the UDF using SQL in the command line:

```
snow sql -q "select oreilly_app_tutorial_fasih.oreilly_app.square_num(5)"
-c native_app_connection
```

If everything worked correctly, you will see an output similar to what you see here:

```
select oreilly_app_tutorial_fasih.oreilly_app.square_num(5)
+--------------------------------------------------+
|OREILLY_APP_TUTORIAL_FASIH.OREILLY_APP.SQUARE_NUM(5) |
|--------------------------------------------------|
|25                                                |
+--------------------------------------------------+
```

Now that I have all the pieces in one place, let's add a Streamlit dashboard on top of it. I will first create a new folder, *streamlit*, and a new file in it called *streamlit_ui.py*. Figure 5-12 shows the updated file structure for the app.

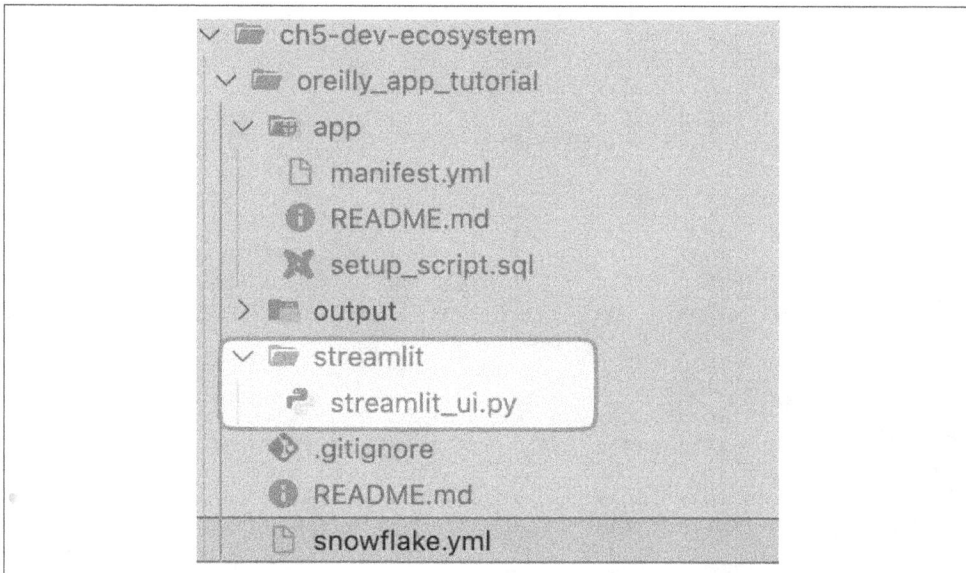

Figure 5-12. Updated folder structure after adding streamlit

The next step is to make sure that the *setup_script.sql* file is updated. We need a STREAMLIT object and proper permission to be able to access it:

```
CREATE STREAMLIT IF NOT EXISTS oreilly_app.oreilly_streamlit
    FROM '/streamlit'
    MAIN_FILE = '/streamlit_ui.py'
;

GRANT USAGE ON STREAMLIT oreilly_app.oreilly_streamlit
TO APPLICATION ROLE OREILLY_APPLICATION_ROLE
;
```

The first part in the code above creates a STREAMLIT object, defines the path, and the main file in that path for Streamlit. The second part grants our application role permissions to use the STREAMLIT object. The *streamlit_ui.py* file looks like this:

```python
# Import Python packages
import streamlit as st
from snowflake.snowpark import Session

# Write directly to the app
st.title("Hello from the awesome O'Reilly Streamlit App")
st.write(
    """
        Input a number between 1 and 100,
        \nThe output will automatically update to show the square of the number.
        \nThe UDF is defined in the Snowflake Native App.
    """
)

# Get the current session
session = Session.builder.getOrCreate()

num_to_square = st.number_input(
    "Enter a number to square (1-100)",
    min_value=1,
    max_value=100,
    value=5,
    step=1,
    placeholder="Type a number between 1 and 100",
)

#  Create a DataFrame
df = session.sql(f"""select
            oreilly_tutorial_app.oreilly_app.square_num({num_to_square})
            as squared_number""")

# Execute the query and convert it into a pandas DataFrame
queried_data = df.to_pandas()

# Display the pandas DataFrame as a Streamlit DataFrame
st.dataframe(queried_data, use_container_width=True)
```

We start by importing the Python packages:

```
# Import Python packages
import streamlit as st
from snowflake.snowpark import Session
```

Then we add a header on top with a title and subtitle:

```
# Write directly to the app
st.title("Hello from the awesome O'Reilly Streamlit App")
st.write(
    """
        Input a number between 1 and 100,
        \nThe output will automatically update to show the square of the number.
        \nThe UDF is defined in the Snowflake Native App.
    """
)
```

Then we get the session information to set the context:

```
# Get the current session
session = Session.builder.getOrCreate()
```

We build the UI by adding a numeric input:

```
num_to_square = st.number_input(
    "Enter a number to square (1-100)",
    min_value=1,
    max_value=100,
    value=5,
    step=1,
    placeholder="Type a number between 1 and 100",
)
```

Then we call our UDF in SQL and input the number we got to get the square of the number:

```
#  Create a DataFrame
df = session.sql(f"""select
            oreilly_tutorial_app.oreilly_app.square_num({num_to_square})
            as squared_number""")

# Execute the query and convert it into a pandas DataFrame
queried_data = df.to_pandas()
```

Once that's done, we display the DataFrame in the Streamlit UI:

```
# Display the pandas DataFrame as a Streamlit DataFrame.
st.dataframe(queried_data, use_container_width=True)
```

The last thing you need to add is the path to Streamlit UI in the artifacts so that snow-cli includes it in the next build and pushes the file to the stage. See the artifacts section in the *snowflake.yml* file (*https://oreil.ly/advanced-snowflake-reposnowflakeyml*). Now, from your terminal, run the app again to update it. Once that's done, you can simply navigate to the Apps tab, open your app, and click on the STREAMLIT object name you chose at the top. You will need an active warehouse to be able to run the Streamlit app. Figure 5-13 shows how the Streamlit UI looks in Snowsight.

> This is just a basic UI to show you what an app would look like with a UI built in Streamlit. You can extend its functionality by adding more components. Streamlit's documentation (*https://docs.streamlit.io*) is a great resource to get the latest and greatest on what's available at your disposal.

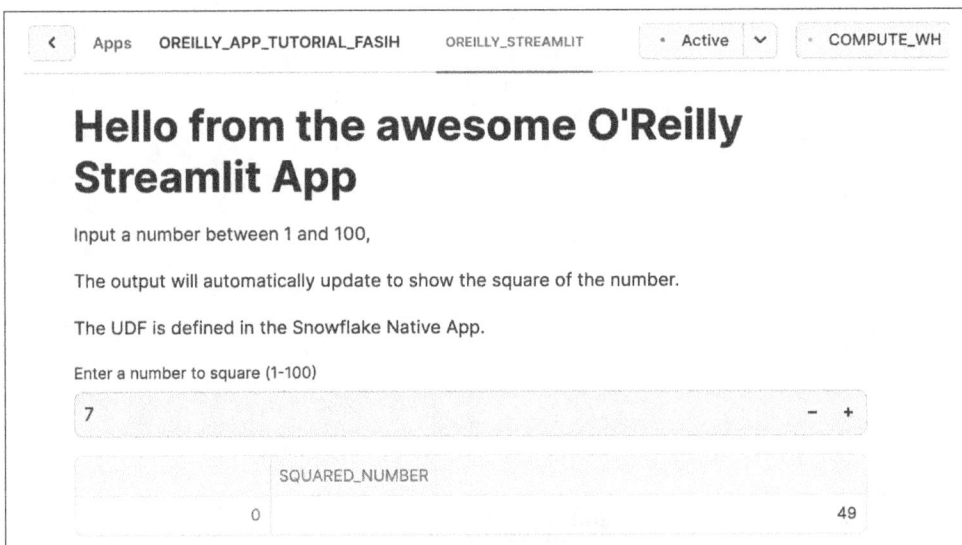

Figure 5-13. Streamlit UI of the app

Now, before you publish your app, you need to add a version to your app. Right now, since we haven't done it, we will see UNVERSIONED everywhere. Figure 5-14 shows what it looks like when an app is unversioned.

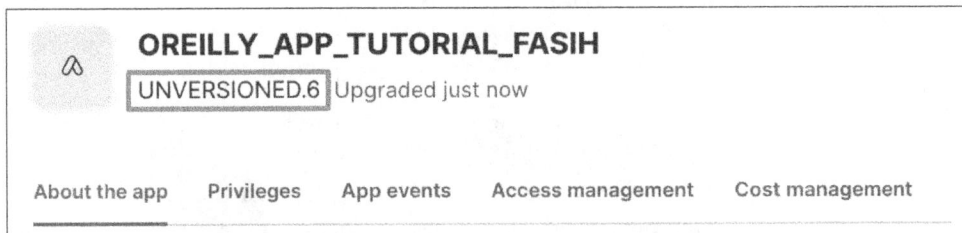

Figure 5-14. An unversioned app

To add a version to my app, I will run the following command in my terminal:

```
snow app version create v1_0 -c native_app_connection
```

Upon success, you will see the following success message:

```
Defining a new version v1_0 in application package oreilly_app_tutorial_pkg_fasih
Version v1_0 created for application package oreilly_app_tutorial_pkg_fasih.
Version create is now complete.
```

To verify if the version was added correctly, you can run the following command:

```
snow app version list -c native_app_connection
```

Figure 5-15 shows how the output of the list would look in the terminal.

```
+---------+-------+-------+---------+------------------------------+-----------+-----------+-------------+-------+---------------+--------------+
| version | patch | label | comment | created_on                   | dropped_on | log_level | trace_level | state | review_status | metric_level |
+---------+-------+-------+---------+------------------------------+-----------+-----------+-------------+-------+---------------+--------------+
| V1_0    | 0     | None  | None    | 2025-07-20 19:11:43.267000-07:00 | None      | OFF       | OFF         | READY | NOT_REVIEWED  | NONE         |
+---------+-------+-------+---------+------------------------------+-----------+-----------+-------------+-------+---------------+--------------+
```

*Figure 5-15. Adding and verifying the version to the app (see this screengrab in full size)
(https://oreil.ly/adsf_0515png)*

Now, on to the last part, publishing the app. Before publishing an app, we need to set the release directive on the app that states which version and patch number is made available to the consumers. To set the default release directive with version v1_0 and patch 0, run the following command in your terminal:

```
snow sql -q "ALTER APPLICATION PACKAGE OREILLY_APP_TUTORIAL_PKG_FASIH
SET DEFAULT RELEASE DIRECTIVE VERSION = v1_0 PATCH = 0" -c oreilly_app_tutorial
```

To publish the app, the steps from the Snowflake documentation are as follows:

1. Sign in to Snowsight.
2. In the navigation menu, select Data Products → Provider Studio.
3. Select "+ Create listing" and then Specified Consumers to privately share the listing with specific accounts.
4. From the "Select role" drop-down menu, select ACCOUNTADMIN.
5. Enter a name for your listing.
6. Select Next.
7. Click + Select to select the application package for the listing.
8. Enter a description for your listing.
9. In the "Add consumer accounts" section, add the account identifier for the account you are using to test the consumer experience of installing the app from a listing.
10. Select Publish.

Figures 5-16 and 5-17 show a summary of these steps.

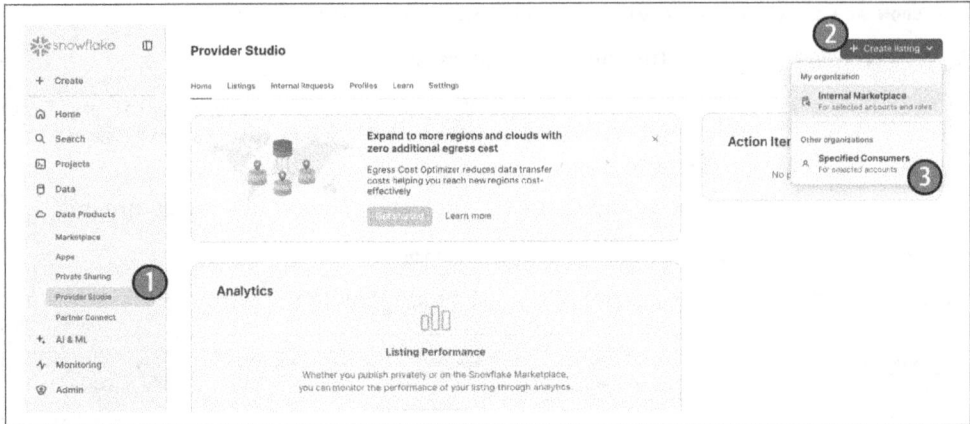

Figure 5-16. Creating a new listing in Snowsight

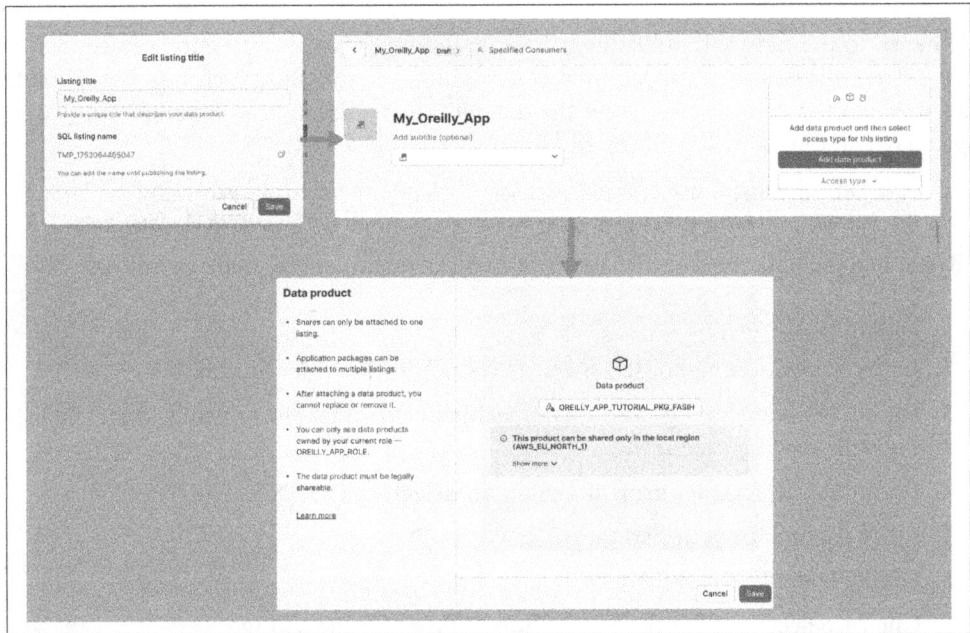

Figure 5-17. Setting up and publishing a new listing in Snowsight

After this screen, you will have a detailed page along with a publishing guide from Snowflake to help you with your listing.

On the consumer side, you can navigate to the data studio and simply accept the incoming app and install it. The following are the steps from the Snowflake documentation that a consumer needs to follow:

1. Sign in to Snowsight.

2. In the navigation menu, select Data Products → Apps.

3. Select the tile for the listing under "Recently shared with you."

4. Select Get.

5. Select Options and enter a customer-facing name for the app. For this tutorial, use "HelloSnowflakeApp".

6. Select the warehouse where you want to install the app.

7. Select Get.

8. Select Open to view your listing or Done to finish.

Summary

With that, I conclude this hands-on example. You looked at how to install Snowflake CLI and set up its connection with your Snowflake account; then you created a new role for the app and set up an app from Snowflake CLI templates. Then you created a simple stored procedure that said hello, followed by a simple UDF that takes a number and squares it. It was published on Snowflake along with a Streamlit dashboard where we can input a number to square it. You also learned about versioning the app, assigning a release directive to it, and finally, publishing the app. These are all the steps you need to be able to create and release custom apps on Snowflake.

In Chapter 6, you will learn more about the AI and ML capabilities of Snowflake and how to deploy an end-to-end ML pipeline.

Snowflake for AI and ML

In this chapter, I will walk you through Snowflake's AI ecosystem, which brings a significant advancement in integrated analytics to Snowflake's platform. The ecosystem is ever-evolving, and it now offers solutions for all AI and ML use cases that Snowflake users may have.

At its center, we have Snowflake Cortex, your gateway to large language models in Snowflake. It includes LLMs trained by companies like Anthropic, Mistral, Reka, Meta, and Google, and Snowflake's proprietary Snowflake Arctic (Snowflake lists all available models (*https://oreil.ly/E9_TK*)). Snowflake Cortex provides native support for large language models, vector processing, and time series analysis, all without requiring data movement or complex infrastructure management. This enables sophisticated generative AI workloads to be executed directly within your existing data architecture. It is complemented with Snowflake Notebooks, which we saw in earlier hands-on examples. It delivers a familiar Jupyter-based environment with enhanced performance for data science workflows. It features built-in Python and SQL execution, simplified package management, and seamless integration with enterprise governance controls.

Additionally, for rapid development, Snowflake offers a Copilot. This intelligent assistant can generate optimized SQL, troubleshoot performance issues, and suggest improvements based on your workloads and access patterns, and it can also deal with unstructured data. In addition to that, Document AI provides automated indexing and extraction services that enable complex document analysis with customized extraction pipelines. You will appreciate the support for custom model deployment through Snowpark Container Services, streamlined machine learning operations (MLOps) with model registry integration, and comprehensive feature store capabilities for production machine learning systems. Let's now detail some of these features and explore how they work.

Snowflake Notebooks

Think of Snowflake Notebooks as your data science workbench inside Snowsight. It's essentially a cell-based development environment where you can mix Python, SQL, and Markdown, however you need to—it's perfect for those moments when you are jumping between data exploration, model building, and documenting your findings, all in one place. Snowflake Notebooks not only allows you to access your data from your Snowflake environment, but it also allows you to upload files from your local machine to Snowflake and access them in notebooks, all while keeping the capabilities to access files from an external stage (cloud storage) and explore datasets from Snowflake Marketplace.

To support different workloads, Snowflake Notebooks supports two different runtimes: the warehouse environment and the container environment. Table 6-1 shows you the comparison of the two runtimes.

Table 6-1. Comparison of Warehouse Runtime and Container Runtime for Snowflake Notebooks (https://oreil.ly/gQaNI)

Supported features	Warehouse Runtime	Container Runtime
Compute	Kernel runs on the notebook warehouse.	Kernel runs on a compute pool node (*https://oreil.ly/2fqxH*).
Environment	Python 3.9	Python 3.10 (preview).
Base image	Streamlit + Snowpark	Snowflake Container Runtime (CPU and GPU images pre-installed with Python libraries).
Additional Python libraries	Install using Snowflake Anaconda or from a Snowflake stage.	Install using pip, conda, or from a Snowflake stage. If needed, specify a particular package version.
Editing support	Python, SQL, and Markdown cells. References outputs from SQL cells in Python cells and vice versa. Uses visualization libraries like Streamlit.	Same as Warehouse Runtime.
Access	Ownership required to access and edit notebooks.	Same as Warehouse Runtime.
Supported notebook features (still in preview)	Git integration (preview); scheduling (preview)	Same as Warehouse Runtime.

As you can see in Table 6-1, the Warehouse Runtime is your quickest path forward. It's basically the standard Snowflake warehouse environment you are already familiar with. I'd recommend using this one unless you are sure that you need Container Runtime.

Container Runtime gives you flexibility. It's designed to handle almost anything you throw at it, whether you are working with SQL analytics, data engineering pipelines, or deep learning models; it can scale according to your needs. An additional nice thing is that you can install any Python package from pip, conda, or your custom

Python package without any additional bureaucracy or approval processes. Think of containers as isolated environments within Snowflake to run your code, with notebooks to help put it all together, and with all the excellent features of the Snowflake engine underneath. The Container Runtime for Snowflake Notebooks can be run on CPUs or GPUs. The GPU version is ideal for ML work, as it comes pre-loaded with all the popular machine learning libraries you'd expect.

The best part of using Snowflake Notebooks is that you can interchangeably use SQL or Python without having to switch environments, keeping all your work in one place. Think of the flexibility it gives you: you can write SQL in one cell, switch to Python in the next, and immediately compare results as you go. You can even query the output of a cell in the analysis of the next cell. No more context switching between different tools or waiting for data exports to finish, and when you want to visualize something, you've got Streamlit built right in, plus access to other helpful packages like Matplotlib, Altair, or seaborn.

Notebooks also supports Git integration, which means you can collaborate effectively with proper version control. Since it all runs on Snowflake's infrastructure, your existing role-based access controls and governance policies will work out of the box, so you don't have to worry about someone accessing data they are not allowed to when sharing notebooks.

Last but not least, you can schedule notebooks to run on their own. This is an effortless way of turning your exploratory work into production pipelines. Once you schedule your notebook, it will create a Snowflake task for you, giving you all the features of a Snowflake task, like task graphs, monitoring, error logging, etc.

In Figure 6-1, you can see the Snowflake notebook creation dialogue box for Warehouse Runtime. You just need to specify the database, schema, warehouse (for queries), and notebook warehouse (for notebook kernel and Python code).

> The role in your notebook will need usage permissions to the database and schema you select to work in. For scheduled execution, it requires the CREATE TASK privilege on the schema where the notebook is located, and it needs the EXECUTE TASK privilege to run tasks.

Then in Figure 6-2, you will see the Snowflake notebook creation dialogue box for Container Runtime. Here, you need to specify the database, schema, runtime (CPU or GPU), compute pool (system default compute pool), and query warehouse (for queries).

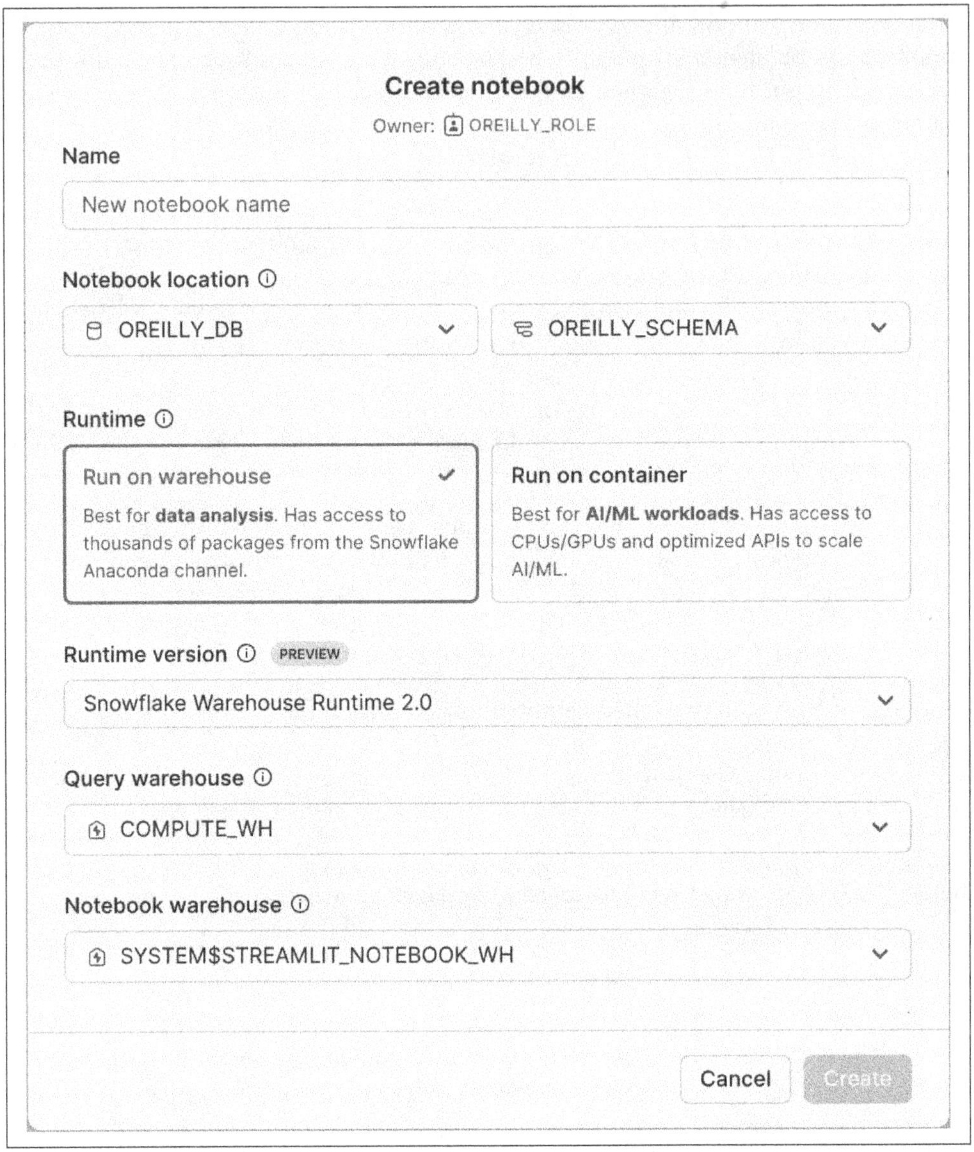

Figure 6-1. Snowflake Notebooks creation dialogue box—Warehouse Runtime

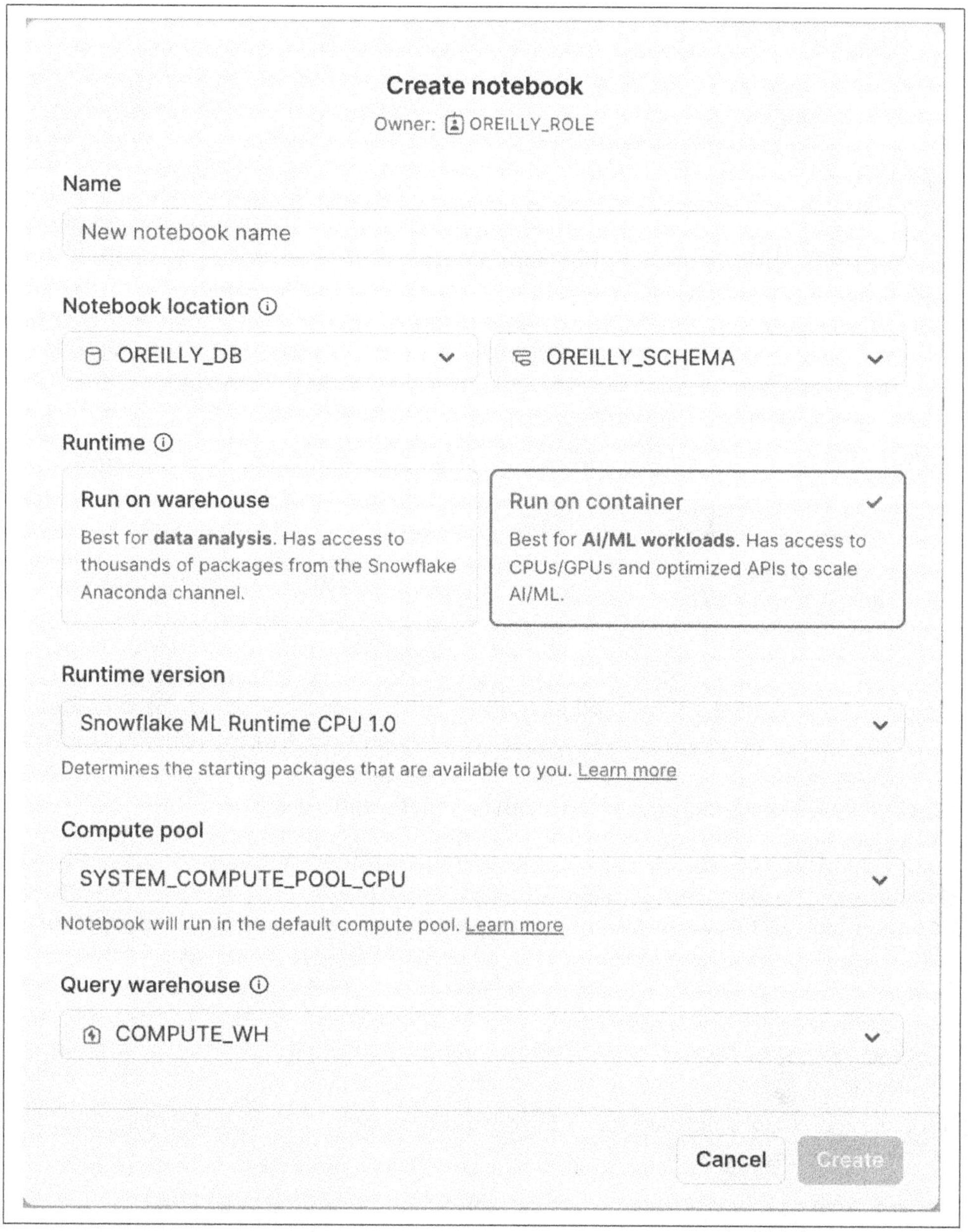

Create notebook

Owner: 🔲 OREILLY_ROLE

Name

New notebook name

Notebook location ⓘ

🗄 OREILLY_DB   ⌄   🗂 OREILLY_SCHEMA   ⌄

Runtime ⓘ

Run on warehouse	**Run on container** ✓
Best for **data analysis**. Has access to thousands of packages from the Snowflake Anaconda channel.	Best for **AI/ML workloads**. Has access to CPUs/GPUs and optimized APIs to scale AI/ML.

Runtime version

Snowflake ML Runtime CPU 1.0   ⌄

Determines the starting packages that are available to you. Learn more

Compute pool

SYSTEM_COMPUTE_POOL_CPU   ⌄

Notebook will run in the default compute pool. Learn more

Query warehouse ⓘ

🔼 COMPUTE_WH   ⌄

Cancel   Create

Figure 6-2. Snowflake notebook creation dialogue box—Container Runtime

Snowflake Cortex

Snowflake Cortex makes it easier to make practical use of AI and LLMs; it's about working smarter, not harder. Snowflake Cortex is a suite of LLM-powered features by Snowflake that can understand unstructured data, answer your questions, and provide you with an intelligent assistant. Under the hood, you've got LLM functions for text processing, Snowflake Copilot acting as your AI assistant, Document AI for extracting data from PDFs and other formats, fine-tuning capabilities for pre-trained models when you need custom behavior, Cortex Search for semantic search across your Snowflake data, and Cortex Analyst for natural language analytics. With this toolset at your disposal, the possibilities of taking your company from a data-driven to an AI-enabled company are endless. You get state-of-the-art models at your disposal within just a few clicks, ready to be customized to your use case. Let's now explore each one of Snowflake Cortex's features in the following subsections.

Snowflake Cortex LLM Functions

Snowflake Cortex LLM functions give you access to the best LLMs out there without any of the usual setup nightmare. I am referring to models from major players such as Anthropic, Mistral, Google, Meta, and Snowflake's own Arctic model, which is quite robust for enterprise use. Snowflake will handle all the hosting and management, so you don't have to worry about API keys, rate limits, or figuring out which endpoint to hit. Your data never leaves Snowflake, and you get the power of the world's best LLMs at your disposal, which means you keep all the performance, scaling, and governance benefits you are already used to with no data movement and no compliance headaches.

Here is what you need to think about when you are planning to use these models: the Cortex LLM SQL functions are built for heavy lifting and are optimized for throughput. If you are processing text from the large SQL tables in a batched manner, these functions should be your go-to functions. If you are optimizing for latency, and if you are building something more interactive where users wait for the responses, you might want to fetch results from the REST API instead. These functions have different endpoints depending on what you are doing: the Cortex Complete API for simple inference, the Cortex Embed API for embeddings, and the Cortex Agents API if you are building more sophisticated agentic workflows.

These functions are available to you as SQL functions and also in Python, in Snowpark ML version 1.1.2 and later. Let's look at a quick example and use these functions in Python using Snowflake Notebooks and SQL in Snowflake worksheets.

First, create a new notebook and make sure you have added `snowflake-ml-python` and `snowflake-snowpark-python` in the packages section of the Snowflake notebook.

Then, for our example, we'll ask about quantum computing (for the output, see Figure 6-3):

```
from snowflake.cortex import complete
print(
    complete(
        'mistral-large',
        'In 100 words, explain quantum computing to a middle school student'
))
```

```
from snowflake.cortex import complete

print(
    complete(
        'mistral-large',
        'In 100 words, explain quantum computing to a middle school student'
))

Quantum computing is like a super-powerful computer that uses the strange and fascinating rules of quantum physics
```

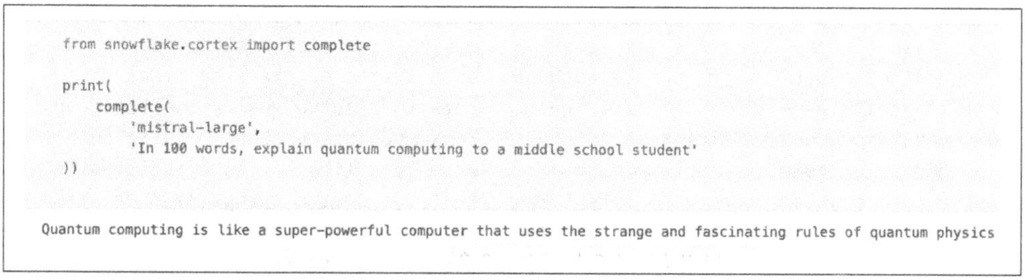

Figure 6-3. Output of running the `complete` *function using Python*

To do the same with SQL, you can simply write the following query (for the output, see Figure 6-4):

```
SELECT
    SNOWFLAKE.CORTEX.COMPLETE(
        'mistral-large',
        'In 100 words, explain quantum computing to a middle school student'
    ) as cortex_complete_sql;
```

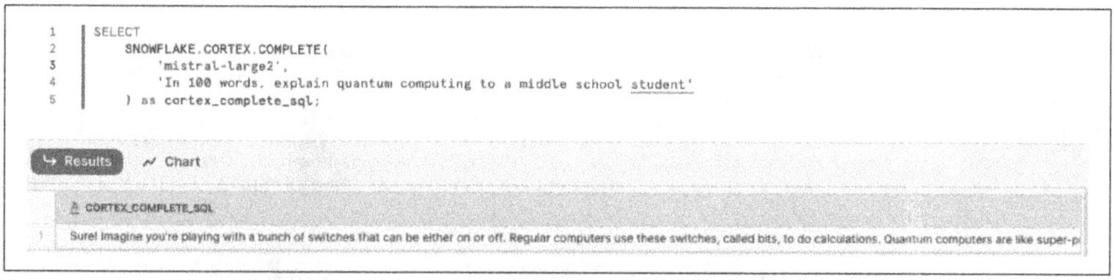

```
1   SELECT
2       SNOWFLAKE.CORTEX.COMPLETE(
3           'mistral-large2',
4           'In 100 words, explain quantum computing to a middle school student'
5       ) as cortex_complete_sql;
```

Results   Chart

CORTEX_COMPLETE_SQL

Sure! Imagine you're playing with a bunch of switches that can be either on or off. Regular computers use these switches, called bits, to do calculations. Quantum computers are like super-p

Figure 6-4. Output of running the COMPLETE *function using SQL*

Table 6-2 shows the comparison of the outputs generated using the two models.

Table 6-2. Comparison of outputs of the complete function using SQL and Python

Function output from Python	Function output from SQL
Quantum computing is like a super-powerful computer that uses the strange and fascinating rules of quantum physics to solve problems. You know how your regular computer or video game console uses bits, which are like tiny switches that can be either on or off, represented by 0s and 1s? Quantum computers use something called qubits, which can be both on and off at the same time! This lets quantum computers process a lot more information and solve complex problems much faster than regular computers. It's like having a magical calculator that can do many calculations at once!	Sure! Imagine you are playing with a bunch of switches that can be either on or off. Regular computers use these switches, called bits, to do calculations. Quantum computers are like super-powered versions of these. Instead of just on or off, their switches, called qubits, can be in both states at the same time! This lets them solve really complex problems much faster than regular computers. It's like having a magic switch that can do two things at once, making quantum computers super powerful for certain tasks.

The following function is the extract_answer() function that takes two parameters as inputs: the source document or an input text, and a question that you need to be answered from that text. The Snowflake documentation defines the syntax:

```
SNOWFLAKE.CORTEX.EXTRACT_ANSWER(
    <source_document>, <question>)
```

In our examples, we will give the input story of "Jack and the Beanstalk" and pose a question related to that to the LLM. Let's do it in Python first; see Figure 6-5.

```
from snowflake.cortex import extract_answer

story = """
    'Once upon a time there lived a poor widow and her son Jack. One day, Jack's mother told him to sell their only cow.
    The next day, when Jack woke up in the morning and looked out of the window, he saw that a huge beanstalk had grown
    While he was eating, the giant came home. The giant was very big and looked very fearsome. Jack was terrified and we
    Climbed the beanstalk and went to the giant's house again. Once again, Jack asked the giant's wife for food, but whi

    After some days, Jack once again climbed the beanstalk and went to the giant's castle. For the third time, Jack met

    The giant had a magical harp that could play beautiful songs. While the giant slept, Jack took the harp and was abou
    """

print(extract_answer(story, "How did the giant start its cry in the story?"))

[
    {
        "answer": "fee - fi - fo - fum, i smell the blood of an englishman.",
        "score": 0.000018566241
    }
]
```

Figure 6-5. Output of running the extract_answer() function using Python

If you run the same in SQL, you will get the same output but with a slightly different score value. What this means is that, regardless of whether you're using Python or SQL, you will get similar outputs, since the model working under the hood is the same. In Figure 6-6, we can see the results from the SQL variant of the extract_answer() function.

```
7   SELECT
8       SNOWFLAKE.CORTEX.EXTRACT_ANSWER(
9           'Once upon a time there lived a poor widow and her son Jack. One day, Jack's mother told him to sell their only
cow. Jack went to the market and on the way he met a man who wanted to buy his cow. Jack asked, "What will you give
me in return for my cow?" The man answered, "I will give you five magic beans!" Jack took the magic beans and gave
the man the cow. But when he reached home, Jack's mother was very angry. She said, "You fool! He took away your cow
and gave you some beans!" She threw the beans out of the window. Jack was very sad and went to sleep without dinner.
10          The next day, when Jack woke up in the morning and looked out of the window, he saw that a huge beanstalk had
grown from his magic beans! He climbed up the beanstalk and reached a kingdom in the sky. There lived a giant and his
wife. Jack went inside the house and found the giant's wife in the kitchen. Jack said, "Could you please give me
something to eat? I am so hungry!" The kind wife gave him bread and some milk.
11          While he was eating, the giant came home. The giant was very big and looked very fearsome. Jack was terrified and
went and hid inside. The giant cried, "Fee-fi-fo-fum, I smell the blood of an Englishman. Be he alive, or be he dead,
I'll grind his bones to make my bread!" The wife said, "There is no boy in here!" So, the giant ate his food and then
went to his room. He took out his sacks of gold coins, counted them and kept them aside. Then he went to sleep. In
the night, Jack crept out of his hiding place, took one sack of gold coins and climbed down the beanstalk. At home,
he gave the coins to his mother. His mother was very happy and they lived well for sometime.
12          Climbed the beanstalk and went to the giant's house again. Once again, Jack asked the giant's wife for food, but
while he was eating the giant returned. Jack leapt up in fright and went and hid under the bed. The giant cried, "Fee-
fifo-fum, I smell the blood of an Englishman. Be he alive, or be he dead, I'll grind his bones to make my bread!" The
wife said, "There is no boy in here!" The giant ate his food and went to his room. There, he took out a hen. He
shouted, "Lay!" and the hen laid a golden egg. When the giant fell asleep, Jack took the hen and climbed down the
beanstalk. Jack's mother was very happy with him.
13
14          After some days, Jack once again climbed the beanstalk and went to the giant's castle. For the third time, Jack
met the giant's wife and asked for some food. Once again, the giant's wife gave him bread and milk. But while Jack
was eating, the giant came home. "Fee-fi-fo-fum, I smell the blood of an Englishman. Be he alive, or be he dead, I'll
grind his bones to make my bread!" cried the giant. "Don't be silly! There is no boy in here!" said his wife.
15
16          The giant had a magical harp that could play beautiful songs. While the giant slept, Jack took the harp and was
about to leave. Suddenly, the magic harp cried, "Help master! A boy is stealing me!" The giant woke up and saw Jack
with the harp. Furious, he ran after Jack. But Jack was too fast for him. He ran down the beanstalk and reached home.
The giant followed him down. Jack quickly ran inside his house and fetched an axe. He began to chop the beanstalk.
The giant fell and died.'
17          ,
18          'How did the giant start its cry in the story?'
19      ) AS EXTRACT_ANSWER_SQL
```

→ Results   ∿ Chart   Q ▥ ⬇ ⬓ ⏱

[ ] EXTRACT_ANSWER_SQL

[{ "answer": "fee - fi - fo - fum, I smell the blood of an englishman", "score": 0.00041811288 }]

Figure 6-6. Output of running the extract_answer() function using SQL

Now, for the following examples, we will only look at the Python version.

Similar to the previous functions, we have a summarize() function to summarize the long documents into digestible bits and pieces. Let's summarize the same story using this function (Figure 6-7). The Python code is straightforward in this case:

```
from snowflake.cortex import summarize
print(summarize(story))
```

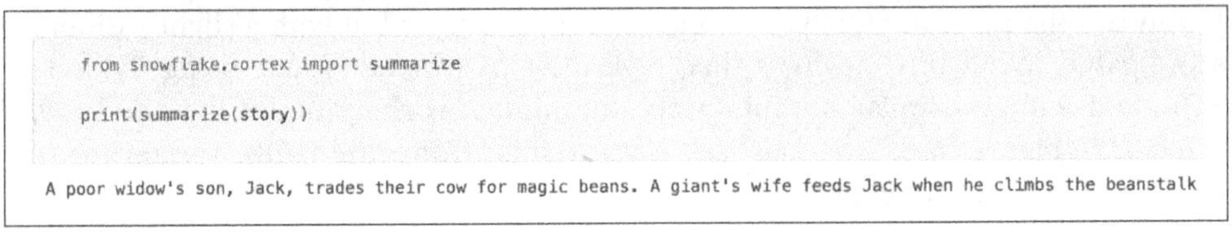

```
from snowflake.cortex import summarize

print(summarize(story))
```

A poor widow's son, Jack, trades their cow for magic beans. A giant's wife feeds Jack when he climbs the beanstalk

Figure 6-7. Output of running the `summarize()` *function using Python*

If you look at the full output, it is a much smaller variant of the original text summarizing the crux of the story:

```
Output:
A poor widow's son, Jack, trades their cow for magic beans. A giant's wife feeds
Jack when he climbs the beanstalk to the giant's kingdom. Jack steals gold coins
and a golden goose. Repeating this, Jack takes the giant's magical harp and is
chased down, chopping the beanstalk to escape, killing the giant.
```

Next, we will look at the `sentiment()` function, used to extract the "happiness index" from a particular review, and we will try to classify it using the `classify_text()` function into "positive, negative, neutral" (Figure 6-8). Again, the code for this is very straightforward:

```
print("Sentiment: ", sentiment(review))
print("Classification: ",
    classify_text(
        review,
        ["positive", "negative", "neutral"]
    )
)
```

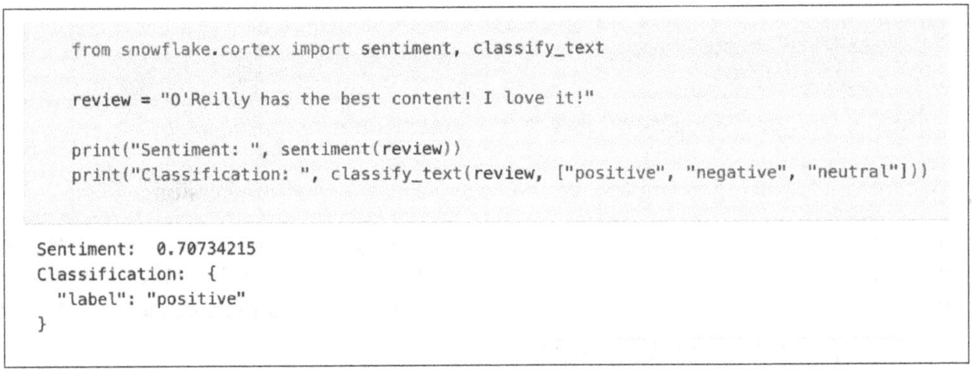

```
from snowflake.cortex import sentiment, classify_text

review = "O'Reilly has the best content! I love it!"

print("Sentiment: ", sentiment(review))
print("Classification: ", classify_text(review, ["positive", "negative", "neutral"]))


Sentiment:  0.70734215
Classification:  {
  "label": "positive"
}
```

Figure 6-8. Output of running the `sentiment()` *and* `classify_text()` *functions using Python*

In Figure 6-8, you can see that the review is positive, resulting in a sentiment score of 0.707 on a scale of −1 to +1, where higher numbers indicate a more positive sentiment. Snowflake Cortex's `classify_text()` function does a good job of classifying it correctly as "positive".

You can use all of these functions in SQL as well. I am not covering the SQL examples in this book, but you can refer to the Snowflake documentation and find them in the large language model functions (*https://oreil.ly/lj1Ig*).

Snowflake Cortex Analyst

When the AI boom began, everyone was seeking a way to automate their workflows and integrate AI into their existing tools. People were quick to connect their databases to their favorite AI tool and ask questions, but questions remained regarding the accuracy of text-to-SQL conversions, especially when there was no defined way of letting a model know what data your database, schema, and tables hold and how they are connected. There were some excellent solutions, but they always had their limitations. Enter Snowflake Cortex Analyst, Snowflake's answer to the age-old problem of business users wanting to ask questions about data without having to learn SQL or bug the analytics team every five minutes.

The best analogy I can think of is to consider it a very reliable translator that converts natural language questions, such as "What were our sales in Q3?" into effective SQL queries that work. The natural question here is, "If others couldn't do it well, how can Snowflake succeed?", and the answer to that is Snowflake's secret sauce: semantic models. Instead of just throwing your database schema at an LLM and hoping for the best, Cortex Analyst uses predefined semantic models.

A semantic model is a YAML file that explains what your data means in business terms. You define exactly how everything is defined, how everything is connected, the dimensions, the metrics, etc. This is a game-changer, as now you don't have to craft a delicate and very engineered prompt and try to keep up with ever-evolving prompt engineering best practices, because now, you can programmatically define it in one place. Raw schemas will never tell you that calculating "revenue" for your business should exclude refunds or cater to discounts that are in percentages in another column, or that "active users" are only users active on your platform in the last week or the previous 90 days. The semantic model bridges that gap between how databases store data and how humans think about it.

On top of that, Snowflake provides API access to Cortex Analyst, and this is where the magic happens. Now you can plug it into whatever your business users are already using—Slack, Teams, etc.—and have your insights delivered to you directly from Snowflake. Like everything else on Snowflake, Cortex Analyst also does all of it while handling the administrative complexity for you so that you can focus on the actual problems. Anyone who's tried building a decent text-to-SQL system knows it's a nightmare; you juggle accuracy (writing queries that make sense and work in the first go), speed (nobody wants to wait for a minute for an answer), and costs (LLM calls add up fast, and the bills even faster). People try to use different LLMs, but it's hard to keep up with everything. Snowflake's Cortex Analyst solves that too, as under the hood, it runs the latest Llama and Mistral models by default, all hosted securely within Snowflake (meaning your data does not leave Snowflake). If you want to use OpenAI's GPT models through Azure, well, now you can do that too, with a small (but worth mentioning) caveat that metadata and prompts do go outside of Snowflake's architecture. Snowflake automatically picks the best model combination for each query, which, in my opinion, is pretty slick.

It is not available in all regions natively, but you can still use it by leveraging cross-region inference. You can head to Snowflake's documentation for Cortex Analyst (*https://oreil.ly/9YyMa*) for more details.

Snowflake Cortex Fine-Tuning

Fine-tuning, as the name suggests, is using what's readily available on the market and customizing it for your use cases. What it means for LLMs is to take one of the pre-trained models and adapt it to your use case by training it on your smaller but tailored dataset. This enables LLMs to deliver specialized performance with significantly improved accuracy, eliminating the need for manual training. Snowflake Cortex fine-tuning is similar. It's a way to turn a very competent generalist into a domain expert, all within Snowflake, while avoiding any unnecessary data movement.

There's a classic example that hits home: you have a massive language model that can extract medical conditions perfectly from clinical notes, but on the other hand, it is a whopping 405 B parameter monster that will bankrupt you when deployed to production. Meanwhile, the smaller 1 B parameter model is what you can actually afford. Throwing the smaller model at the task will make it respond like a deer staring directly into the headlights of an oncoming car, overwhelmed and frozen. Fine-tuning lets you teach that small model to behave like the big one, with the same quality but at a fraction of the cost. The vital thing to know about fine-tuning is that it shouldn't be confused with prompt engineering. Clever prompts can do wonders, but then you are not telling the model anything new, and you are stuck with the knowledge that the model already possesses. Fine-tuning, however, is like teaching existing models something new—new knowledge, new tricks, exposing a new domain to it that wasn't a part of its training before. Under the hood, Cortex fine-tuning uses parameter-efficient fine-tuning (PEFT). It's a fine-tuning technique that only adjusts the parts of the model that matter for your task, making it a very efficient technique, in terms of both time and cost. So, instead of retraining billions of parameters, you will be tweaking a small subset of them.

Not every LLM available for you to use in Snowflake is also available for fine-tuning. You can refer to the Snowflake documentation (*https://oreil.ly/bFJ3I*) to see the base models that you can fine-tune.

> I will not be fine-tuning an LLM for the scope of this book, but I highly recommend two resources from Snowflake to learn it and see hands-on examples: Snowflake's "Introduction to Generative AI with Snowflake" (*https://oreil.ly/awXjE*) class on Coursera and Snowflake's AI Data Cloud Academy (*https://oreil.ly/XZ2CB*).

Snowflake Cortex Search

Snowflake Cortex Search is Snowflake's take on unstructured data retrieval. Similar to how Snowflake Cortex Analyst utilizes a semantic model on structured data, Snowflake Cortex Search employs text embeddings with semantic and keyword search to retrieve data from a given set of documents. Think of it as a really smart search that doesn't just match exact keywords. It understands what you are looking for even when you are a bit fuzzy with your words. In fact, it's defined as a high-quality "fuzzy search" by Snowflake. Under the hood, it runs both vector and keyword search simultaneously, so that you can get the best of both worlds.

If you are building any kind of AI chat use case or retrieval-augmented generation (RAG)[1] application, you know the pain of getting good retrieval working. You need your LLM to find the right context from your data, but setting up embeddings, tuning search parameters, keeping indexes fresh—all of it becomes a full-fledged infrastructure project before you even get to the fun AI stuff. Snowflake Cortex Search eliminates all that setup headache. You point it at your text data, and within minutes, you have a production-ready search engine at your disposal. No embedding models to choose, no vector databases to set up or maintain, no endless parameter tweaking to get a decent result. Snowflake automatically indexes your data, so when your data changes, your search updates automatically. It's one of those "why didn't this exist sooner" features; it removes friction from building AI applications on your Snowflake data.

If you are wondering when to use Cortex Search, the top use cases are when you need a RAG engine for chat-based applications or when you want a high-end search back-end for your application. For the RAG-based systems, when you have to retrieve data from a knowledge base, Cortex Search comes in handy. Figure 6-9 shows how you can combine Cortex Search with Cortex LLM functions to create state-of-the-art chatbots with RAG.

---

1 In the context of artificial intelligence, RAG is a technique that enhances the capabilities of LLMs by combining them with an external knowledge base to provide more accurate, relevant, and up-to-date responses.

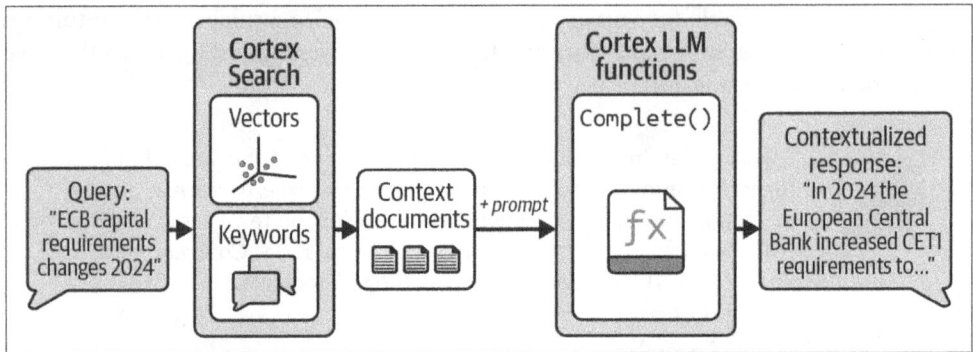

Figure 6-9. Combining Cortex Search and Cortex LLM functions

The embedding models that are available to you at your disposal from Snowflake are listed in the Snowflake documentation (*https://oreil.ly/eyoAw*).

Document AI

Unstructured data is everywhere, and it is often a mess to work with, especially when you have to extract insights out of it. It might work for a couple of documents, but what if you have thousands of documents, all with slightly different formats? That's where Snowflake's Document AI comes in: it's Snowflake's take on getting useful information out of messy documents using their proprietary LLM, called Arctic-TILT.

Document AI is capable of extracting text from documents, but what's even cooler is that it can pull information from logos, handwritten signatures, checkboxes—you name it. This enables any solution you build with Document AI to scale across various use cases. Whether you are dealing with invoices, complex contracts, structured agreements, or whatever other document chaos your organization throws around, you can set up automated pipelines to process them continuously, eliminating the need to enter the data manually.

The model is capable of performing *zero-shot extraction*. Zero-shot extraction means that the base model is capable of locating and extracting the information from unseen documents without any tailored training on that dataset. This is possible because it has been trained on such a massive variety of documents. It's like having an experienced data entry person who has (more or less) seen it all.

And that's not all. If you want to take it a step further, you can fine-tune the model on your specific documents to achieve even better results. Snowflake won't share your data or your fine-tuned model anywhere, so it stays private to you, while you can leverage the pre-trained model it provides. It is essentially solving that age-old problem of "we have all this valuable information locked up in PDFs and paper forms, but getting it into our systems is a nightmare." Well, with Snowflake, not anymore!

To follow a hands-on tutorial about Document AI, refer to the user guide available in the Snowflake documentation (*https://oreil.ly/y6okB*).

Snowflake Copilot

Snowflake Copilot is often confused with Snowflake Cortex Analyst. I will start by explaining the differences. We have learned that Cortex Analyst works with your defined semantic model and that it can be seen as your text-to-SQL AI solution for Snowflake's data. Snowflake Copilot, on the other hand, can be seen as your AI pair-programming buddy. You can see it as an assistant who is there to tell you more about Snowflake, teach you SQL, help you understand complex queries, etc.

The real value of Snowflake Copilot shows up in your day-to-day workflow. For example, if you are starting with an unfamiliar dataset, you can ask Copilot to explain what type of data you are looking at, and it can also suggest where to start exploring. If you inherit some legacy code and want to understand it, you can ask Copilot to break it down for you, and even better, to suggest improvements and generate SQL for you. It is a great learning tool for you to become familiar with Snowflake and explore documentation and function syntax quickly, as well as to debug and optimize slow-running queries. In Figure 6-10, you can see where to access the Snowflake Copilot.

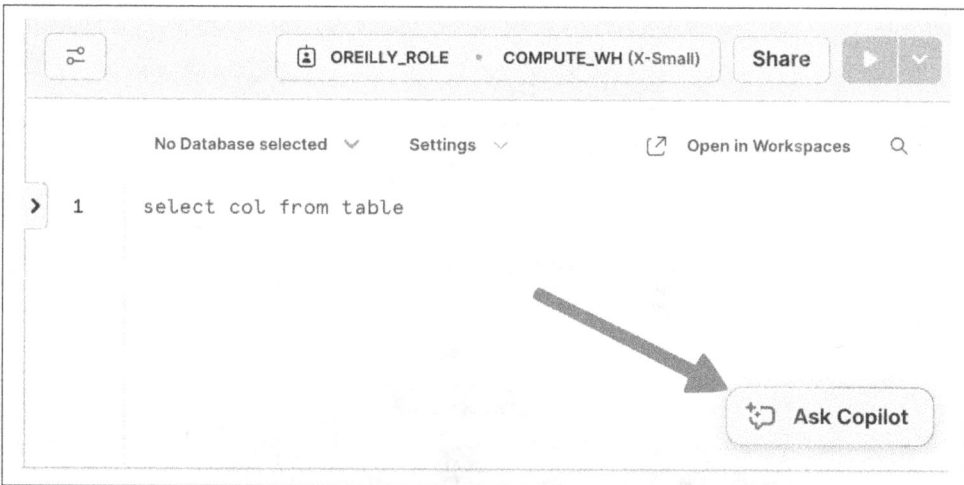

Figure 6-10. Use the Ask Copilot button on Snowflake worksheets to interact with Copilot

In Figure 6-11, you can see the Snowflake Copilot's welcome screen. You can select the context (database and schema) for Snowflake Copilot from the options, and start with the question templates already provided by Copilot.

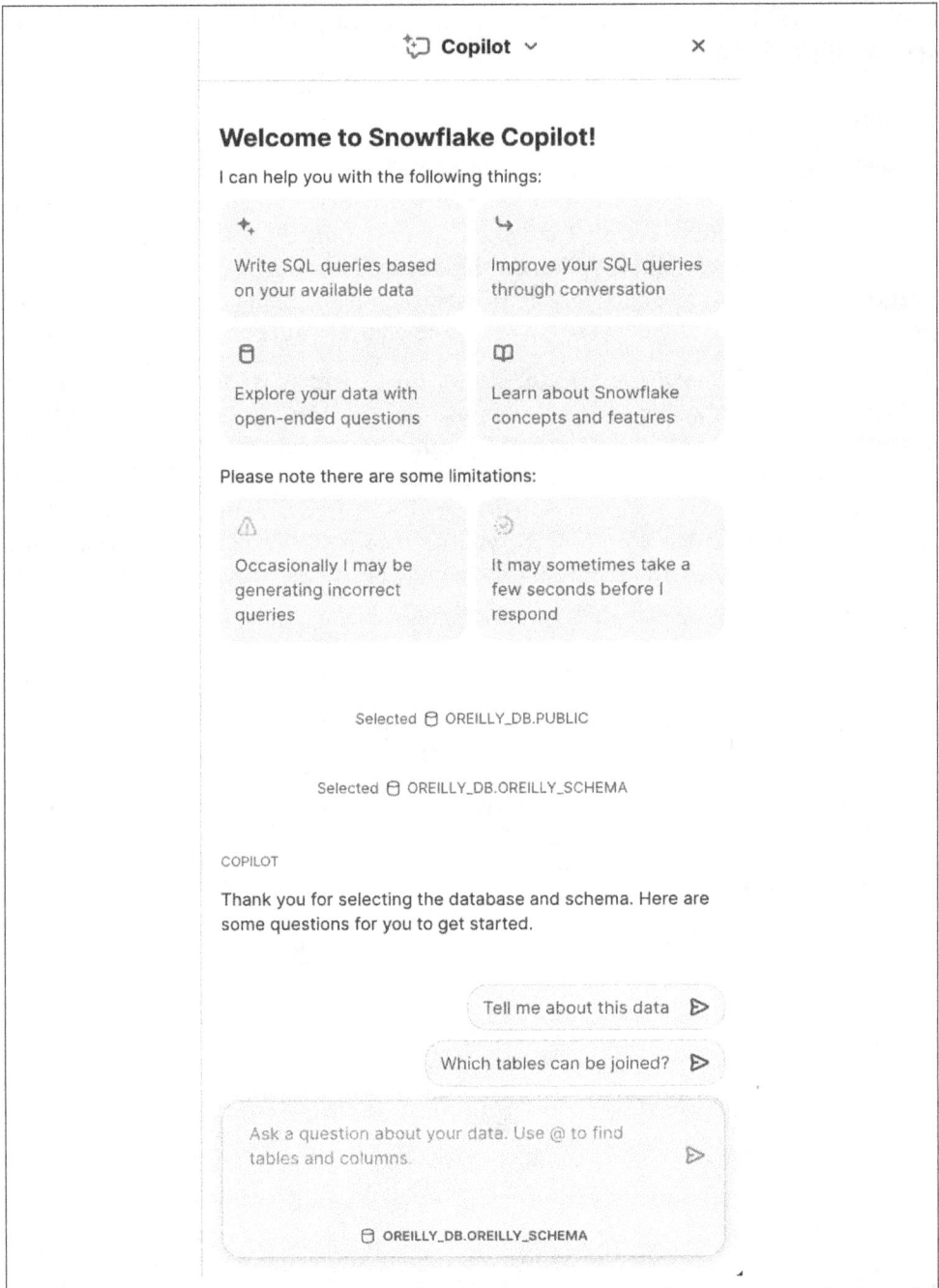

Figure 6-11. Snowflake Copilot's welcome screen after selecting the database and schema

Hands-on Example: End-to-End Machine Learning with Snowflake

In this section, I will tackle the famous diamond price prediction problem. The dataset contains information about various diamonds, including their "four Cs," carat (weight), cut, color, and clarity, and some more data. The goal here is to build a model that can accurately predict a diamond's price based on its characteristics. To begin, I will load the data using Snowsight. Then, using Snowflake Notebooks, I will explore the dataset, normalize it, and perform exploratory data analysis (EDA) on it. After that, I will use scikit-learn to run machine learning models on it. Depending on the performance, I will choose the best model and save it in the Snowflake ML Model Registry. Lastly, I will perform inference using my saved model in the registry. This will show you how different parts of the Snowflake AI and ML ecosystem come together and give you flexible tooling to set you up for success in your machine learning and AI workloads. Let's jump right in and set things up first.

The first step here is to set up our environment for machine learning. Let's open up a new worksheet in Snowsight and create a new database and a new role, which we will be using for this tutorial:

```
USE ROLE OREILLY_ROLE;
CREATE DATABASE ML_TUTORIAL;
CREATE SCHEMA ML_TUTORIAL.DIAMONDS;
CREATE OR REPLACE ROLE ML_DEV;
```

Grant some privileges to the new ML_DEV role to allow it some working freedom:

```
GRANT ROLE ML_DEV TO USER OREILLY;
GRANT ALL ON DATABASE ML_TUTORIAL TO ROLE ML_DEV;
GRANT ALL ON SCHEMA ML_TUTORIAL.DIAMONDS TO ROLE ML_DEV;
GRANT IMPORTED PRIVILEGES ON DATABASE SNOWFLAKE TO ROLE ML_DEV;
GRANT CREATE NOTEBOOK ON SCHEMA ML_TUTORIAL.DIAMONDS TO ROLE ML_DEV;
```

Now, let's create a new virtual warehouse for our machine learning workloads. A separate warehouse for such workloads ensures isolated costs for projects, and we can configure it to be more powerful. If you use a shared resource for different workloads, you must consider the amount of computing power it requires and when it is needed. You don't want an expensive warehouse performing a few lightweight SQL tasks:

```
CREATE WAREHOUSE ML_TUTORIAL_WH WITH
    WAREHOUSE_SIZE = 'MEDIUM'
    AUTO_SUSPEND = 300
    AUTO_RESUME = TRUE
    MIN_CLUSTER_COUNT = 1
    MAX_CLUSTER_COUNT = 3
    SCALING_POLICY = 'STANDARD'
    ;
```

```
GRANT USAGE ON WAREHOUSE ML_TUTORIAL_WH TO ROLE ML_DEV;
GRANT OPERATE ON WAREHOUSE ML_TUTORIAL_WH TO ROLE ML_DEV;
```

Now that we have some compute at hand, let's just verify our setup really quickly before we move forward:

```
USE ROLE ML_DEV;
USE WAREHOUSE ML_TUTORIAL_WH;
USE DATABASE ML_TUTORIAL;
USE SCHEMA DIAMONDS;
SELECT CURRENT_ROLE(), CURRENT_WAREHOUSE(), CURRENT_DATABASE(), CURRENT_SCHEMA();
```

If everything worked well, you should see an output like the one shown in Figure 6-12.

A CURRENT_ROLE()	A CURRENT_WAREHOUSE()	A CURRENT_DATABASE()	A CURRENT_SCHEMA()
1 ML_DEV	ML_TUTORIAL_WH	ML_TUTORIAL	DIAMONDS

Figure 6-12. Lightweight verification of the setup

Now it's time to load data to a Snowflake table; we have several ways to do it. We saw earlier in this chapter that Snowflake Notebooks can connect to a Git repository and read files directly to it, but just like SPCS is not available in trial accounts, external access in Snowflake is not available either. You can contact your account representative at Snowflake to enable it on your trial account, but for the sake of this tutorial, we won't be using any external access features.

> **Why would we need external access features for the hands-on tutorials?**
>
> External access allows Snowflake to access network locations external to Snowflake. We would need it in order to connect our Snowflake notebook to GitHub and load the data and the scripts directly into Snowflake.

Now that we've covered that, let's go ahead and load the data manually. I have uploaded the data file to the GitHub repository (*https://oreil.ly/advanced-snowflake-repoch6-1*) of this tutorial, which you can download to your local machine. Let's upload the file to Snowflake. As we learned before, we can now upload our file directly to Snowflake and load the data into Snowflake. Let's put that to use. In case you need a reminder, Figure 6-13 shows where you can find that option.

Click on the From File option, and it will display another pop-up, where you can drag and drop or select your local file. Figure 6-14 shows how that UI component looks.

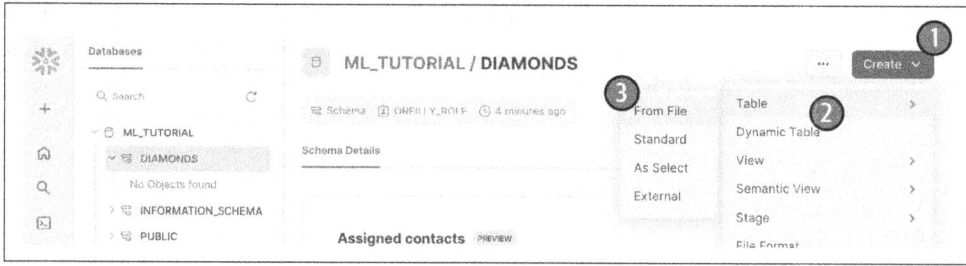

Figure 6-13. Options to upload the file manually via Snowsight

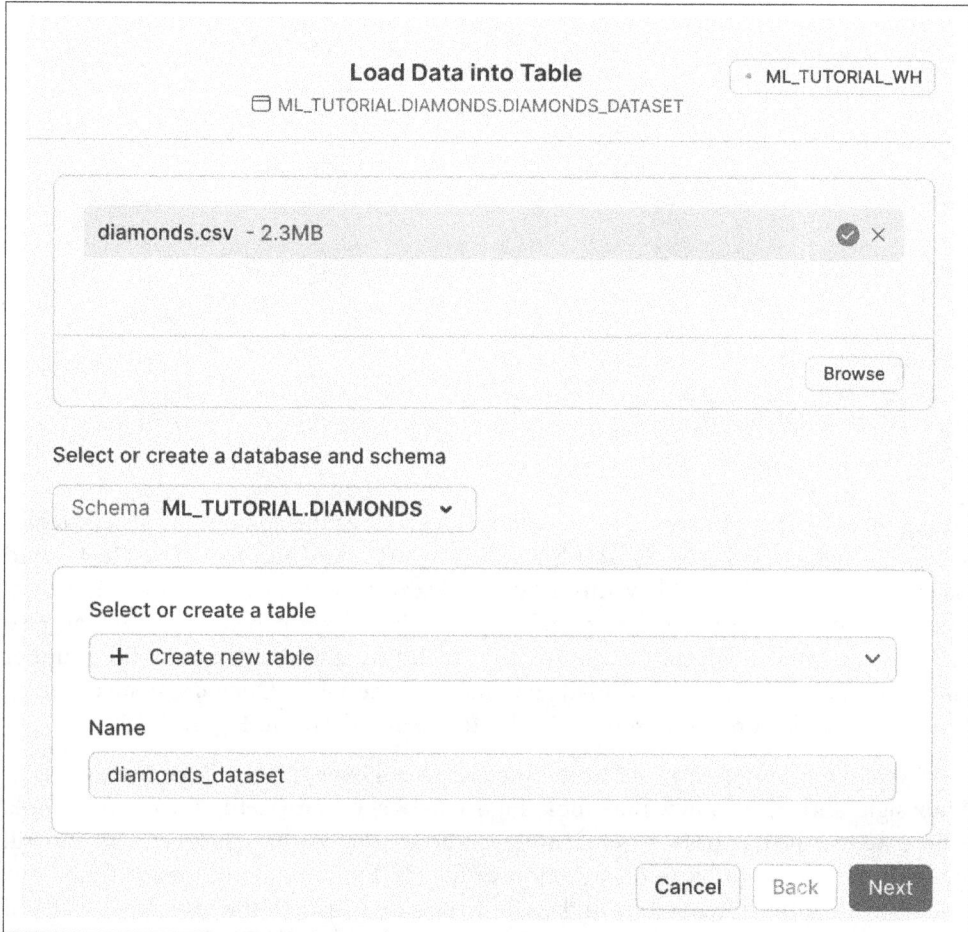

Figure 6-14. UI to upload the file

As you can see in Figure 6-14, it's here that you have to select the schema to create that table in and also give it a name. I have named it "diamonds_dataset" (not very creative, but that's the best I could come up with). When you click Next, Snowflake will upload the file and show you the schema it inferred from the file. Make sure that the file format is set to "Delimited Files (CSV or TSV)" to ensure that the schema is inferred correctly. See Figure 6-15 to look at the schema that Snowflake inferred.

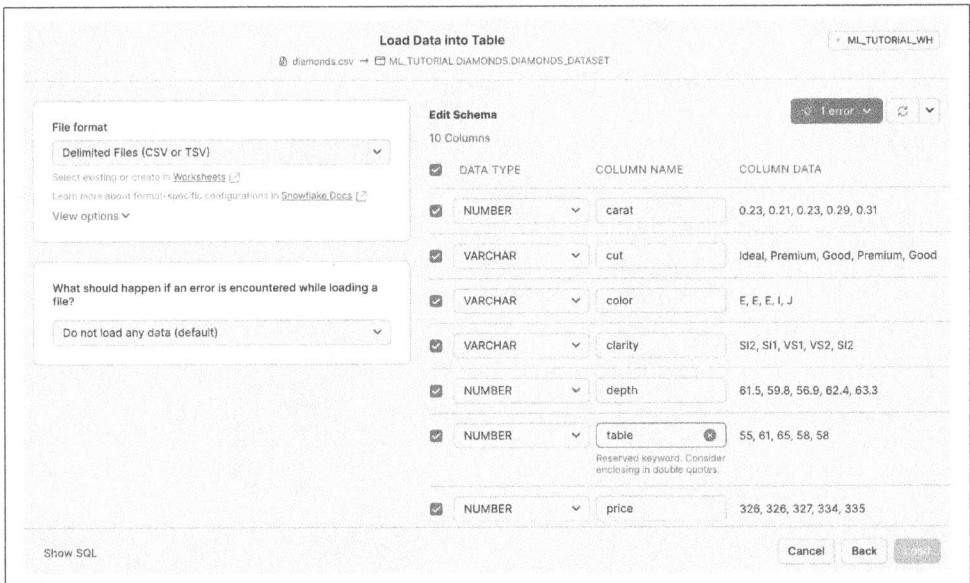

Figure 6-15. Snowflake's inferred schema from the file (see this screengrab in full size) (https://oreil.ly/adsf_0615png)

In Figure 6-15, you can see that you will get an error, as the column is named "table", which is a reserved keyword, and Snowflake won't allow you to upload it. I could have fixed it in the file, but hey, this is how we learn. You can see in Figure 6-16 (highlighted) that I have renamed it to "table_perc" since it's a percentage. You can also click on the bottom left button, Show SQL, to see what Snowflake is running under the hood. Let's click Load and load the data into the table. Once done successfully, you should see a completion screen similar to the one shown in Figure 6-17.

Now that the boring part is out of the way, let's head over to Snowflake Notebooks in Snowsight and create a new notebook. Figure 6-18 shows my setup for the notebook, where we use the database, schema, and warehouse that we have just created. We will go with the option of "Run on warehouse" for the Python environment. If, like me, you're creating the notebook from the UI, make sure to switch the role to ML_DEV if you haven't already. You'll also notice a new preview config for "Runtime version" with Snowflake Warehouse Runtime 1.0 and Snowflake Warehouse Runtime 2.0 as options. We will use Snowflake Warehouse Runtime 1.0, which uses Python version 3.9, for the scope of this tutorial.

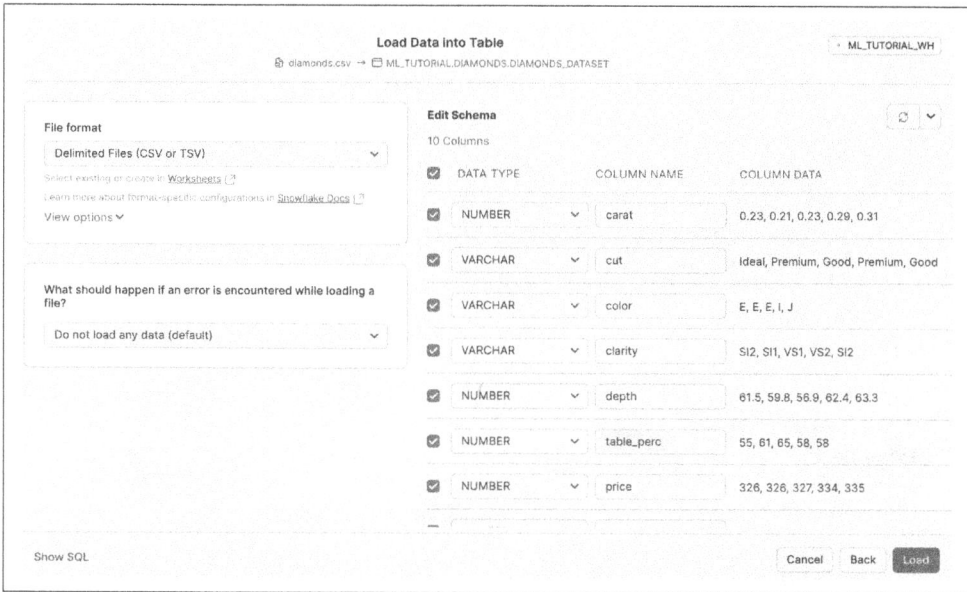

Figure 6-16. *Updating the reserved keyword from the inferred schema in Snowflake UI (see this screengrab in full size) (https://oreil.ly/adsf_0616png)*

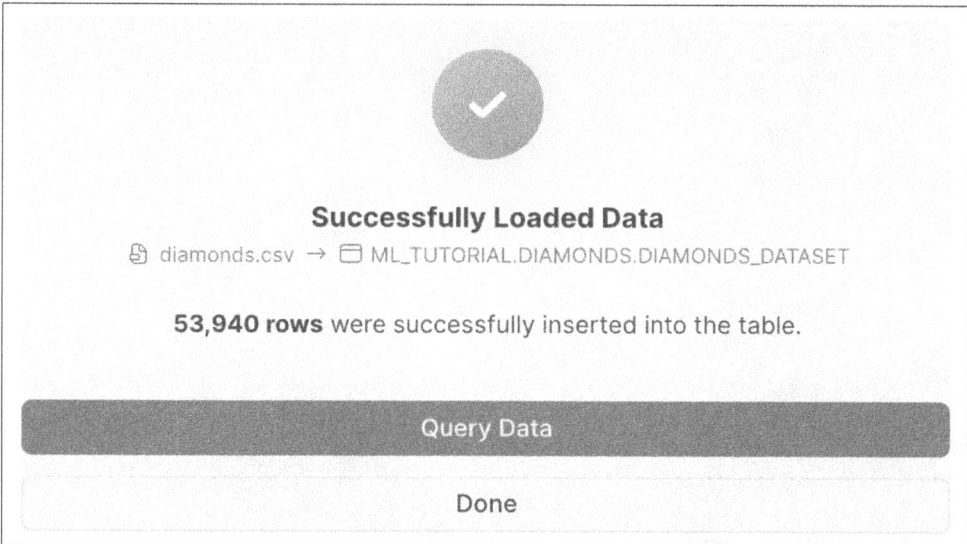

Figure 6-17. *Data load completion screen*

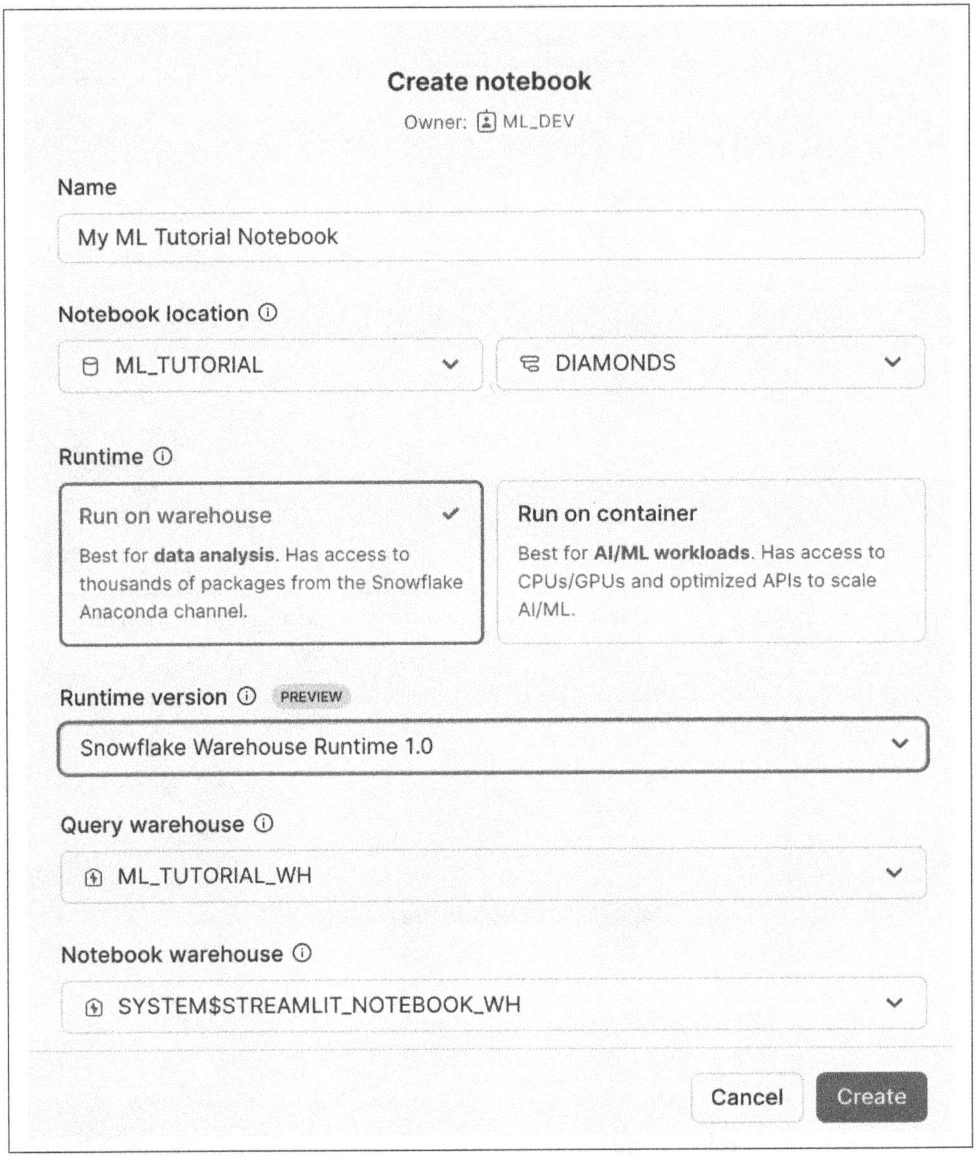

Figure 6-18. Create notebook dialogue

Now you have an empty (well, with some pre-filled code) notebook that you will be using for this tutorial. You can remove all the cells that preexisted in the notebook. Figure 6-19 shows how notebooks look when they are created.

```
Python ∨ as cell1  •                                                    ▶  🗄  ⋮

  1   # Import python packages
  2   import streamlit as st
  3   import pandas as pd
  4
  5   # We can also use Snowpark for our analyses!
  6   from snowflake.snowpark.context import get_active_session
  7   session = get_active_session()
  8
```

```
SQL ∨ as cell2  •

  1   -- Welcome to Snowflake Notebooks!
  2   -- Try out a SQL cell to generate some data.
  3   SELECT 'FRIDAY' as SNOWDAY, 0.2 as CHANCE_OF_SNOW
  4   UNION ALL
  5   SELECT 'SATURDAY',0.5
  6   UNION ALL
  7   SELECT 'SUNDAY', 0.9;
```

```
Python ∨ as cell3  •

  1   # Then, we can use the python name to turn cell2 into a Pandas dataframe
  2   my_df = cell2.to_pandas()
  3
  4   # Chart the data
  5   st.subheader("Chance of SNOW ❄")
  6   st.line_chart(my_df, x='SNOWDAY', y='CHANCE_OF_SNOW')
  7
  8   # Give it a go!
  9   st.subheader("Try it out yourself and show off your skills 🏂")
```

Figure 6-19. Pre-filled code in a newly created Snowflake notebook

Once you remove it, you may choose to add the following code in the first cell and try
running it, and load the libraries:

```
# Library Imports

## Snowflake Snowpark
import snowflake.snowpark as snowpark
from snowflake.snowpark import Session
from snowflake.snowpark.functions import col, upper, regexp_replace
from snowflake.snowpark.types import StructType, StructField, StringType
from snowflake.snowpark.types import IntegerType, FloatType, DecimalType

## Snowflake ML
import snowflake.ml.modeling.preprocessing as snowml_pp
```

```
## Data Science toolkit
import pandas as pd
import numpy as np
import matplotlib.pyplot as plt
import seaborn as sns

## Scikit-learn
from sklearn.model_selection import train_test_split
from sklearn.ensemble import RandomForestRegressor
from sklearn.linear_model import LinearRegression
from sklearn.metrics import mean_squared_error, r2_score, mean_absolute_error

import warnings
warnings.filterwarnings('ignore')

print("✔ Libraries imported successfully")
```

Figure 6-20 shows the output of this code.

```
1    # Library Imports
2
3    ## Snowflake Snowpark
4    import snowflake.snowpark as snowpark
5    from snowflake.snowpark import Session
6    from snowflake.snowpark.functions import col, upper, regexp_replace
7    from snowflake.snowpark.types import StructType, StructField, StringType, IntegerT)
8
9
10   ## Snowflake ML
11   import snowflake.ml.modeling.preprocessing as snowml_pp
12
13
14   ## Data Science toolkit
15   import pandas as pd
16   import numpy as np
17   import matplotlib.pyplot as plt
18   import seaborn as sns
19
20
21   ## Scikit-learn
22   from sklearn.model_selection import train_test_split
23   from sklearn.ensemble import RandomForestRegressor
24   from sklearn.linear_model import LinearRegression
25   from sklearn.metrics import mean_squared_error, r2_score, mean_absolute_error
26
27
28   import warnings
29   warnings.filterwarnings('ignore')
30
31
32   print("✔ Libraries imported successfully")
```

ModuleNotFoundError: Line 11: Module Not Found: snowflake.ml. To import packages from Anaconda, install them first using the package selector at the top of the page.

Figure 6-20. Error on loading the libraries

Oops! What happened there? Take a moment to think why the library is not there. Isn't Snowflake claiming that it provides us with all the libraries in the Anaconda channel?

Snowflake does indeed provide all the libraries in the Anaconda channel, but you always have to add them to your notebook in order to be able to use them. Snowflake doesn't pre-load everything for you, and that is because not everyone needs everything. You can choose what you want Snowflake to load. Let's add all of them now. You can do so in the Packages drop-down menu on the top. Figure 6-21 shows how you can look for and add libraries.

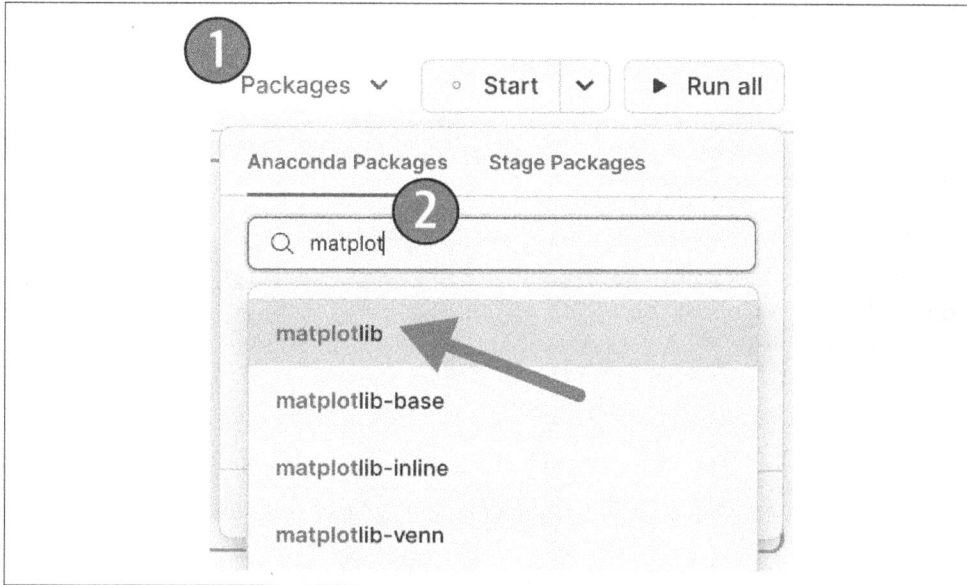

Figure 6-21. Adding required packages to the notebooks

Once this is done, you might get a prompt to restart your session. It is best practice to restart your session after loading the packages. Figure 6-22 shows the warning.

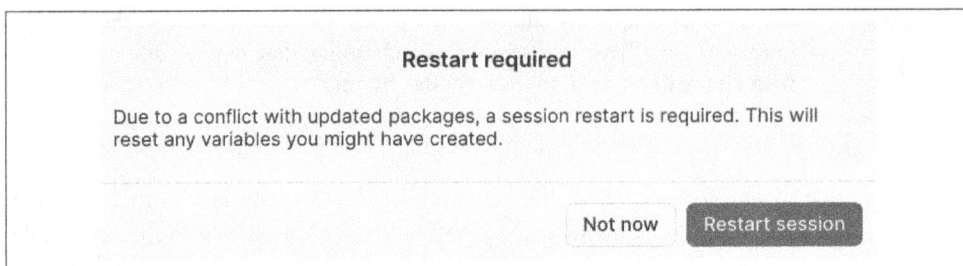

Figure 6-22. Prompt nudging to restart the Notebooks session after updating packages

Now that that's out of the way, let's start the session and load the dataset:

```
# Get current session
session = snowpark.Session.builder.getOrCreate()

session.use_role("ML_DEV")
print(f"Snowpark version: {snowpark.__version__}")
print(f"Current context: {session.get_current_database()}\
.{session.get_current_schema()}")
print(f"Current Role: {session.get_current_role()} ")
print(f"Current Warehouse: {session.get_current_warehouse()}")
```

When verifying the context, you should get the output shown in Figure 6-23 when you run the preceding code.

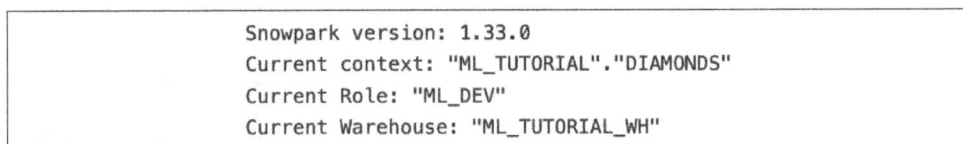

```
Snowpark version: 1.33.0
Current context: "ML_TUTORIAL"."DIAMONDS"
Current Role: "ML_DEV"
Current Warehouse: "ML_TUTORIAL_WH"
```

Figure 6-23. Checking the context being used within Snowflake Notebooks

The next step? Load the data:

```
# Now it's time to upload and load the diamonds dataset

diamonds_df = session.table("diamonds_dataset")

diamonds_df.show(10)
```

The show() function of Snowpark is similar to the head() function from pandas. Figure 6-24 shows the output of the show() function and the dataset loaded into a Snowpark DataFrame.

Note that the values in CUT are in title case and contain spaces. We don't want that; let's fix those by converting them to all uppercase and removing the spaces between them:

```
diamonds_df = diamonds_df.withColumn(
    "CUT",
    regexp_replace(upper(col("CUT")), '[^a-zA-Z0-9]+', '')
)
diamonds_df.show(10)
```

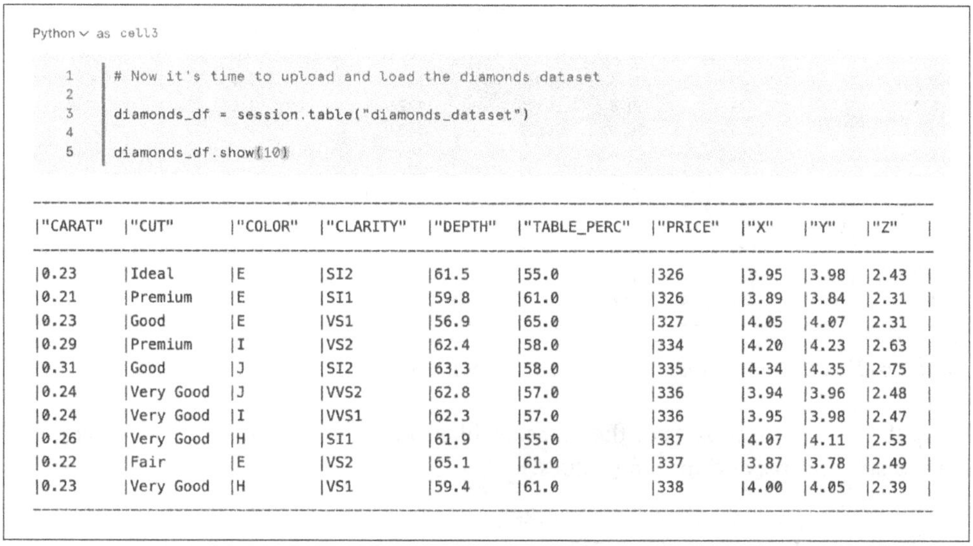

```
Python ∨ as cell3

1   # Now it's time to upload and load the diamonds dataset
2
3   diamonds_df = session.table("diamonds_dataset")
4
5   diamonds_df.show(10)
```

"CARAT"	"CUT"	"COLOR"	"CLARITY"	"DEPTH"	"TABLE_PERC"	"PRICE"	"X"	"Y"	"Z"
0.23	Ideal	E	SI2	61.5	55.0	326	3.95	3.98	2.43
0.21	Premium	E	SI1	59.8	61.0	326	3.89	3.84	2.31
0.23	Good	E	VS1	56.9	65.0	327	4.05	4.07	2.31
0.29	Premium	I	VS2	62.4	58.0	334	4.20	4.23	2.63
0.31	Good	J	SI2	63.3	58.0	335	4.34	4.35	2.75
0.24	Very Good	J	VVS2	62.8	57.0	336	3.94	3.96	2.48
0.24	Very Good	I	VVS1	62.3	57.0	336	3.95	3.98	2.47
0.26	Very Good	H	SI1	61.9	55.0	337	4.07	4.11	2.53
0.22	Fair	E	VS2	65.1	61.0	337	3.87	3.78	2.49
0.23	Very Good	H	VS1	59.4	61.0	338	4.00	4.05	2.39

Figure 6-24. Loading the data into Snowpark DataFrame

Now, if you look at the dataset, as shown in Figure 6-25, we can see that the CUT column has all uppercase values without any spaces. Let's keep rolling.

```
1   # Note that the CUT values are in Camel Case and there are spaces between them.
2   # Let's fix those first
3   # Then let's remove the spaces
4
5   diamonds_df = diamonds_df.withColumn(
6       "CUT",
7       regexp_replace(upper(col("CUT")), '[^a-zA-Z0-9]+', '')
8   )
9   diamonds_df.show(10)
```

"CARAT"	"COLOR"	"CLARITY"	"DEPTH"	"TABLE_PERC"	"PRICE"	"X"	"Y"	"Z"	"CUT"
0.23	E	SI2	61.5	55.0	326	3.95	3.98	2.43	IDEAL
0.21	E	SI1	59.8	61.0	326	3.89	3.84	2.31	PREMIUM
0.23	E	VS1	56.9	65.0	327	4.05	4.07	2.31	GOOD
0.29	I	VS2	62.4	58.0	334	4.20	4.23	2.63	PREMIUM
0.31	J	SI2	63.3	58.0	335	4.34	4.35	2.75	GOOD
0.24	J	VVS2	62.8	57.0	336	3.94	3.96	2.48	VERYGOOD
0.24	I	VVS1	62.3	57.0	336	3.95	3.98	2.47	VERYGOOD
0.26	H	SI1	61.9	55.0	337	4.07	4.11	2.53	VERYGOOD
0.22	E	VS2	65.1	61.0	337	3.87	3.78	2.49	FAIR
0.23	H	VS1	59.4	61.0	338	4.00	4.05	2.39	VERYGOOD

Figure 6-25. CUT column is in uppercase and without any spaces

Now, let's check some stats of the datasets, like total records, total unique values, column distributions, and missing values:

```
# Let's do some basic dataset checks
print("=== DATASET OVERVIEW ===")
print(f"Total records: {diamonds_df.count()}")
print(f"Total columns: {len(diamonds_df.columns)}")

# Display basic statistics
diamonds_df.describe().show()

# Check for missing values
print("\n=== CHECK MISSING VALUES ===")
for col_name in diamonds_df.columns:
    null_count = diamonds_df.filter(col(col_name).is_null()).count()
    print(f"{col_name}: {null_count} missing values")
```

Figure 6-26 shows the result of the preceding code and a basic dataset overview.

```
=== DATASET OVERVIEW ===
Total records: 53940
Total columns: 10
_____

|"SUMMARY"     |"CARAT"                |"COLOR"  |"CLARITY"  |"DEPTH"
_____

|count         |53940.0                |53940    |53940      |53940.0
|mean          |0.79793975             |NULL     |NULL       |61.7494049
|stddev        |0.4740112443813965     |NULL     |NULL       |1.43262131
|min           |0.2                    |D        |I1         |43.0
|max           |5.01                   |J        |VVS2       |79.0
_____


=== CHECK MISSING VALUES ===
CARAT: 0 missing values
COLOR: 0 missing values
CLARITY: 0 missing values
DEPTH: 0 missing values
TABLE_PERC: 0 missing values
PRICE: 0 missing values
X: 0 missing values
Y: 0 missing values
Z: 0 missing values
CUT: 0 missing values
```

Figure 6-26. Basic dataset overview

Going strong so far! Now, let's visually see some distributions and relations within the dataset. It's always good to plot them out. It helps uncover some trends and gets you more familiar with how the dataset is distributed. Let's use the libraries we have loaded before for data visualization and plot some charts. The code will look like this:

```
# Convert to Pandas for visualization
diamonds_pd = diamonds_df.to_pandas()

# Set up the plotting style
plt.style.use('default')
fig, axes = plt.subplots(2, 3, figsize=(18, 12))
fig.suptitle('Diamond Dataset - Exploratory Data Analysis',
             fontsize=16,
             fontweight='bold'
             )

# Price distribution
axes[0, 0].hist(
    diamonds_pd['PRICE'],
    bins=50,
    alpha=0.7,
    color='skyblue',
```

```
        edgecolor='black'
    )
    axes[0, 0].set_title('Price Distribution')
    axes[0, 0].set_xlabel('Price ($)')
    axes[0, 0].set_ylabel('Frequency')

    # Carat distribution
    axes[0, 1].hist(
        diamonds_pd['CARAT'],
        bins=50,
        alpha=0.7,
        color='lightgreen',
        edgecolor='black'
    )
    axes[0, 1].set_title('Carat Distribution')
    axes[0, 1].set_xlabel('Carat')
    axes[0, 1].set_ylabel('Frequency')

    # Price vs Carat scatter plot
    axes[0, 2].scatter(
        diamonds_pd['CARAT'],
        diamonds_pd['PRICE'],
        alpha=0.5,
        color='coral'
    )
    axes[0, 2].set_title('Price vs Carat')
    axes[0, 2].set_xlabel('Carat')
    axes[0, 2].set_ylabel('Price ($)')

    # Cut distribution
    cut_counts = diamonds_pd['CUT'].value_counts()
    axes[1, 0].bar(
        cut_counts.index,
        cut_counts.values,
        color='gold',
        alpha=0.7
    )
    axes[1, 0].set_title('Cut Distribution')
    axes[1, 0].set_xlabel('Cut')
    axes[1, 0].set_ylabel('Count')
    axes[1, 0].tick_params(axis='x', rotation=45)

    # Color distribution
    color_counts = diamonds_pd['COLOR'].value_counts()
    axes[1, 1].bar(
        color_counts.index,
        color_counts.values,
        color='lightpink',
        alpha=0.7
    )
    axes[1, 1].set_title('Color Distribution')
    axes[1, 1].set_xlabel('Color')
```

```
axes[1, 1].set_ylabel('Count')

# Clarity distribution
clarity_counts = diamonds_pd['CLARITY'].value_counts()
axes[1, 2].bar(
    clarity_counts.index,
    clarity_counts.values,
    color='lightblue',
    alpha=0.7
)
axes[1, 2].set_title('Clarity Distribution')
axes[1, 2].set_xlabel('Clarity')
axes[1, 2].set_ylabel('Count')
axes[1, 2].tick_params(axis='x', rotation=45)

plt.tight_layout()
plt.show()
```

It's an extended code, but that's only to keep things tidy and utilize some screen space—after all, I was in no rush. This will place the visuals in a nice grid of 2 × 3. Figure 6-27 shows the results of running the preceding code.

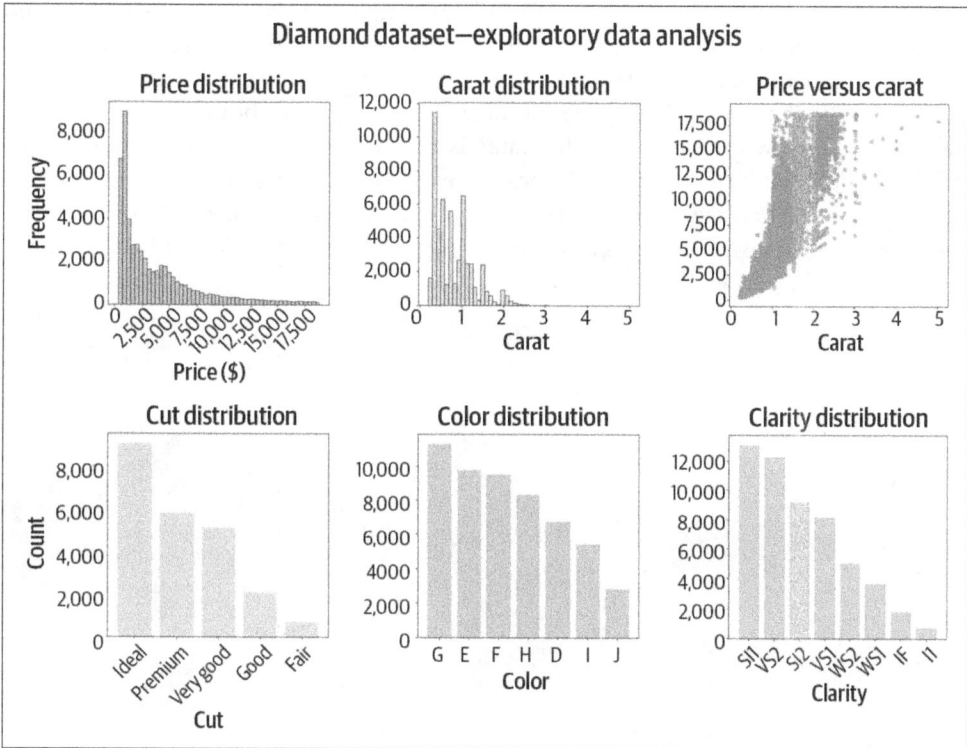

Figure 6-27. EDA plots of our dataset

You can see that the data is not showing something right off the bat. We have to dig a bit deeper. The diamond types are not equally distributed, so it might be a bit harder to be accurate about certain diamond types when we predict prices. Let's look at the correlation of different variables with one another. We can do so by using seaborn's heatmap. See the following code:

```
# Correlation heatmap for numerical features
numerical_features = ['CARAT', 'DEPTH', 'TABLE_PERC', 'X', 'Y', 'Z', 'PRICE']
correlation_matrix = diamonds_pd[numerical_features].corr()

plt.figure(figsize=(10, 8))
sns.heatmap(correlation_matrix, annot=True, cmap='coolwarm', center=0,
            square=True, linewidths=0.5)
plt.title('Correlation Matrix - Numerical Features')
plt.tight_layout()
plt.show()
```

This will give you a beautiful correlation matrix of all the numerical features, including your target variable, PRICE. Figure 6-28 shows the correlation matrix plotted by the preceding code.

This gives us something right away. We can see a high correlation between price and carat. It is common knowledge that more carats means an expensive diamond, but plotting this data makes it beautiful. Also, imagine if there were negative values in your dataset—then you'd have a whole new thing to worry about: "Is the dataset I have correct? How do we collect the data? Is this a human error or is the machine collecting data sending in garbage?" Sometimes asking the obvious questions and visualizing the obvious correlations or trends gives you the confidence that you can trust the data; thus, no visualization is a waste. Enough philosophy, back to the tutorial.

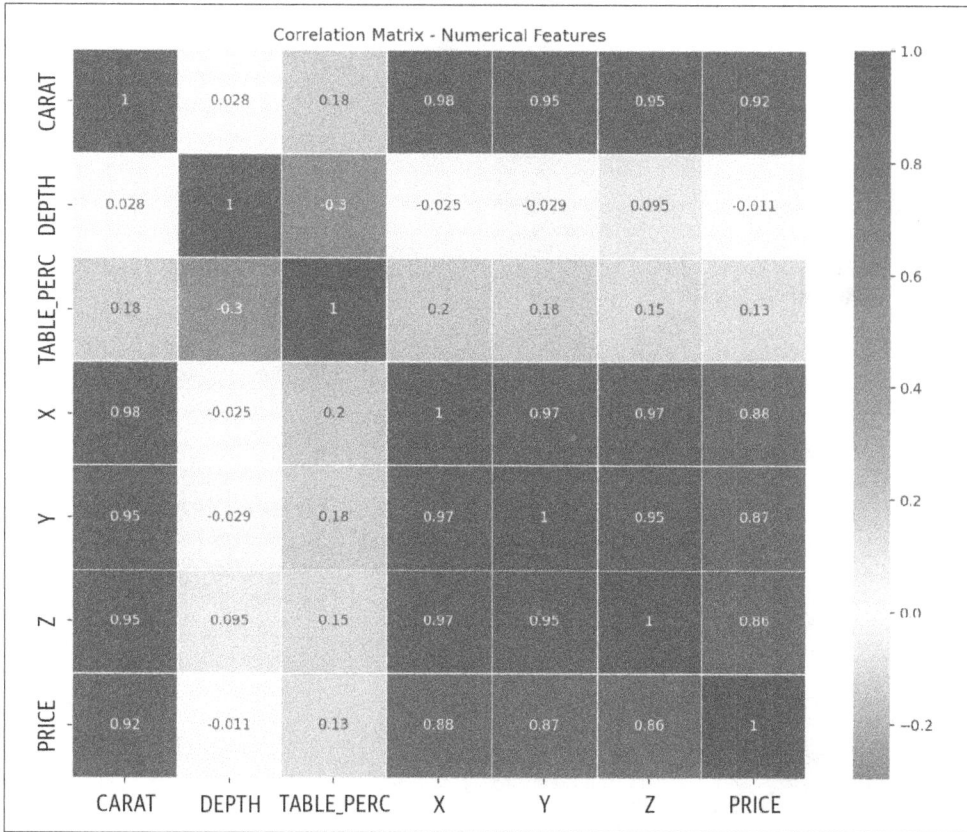

Figure 6-28. Correlation matrix of all numerical variables

Now that I'm satisfied with the dataset, and it appears as expected, I want to prepare it for machine learning algorithms. What I mean by that is that the computer doesn't understand the difference between a "VERYGOOD" cut and an "IDEAL" cut. I need to convert it to numbers, and at the same time, I want to scale my numeric values too. Why? Because you never know when those will be useful.Let's see how we would do it:

```
categorical_columns_names = [
    "CUT",
    "COLOR",
    "CLARITY"
]
categorical_columns_encoded_names = [
    "CUT_ORDINAL",
    "COLOR_ORDINAL",
    "CLARITY_ORDINAL"
]
numerical_columns = [
```

```python
        "CARAT",
        "DEPTH",
        "TABLE_PERC",
        "X",
        "Y",
        "Z"
    ]
    numerical_columns_scaled_names = [
        "CARAT_SCALED",
        "DEPTH_SCALED",
        "TABLE_PERC_SCALED",
        "X_SCALED",
        "Y_SCALED",
        "Z_SCALED"
    ]


    categories = {
        "CUT": np.array([
            "IDEAL",
            "PREMIUM",
            "VERYGOOD",
            "GOOD",
            "FAIR"
        ]),
        "CLARITY": np.array([
            "IF",
            "VVS1",
            "VVS2",
            "VS1",
            "VS2",
            "SI1",
            "SI2",
            "I1",
            "I2",
            "I3"
        ]),
        "COLOR": np.array([
            "D",
            "E",
            "F",
            "G",
            "H",
            "I",
            "J"
        ]),
    }


    # Normalize the CARAT column using MinMax scalar
    numeric_scalar = snowml_pp.MinMaxScaler(
        input_cols=numerical_columns,
```

```
        output_cols=numerical_columns_scaled_names,
)

scaled_diamonds_df = numeric_scalar.fit(diamonds_df).transform(diamonds_df)

# Select new columns
carat_scaled = scaled_diamonds_df.col("CARAT_SCALED")
depth_scaled = scaled_diamonds_df.col("DEPTH_SCALED")
table_perc_scaled = scaled_diamonds_df.col("TABLE_PERC_SCALED")
x_scaled = scaled_diamonds_df.col("X_SCALED")
y_scaled = scaled_diamonds_df.col("Y_SCALED")
z_scaled = scaled_diamonds_df.col("Z_SCALED")

# Add them to the dataframe
scaled_diamonds_df = scaled_diamonds_df\
    .with_column("CARAT_SCALED", carat_scaled)\
    .with_column("DEPTH_SCALED", depth_scaled)\
    .with_column("TABLE_PERC_SCALED", table_perc_scaled)\
    .with_column("X_SCALED", x_scaled)\
    .with_column("Y_SCALED", y_scaled)\
    .with_column("Z_SCALED", z_scaled)

categorical_encoder = snowml_pp.OrdinalEncoder(
    input_cols=categorical_columns_names,
    output_cols=categorical_columns_encoded_names,
    categories=categories,
)

encoded_diamonds_df = categorical_encoder\
    .fit(scaled_diamonds_df)\
    .transform(scaled_diamonds_df)

cut_ordinal = encoded_diamonds_df.col("CUT_ORDINAL")
color_ordinal = encoded_diamonds_df.col("COLOR_ORDINAL")
clarity_ordinal = encoded_diamonds_df.col("CLARITY_ORDINAL")

final_dataset = encoded_diamonds_df\
    .with_column("CUT_ORDINAL", cut_ordinal)\
    .with_column("COLOR_ORDINAL", color_ordinal)\
    .with_column("CLARITY_ORDINAL", clarity_ordinal)


final_dataset.show(10)
```

I first defined the existing columns in the dataset and their new names, then I used the MinMax scalar for the numeric and OrdinalEncoder for the categorical columns. You can choose to do one-hot encoding also, but I'm not going to do it here since our aim is not to build the best-of-class ML model, but rather to understand how different pieces will tie together within Snowflake. Figure 6-29 shows the scaled numeric columns added to the dataset, and Figure 6-30 shows the categorical encoded columns added to the dataset.

```
|"CARAT_SCALED"          |"DEPTH_SCALED"         |"TABLE_PERC_SCALED"      |"X_SCALED"            |"Y_SCALED"
-----------------------------------------------------------------------------------------------------------------------------
|0.00623700623700622     |0.513888888888888824   |0.230769230769230760     |0.3677839851024209    |0.0675721561969∠
|0.00207900207900212     |0.466666666666666605   |0.346153846153846152     |0.3621973929236499    |0.0651952461799€
|0.00623700623700622     |0.386111111111111054   |0.423076923076923080     |0.3770949720670391    |0.0691001697792€
|0.01871101871101872     |0.538888888888888822   |0.288461538461538456     |0.3910614525139665    |0.0718166383701`
|0.02286902286902282     |0.563888888888888821   |0.288461538461538456     |0.4040968342644321    |0.0738539898132∠
|0.00831600831600832     |0.549999999999999933   |0.269230769230769224     |0.3668528864059591    |0.0672325976230€
|0.00831600831600832     |0.536111111111111045   |0.269230769230769224     |0.3677839851024209    |0.0675721561969∠
|0.01247401247401252     |0.524999999999999934   |0.230769230769230760     |0.3789571694599628    |0.0697792869269€
|0.00415800415800412     |0.613888888888888818   |0.346153846153846152     |0.3603351955307263    |0.064176570458∠€
|0.00623700623700622     |0.455555555555555494   |0.346153846153846152     |0.3724394785847300    |0.0687606112054`
-----------------------------------------------------------------------------------------------------------------------------
```

Figure 6-29. Newly added numerical columns after `MinMax` *scaling*

```
     |"CUT_ORDINAL"   |"COLOR_ORDINAL"   |"CLARITY_ORDINAL"   |
     ----------------------------------------------------------------
  2  |0.0             |1.0               |6.0                 |
  5  |1.0             |1.0               |5.0                 |
  5  |3.0             |1.0               |3.0                 |
  1  |1.0             |5.0               |4.0                 |
  9  |3.0             |6.0               |6.0                 |
  0  |2.0             |6.0               |2.0                 |
  3  |2.0             |5.0               |1.0                 |
  7  |2.0             |4.0               |5.0                 |
  1  |4.0             |1.0               |4.0                 |
  7  |2.0             |4.0               |3.0                 |
     ----------------------------------------------------------------
```

Figure 6-30. Newly added categorical columns after ordinal encoding

Now that we have the complete dataset, it is always good to make a copy of it, and in Snowflake, we can save it as a table so it's accessible via SQL also when needed:

```
# Save the engineered dataset
final_dataset.write.mode("overwrite").save_as_table(
    "DIAMONDS_FEATURE_ENGINEERED")
```

In Figure 6-31, we can see that the table is created in the database, and in Figure 6-32, we can see that the new columns that we created are a part of the table.

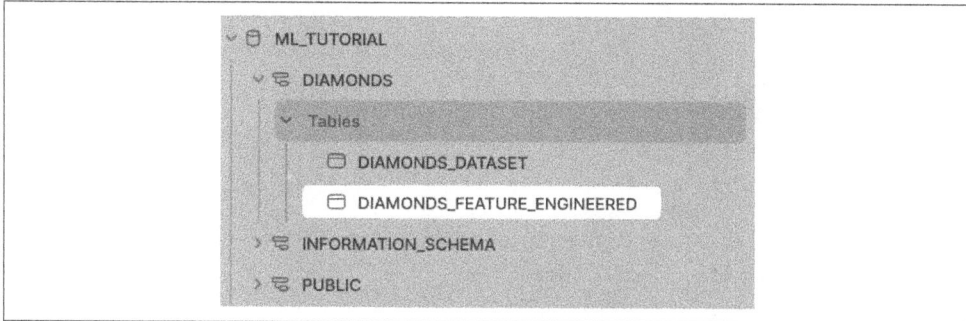

Figure 6-31. Table with feature-engineered dataset in the database

ML_TUTORIAL / DIAMONDS / DIAMONDS_FEATURE_ENGINEERED

Table   ML_DEV   1 minute ago   53.9K   1.0MB

Table Details   Columns   Data Preview   Copy History   Lineage

19 Columns

NAME ↑	TYPE	DESCRIPTION ⓘ	TAGS ⓘ
CLARITY_ORDINAL	# Float		—
COLOR	A Varchar		—
COLOR_ORDINAL	# Float		—
CUT	A Varchar		—
CUT_ORDINAL	# Float		—
DEPTH	# Number		—
DEPTH_SCALED	# Number		—
PRICE	# Number		—
TABLE_PERC	# Number		—
TABLE_PERC_SCA...	# Number		—
X	# Number		—
X_SCALED	# Number		—
Y	# Number		—
Y_SCALED	# Number		—
Z	# Number		—
Z_SCALED	# Number		—

Figure 6-32. Columns in the newly created table

Now, let's prepare the data for ML. In the following code, we will split our dataset into a training set and a test set:

```
feature_columns = [
    "CARAT_SCALED",
    "DEPTH_SCALED",
    "TABLE_PERC_SCALED",
    "X_SCALED",
    "Y_SCALED",
    "Z_SCALED",
    "CUT_ORDINAL",
    "COLOR_ORDINAL",
    "CLARITY_ORDINAL",
]

target_column = "PRICE"

# Get the data as pandas DataFrame for ML
ml_data = final_dataset.select(feature_columns + [target_column]).to_pandas()

# Prepare features and target
X = ml_data[feature_columns]
y = ml_data[target_column]

print(f"Feature matrix shape: {X.shape}")
print(f"Target vector shape: {y.shape}")

# Split the data
X_train, X_test, y_train, y_test = train_test_split(
    X, y, test_size=0.2, random_state=42
)

print(f"Training set: {X_train.shape[0]} samples")
print(f"Test set: {X_test.shape[0]} samples")

# Display feature statistics
print("\n=== FEATURE STATISTICS ===")
print(X_train.describe())
```

The dataset is now split, and we can see the distribution in Figure 6-33, which is generated from the preceding code.

```
=== PREPARING DATA FOR ML ===
Feature matrix shape: (53940, 9)
Target vector shape: (53940,)
Training set: 43152 samples
Test set: 10788 samples
=== FEATURE STATISTICS ===
       CARAT_SCALED  DEPTH_SCALED  ...  COLOR_ORDINAL  CLARITY_ORDINAL
count  4.315200e+04  4.315200e+04  ...   43152.000000     43152.000000
mean   1.243728e-01  5.206402e-01  ...       2.591073         3.947094
std    9.840780e-02  3.967342e-02  ...       1.698757         1.646426
min    2.000000e-17 -3.200000e-17  ...       0.000000         0.000000
25%    4.158004e-02  5.000000e-01  ...       1.000000         3.000000
50%    1.039501e-01  5.222222e-01  ...       3.000000         4.000000
75%    1.746362e-01  5.416667e-01  ...       4.000000         5.000000
max    1.000000e+00  1.000000e+00  ...       6.000000         7.000000
[8 rows x 9 columns]
```

Figure 6-33. Data preparation for ML

Now that I have divided the dataset, I am ready to train the machine learning models. I will be training a linear regression model and a random forest regressor. You may choose to train as many models as you wish:

```
# Train multiple models
print("=== TRAINING MACHINE LEARNING MODELS ===")

models = {}
predictions = {}
metrics = {}

# 1. Linear regression
print("Training Linear Regression...")
lr_model = LinearRegression()
lr_model.fit(X_train, y_train)
lr_pred = lr_model.predict(X_test)

models['Linear Regression'] = lr_model
predictions['Linear Regression'] = lr_pred

# 2. Random forest
print("Training Random Forest...")
rf_model = RandomForestRegressor(n_estimators=100, random_state=42, n_jobs=-1)
rf_model.fit(X_train, y_train)
rf_pred = rf_model.predict(X_test)

models['Random Forest'] = rf_model
predictions['Random Forest'] = rf_pred
```

```
print("All models trained successfully")
```

The output of the code will just mention that the models have been trained; the natural next step is to see how they perform on the test set and generate evaluation metrics. I will use several evaluation metrics to be sure that the best model is actually the best. This is how I will do it:

```
# Evaluate models
print("=== MODEL EVALUATION ===")

def calculate_metrics(y_true, y_pred, model_name):
    mse = mean_squared_error(y_true, y_pred)
    rmse = np.sqrt(mse)
    mae = mean_absolute_error(y_true, y_pred)
    r2 = r2_score(y_true, y_pred)

    return {
        'Model': model_name,
        'MSE': mse,
        'RMSE': rmse,
        'MAE': mae,
        'R-squared': r2
    }

# Calculate metrics for all models
results = []
for model_name, pred in predictions.items():
    result = calculate_metrics(y_test, pred, model_name)
    results.append(result)
    metrics[model_name] = result

# Display results
results_df = pd.DataFrame(results)
print("Model Performance Comparison:")
print("=" * 80)
print(results_df.to_string(index=False, float_format='%.4f'))

# Find best model
best_model_name = results_df.loc[results_df['R-squared'].idxmax(), 'Model']
print(f"\n🏆 Best performing model: {best_model_name}")
print(f"R-squared Score: {results_df.loc[results_df['R-squared'].idxmax(),
                                          'R-squared']:.4f}")
```

The output is shown in Figure 6-34, and you can clearly see from the evaluation scores that I have a clear winner here between these two.

```
=== MODEL EVALUATION ===
Model Performance Comparison:

================================================================================
              Model         MSE       RMSE      MAE  R-squared
Linear Regression 1499636.6903 1224.5965 805.2744     0.9057
    Random Forest  292993.6191  541.2888 266.2805     0.9816
🏆 Best performing model: Random Forest
R-squared Score: 0.9816
```

Figure 6-34. Evaluation scores of the ML models

I am curious to see which features were necessary, so I will plot the feature importance now. That doesn't have much to do with ML; it's more for the inquisitive minds out there. Figure 6-35 shows how the following code generates the bar graph:

```python
# Feature importance analysis (for random forest)
print("=== FEATURE IMPORTANCE ANALYSIS ===")

if 'Random Forest' in models:
    rf_model = models['Random Forest']
    feature_importance = pd.DataFrame({
        'Feature': feature_columns,
        'Importance': rf_model.feature_importances_
    }).sort_values('Importance', ascending=False)

    print("Feature Importance (Random Forest):")
    print(feature_importance.to_string(index=False, float_format='%.4f'))

    # Plot feature importance
    plt.figure(figsize=(12, 8))
    plt.barh(feature_importance['Feature'], feature_importance['Importance'])
    plt.title('Feature Importance - Random Forest Model')
    plt.xlabel('Importance')
    plt.ylabel('Features')
    plt.gca().invert_yaxis()
    plt.tight_layout()
    plt.show()
```

```
=== FEATURE IMPORTANCE ANALYSIS ===
Feature Importance (Random Forest):
             Feature  Importance
        CARAT_SCALED      0.6159
            Y_SCALED      0.2725
     CLARITY_ORDINAL      0.0630
       COLOR_ORDINAL      0.0311
            X_SCALED      0.0052
            Z_SCALED      0.0051
        DEPTH_SCALED      0.0032
   TABLE_PERC_SCALED      0.0023
         CUT_ORDINAL      0.0018
```

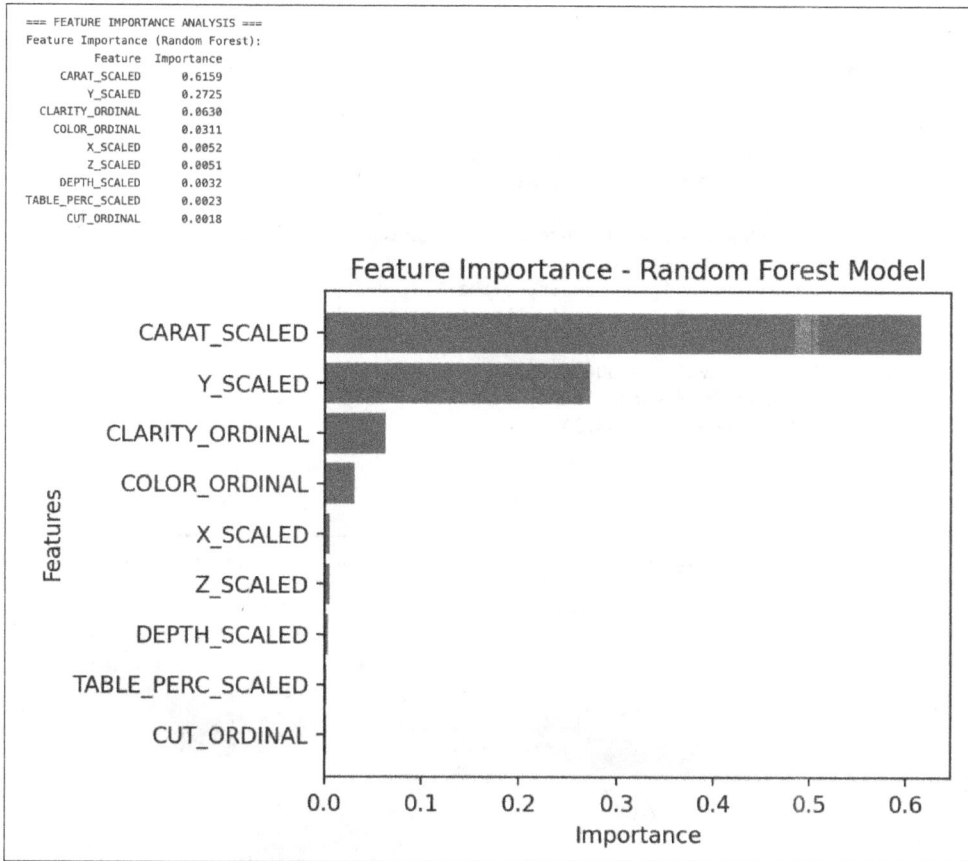

Figure 6-35. Feature importance of our best model

Now, let's see what my model predicted and the actual price on a chart to see how it looks, and if we might have missed something. Also, let's look at the residual plots to see what contributes more to the error within the models (Figure 6-36). The purpose here is to understand how my model does on the unseen data:

```python
# Visualize predictions versus actual values
print("=== PREDICTION VISUALIZATION ===")

fig, axes = plt.subplots(1, 2, figsize=(16, 6))

for i, (model_name, pred) in enumerate(predictions.items()):
    axes[i].scatter(y_test, pred, alpha=0.6, s=30)
    axes[i].plot([y_test.min(), y_test.max()],
                               [y_test.min(), y_test.max()],
                 'r--', lw=2)
    axes[i].set_xlabel('Actual Price ($)')
    axes[i].set_ylabel('Predicted Price ($)')
    axes[i].set_title(f'{model_name}\nR² = {metrics[model_name]["R-squared"]:.4f}')
```

```
        axes[i].grid(True, alpha=0.3)

plt.tight_layout()
plt.show()

# Residual plots
fig, axes = plt.subplots(1, 2, figsize=(16, 6))

for i, (model_name, pred) in enumerate(predictions.items()):
    residuals = y_test - pred
    axes[i].scatter(pred, residuals, alpha=0.6, s=30)
    axes[i].axhline(y=0, color='r', linestyle='--', lw=2)
    axes[i].set_xlabel('Predicted Price ($)')
    axes[i].set_ylabel('Residuals ($)')
    axes[i].set_title(f'{model_name} - Residual Plot')
    axes[i].grid(True, alpha=0.3)

plt.tight_layout()
plt.show()
```

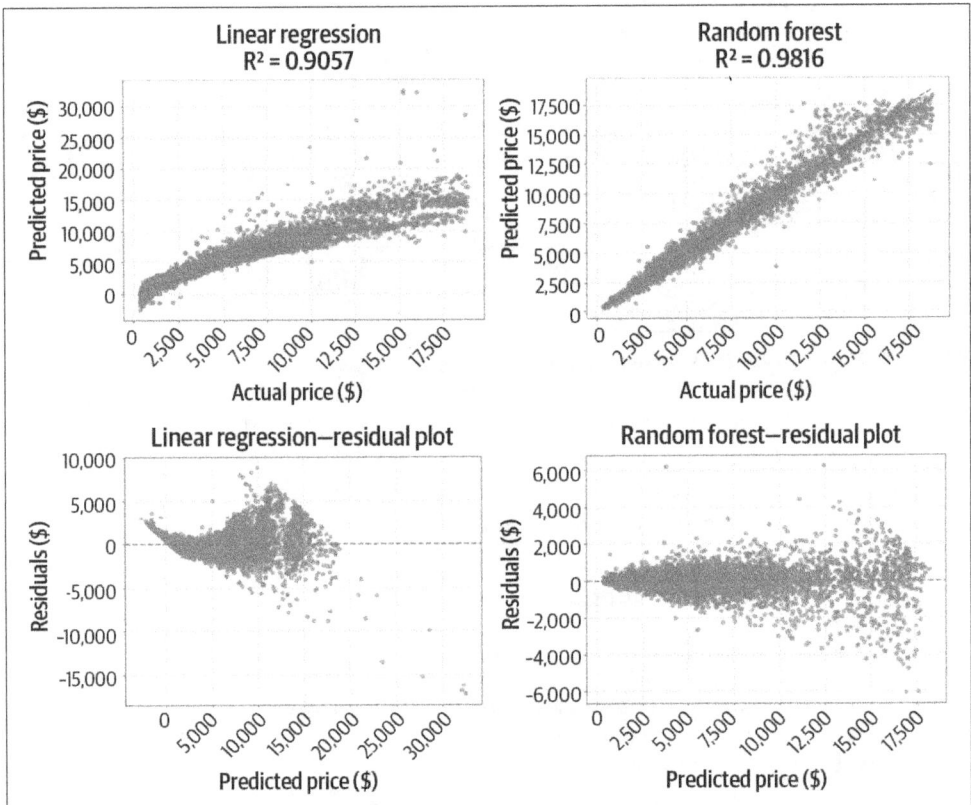

Figure 6-36. Visualizing predicted versus actual values along with residual plots

Looks quite good, I would say. Let's now use the Snowpark library and save the results and predictions in a table. It is, again, a good practice to do so, especially if you want to go deeper and perform an error analysis. Here, we will create the datasets and save them to Snowflake:

```python
# Save predictions back to Snowflake
print("=== SAVING RESULTS TO SNOWFLAKE ===")

# Prepare test results
test_results = X_test.copy()
test_results['ACTUAL_PRICE'] = y_test.values
test_results['LR_PREDICTION'] = predictions['Linear Regression']
test_results['RF_PREDICTION'] = predictions['Random Forest']
test_results['LR_ERROR'] = np.abs(
    y_test.values - predictions['Linear Regression']
)
test_results['RF_ERROR'] = np.abs(
    y_test.values - predictions['Random Forest']
)

# Convert to Snowpark DataFrame and save
test_results_df = session.create_dataframe(test_results)
test_results_df.write.mode("overwrite").save_as_table("MODEL_PREDICTIONS")

# Save model metrics
metrics_data = []
for model_name, metric_dict in metrics.items():
    metrics_data.append([
        model_name,
        metric_dict['MSE'],
        metric_dict['RMSE'],
        metric_dict['MAE'],
        metric_dict['R-squared']
    ])

metrics_schema = StructType([
    StructField("MODEL_NAME", StringType()),
    StructField("MSE", FloatType()),
    StructField("RMSE", FloatType()),
    StructField("MAE", FloatType()),
    StructField("R2_SCORE", FloatType())
])

metrics_df = session.create_dataframe(metrics_data, metrics_schema)
metrics_df.write.mode("overwrite").save_as_table("MODEL_METRICS")

print("✓ Results saved to Snowflake tables:")
print("- MODEL_PREDICTIONS: Test set predictions and errors")
print("- MODEL_METRICS: Model performance metrics")

# Display saved metrics
```

```
    print("\nSaved Model Metrics:")
    session.table("MODEL_METRICS").show()
```

I will show you what I have saved in the MODEL_METRICS table. Let's see Figure 6-37.

```
=== SAVING RESULTS TO SNOWFLAKE ===
☑ Results saved to Snowflake tables:
 - MODEL_PREDICTIONS: Test set predictions and errors
 - MODEL_METRICS: Model performance metrics
Saved Model Metrics:
-------------------------------------------------------------------------------------------------------
|"MODEL_NAME"       |"MSE"             |"RMSE"             |"MAE"              |"R2_SCORE"
-------------------------------------------------------------------------------------------------------
|Linear Regression  |1499636.6903304923 |1224.5965418579674 |805.2743660190143 |0.9056643685073493
|Random Forest      |292993.6191201445  |541.2888499869035  |266.2804537702827 |0.9815690438482638
-------------------------------------------------------------------------------------------------------
```

Figure 6-37. Contents of the MODEL_METRICS table

These metrics can be helpful later, when we modify our data preparation and assess whether these models improve or how a third model performs with these two as benchmarks. Now, let's infer using the random forest model that I have created. I have made a function that reads the model, takes in the parameters, and predicts the price of a diamond:

```
# Create a simple prediction function for new diamonds
print("=== CREATING PREDICTION FUNCTION ===")

def predict_diamond_price(
        carat_scaled,
        depth_scaled,
        table_perc_scaled,
        x_scaled,
        y_scaled,
        z_scaled,
        cut_ordinal,
        color_ordinal,
        clarity_ordinal):
    """
    Predict diamond price using the trained Random Forest model
    """

    # Prepare feature vector
    features = np.array([[
        carat_scaled,
        depth_scaled,
        table_perc_scaled,
        x_scaled,
        y_scaled,
        z_scaled,
        cut_ordinal,
        color_ordinal,
```

```
        clarity_ordinal
    ]])

    # Make prediction using the best model
    best_model = models['Random Forest']  # Using RF as it performed better
    prediction = best_model.predict(features)[0]

    return round(prediction, 2)

# Test the prediction function
predict_this_diamond = {
    'carat_scaled': 0.1746,
    'depth_scaled': 0.5499,
    'table_perc_scaled': 0.2692,
    'x_scaled': 0.5996,
    'y_scaled': 0.1100,
    'z_scaled': 0.1276,
    'cut_ordinal': 2,
    'color_ordinal': 4,
    'clarity_ordinal': 5,
}

predicted_price = predict_diamond_price(**predict_this_diamond)
print(f"\nTest prediction for diamond with specs: {predict_this_diamond}")
print(f"Predicted price: {predicted_price:,.2f}")
```

We create dummy data for a diamond and feed it to the model to get the price. The price we get as an output feels quite right. In Figure 6-38, we can see the predicted price of this diamond.

```
33   predicted_price = predict_diamond_price(**predict_this_diamond)
34   print(f"☑ Prediction function created successfully!")
35   print(f"\nTest prediction for diamond with specs: {predict_this_diamond}")
36   print(f"Predicted price: {predicted_price:..2f}")

=== CREATING PREDICTION FUNCTION ===
☑ Prediction function created successfully!
Test prediction for diamond with specs: {'carat_scaled': 0.1746, 'depth_scaled': 0.5499, 'table_perc_
Predicted price: 4,631.80
```

Figure 6-38. Inferring using the model

Now, let's save the model to the Snowflake ML Model Registry that you looked at in Chapter 4. Remember how you have to create a version of a model, providing its input and output details to create a registry that will serve as your artifact within Snowflake. Let's see how to do it:

```
# Deploy model using Snowflake ML Model Registry
print("=== DEPLOYING MODEL TO SNOWFLAKE ML MODEL REGISTRY ===")

from snowflake.ml.registry import Registry
from snowflake.ml.model import model_signature
```

```
import joblib
import os

# Initialize the model registry
registry = Registry(
    session=session,
    database_name="ML_TUTORIAL",
    schema_name="DIAMONDS"
)

# Create model signature for better tracking
#from snowflake.ml.model.models import Model

# Prepare model metadata
model_name = "diamond_price_predictor"
model_version = "v1"
model_comment = "Random Forest model for diamond price prediction " \
        "with feature engineering"

# Log the model to registry
print("Registering Random Forest model...")

# Create model signature
sample_input_df = final_dataset.select(feature_columns).limit(1)
signature = model_signature.infer_signature(
    sample_input_df.to_pandas(),
    rf_model.predict(sample_input_df.to_pandas()),
    output_feature_names=["PRICE"]
)

print("Signature Created")

# Register the model
model_ref = registry.log_model(
    model=rf_model,
    model_name=model_name,
    version_name=model_version,
    comment=model_comment,
    signatures={"predict": signature}
)

print(f"Model registered successfully!")
print(f"Model Name: {model_name}")
print(f"Version: {model_version}")
print(f"Model Reference: {model_ref}")
```

Here we can see the output of the preceding code, which shows us that the model is successfully registered, and the metadata:

```
=== DEPLOYING MODEL TO SNOWFLAKE ML MODEL REGISTRY ===
Registering Random Forest model…
Signature Created
Model registered successfully!
```

```
Model Name: diamond_price_predictor
Version: v3
Model Reference: ModelVersion(
  name='DIAMOND_PRICE_PREDICTOR',
  version='V3',
)
```

Your version number might not be V3, but rather V1 if you execute the preceding code. I have done it multiple times now, and since I didn't manually remove the old versions, I must update the version number whenever I need to save it again. In Figure 6-39, you can also see it in Snowsight with all versions deployed for me.

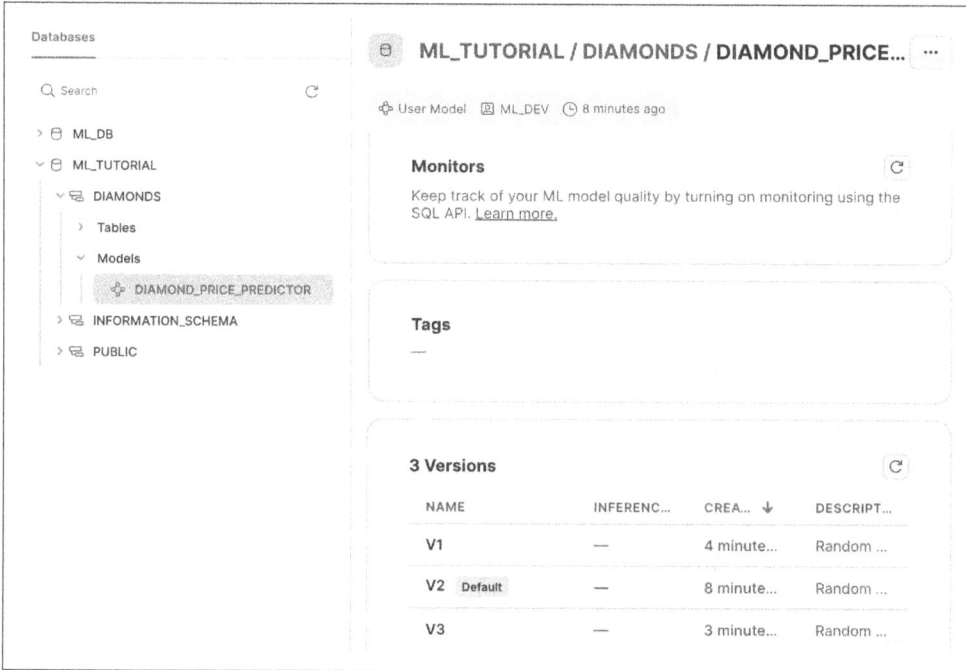

Figure 6-39. Model showing up in Snowsight (see this screengrab in full size) (https://oreil.ly/adsf_0639png)

You can also see in Figure 6-39 that there's a new section called Models in the schema DIAMONDS. When you click on a particular version, Snowsight will take you to another page where you can see all the details of that model, and even the code in SQL and Python for how to use that within your workflows. Quite astonishing, I'd say! I was pleasantly surprised looking at that.

Figure 6-40 shows how that looks.

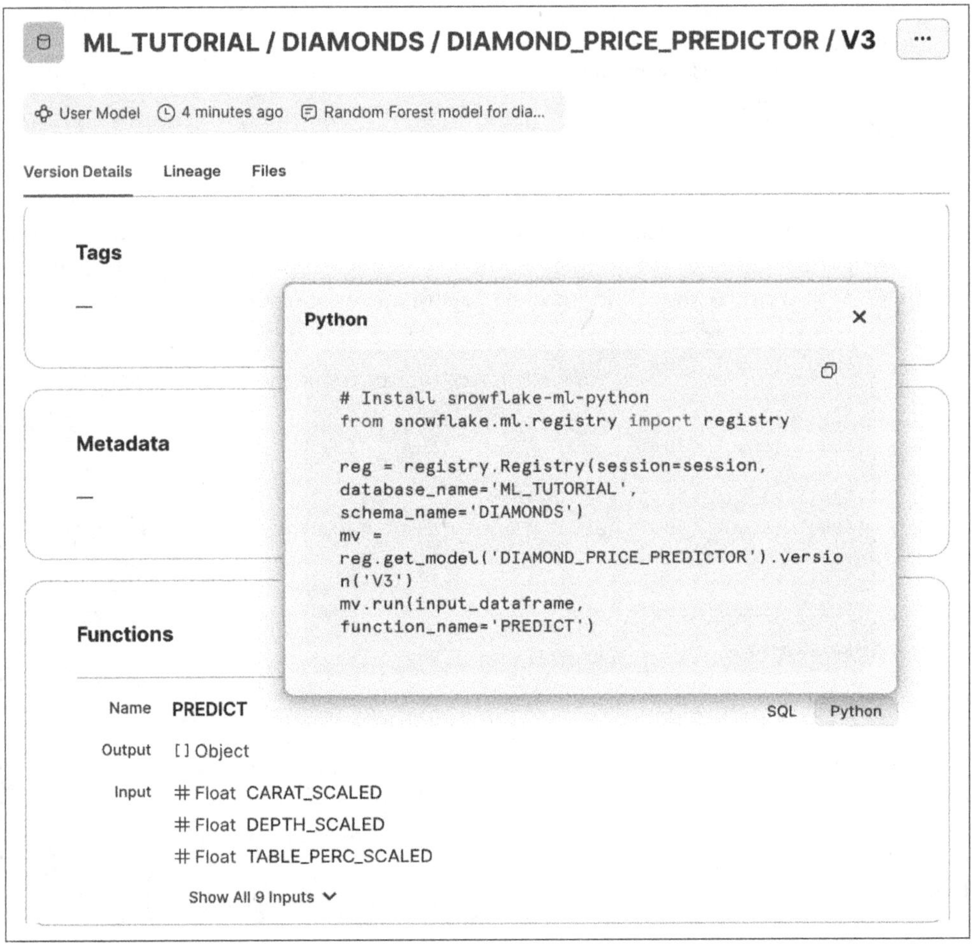

ML_TUTORIAL / DIAMONDS / DIAMOND_PRICE_PREDICTOR / V3 ···

⊹ User Model   ⊙ 4 minutes ago   ⊟ Random Forest model for dia...

Version Details   Lineage   Files

Tags

—

Metadata

—

Functions

| Python | ✕ |

```
# Install snowflake-ml-python
from snowflake.ml.registry import registry

reg = registry.Registry(session=session,
database_name='ML_TUTORIAL',
schema_name='DIAMONDS')
mv =
reg.get_model('DIAMOND_PRICE_PREDICTOR').versio
n('V3')
mv.run(input_dataframe,
function_name='PREDICT')
```

Name	**PREDICT**	SQL	Python
Output	[] Object		
Input	# Float CARAT_SCALED		
	# Float DEPTH_SCALED		
	# Float TABLE_PERC_SCALED		
	Show All 9 Inputs ⌄		

Figure 6-40. Version page of the model

Beyond that, you can also see and download the files it creates under the hood. Basically, you have easier access to all the artifacts. Figure 6-41 shows how that looks.

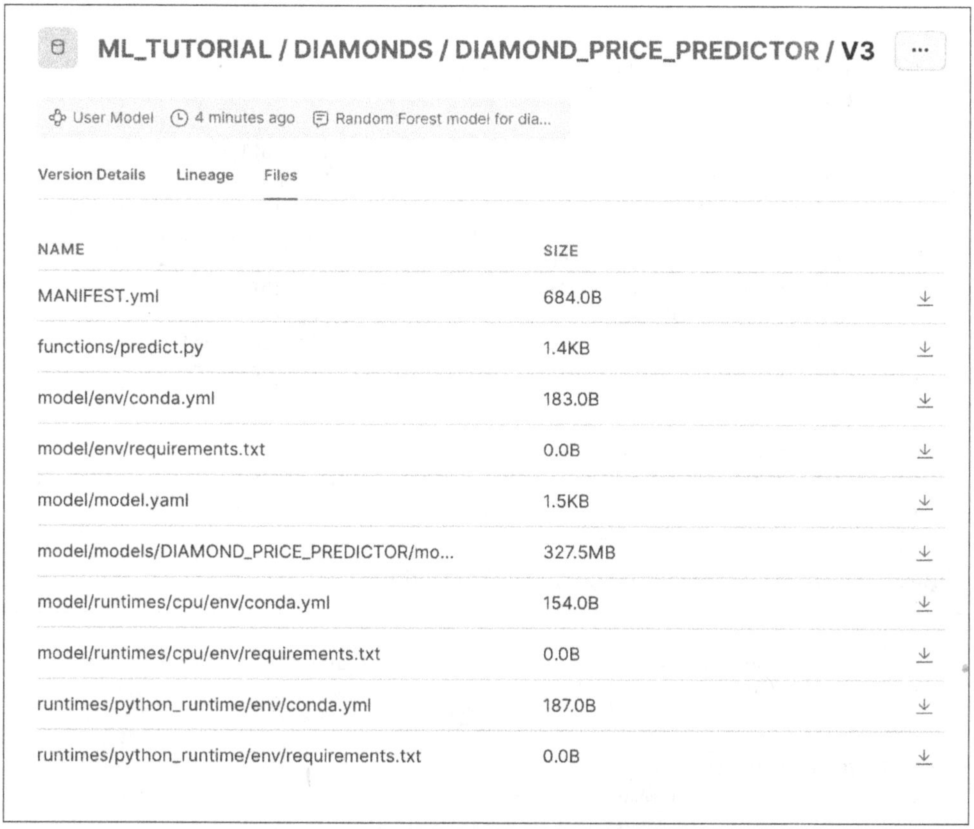

ML_TUTORIAL / DIAMONDS / DIAMOND_PRICE_PREDICTOR / **V3**

User Model   4 minutes ago   Random Forest model for dia...

Version Details   Lineage   Files

NAME	SIZE	
MANIFEST.yml	684.0B	↓
functions/predict.py	1.4KB	↓
model/env/conda.yml	183.0B	↓
model/env/requirements.txt	0.0B	↓
model/model.yaml	1.5KB	↓
model/models/DIAMOND_PRICE_PREDICTOR/mo...	327.5MB	↓
model/runtimes/cpu/env/conda.yml	154.0B	↓
model/runtimes/cpu/env/requirements.txt	0.0B	↓
runtimes/python_runtime/env/conda.yml	187.0B	↓
runtimes/python_runtime/env/requirements.txt	0.0B	↓

Figure 6-41. Artifacts of the model saved with each version you save

Let's now load the model and infer the same diamond using the saved version to see what it produces. Apart from loading the model from the registry, the only extra step here is to add the schema. This is to ensure we stay consistent and avoid errors:

```
# Test the registered model
print("\n=== TESTING REGISTERED MODEL ===")
registered_model = registry.get_model(model_name).version(model_version)

# Create test input
test_input_data = [(
    0.1746,
    0.5499,
    0.2692,
    0.5996,
    0.1100,
    0.1276,
    2,
    4,
    5
```

```
    )]

    test_input_df = session.create_dataframe(
        test_input_data,
        schema=StructType([
            StructField('CARAT_SCALED', DecimalType(38, 17), nullable=True),
            StructField('DEPTH_SCALED', DecimalType(38, 18), nullable=True),
            StructField('TABLE_PERC_SCALED', DecimalType(38, 18), nullable=True),
            StructField('X_SCALED', DecimalType(38, 16), nullable=True),
            StructField('Y_SCALED', DecimalType(38, 17), nullable=True),
            StructField('Z_SCALED', DecimalType(38, 18), nullable=True),
            StructField('CUT_ORDINAL', IntegerType(), nullable=True),
            StructField('COLOR_ORDINAL', IntegerType(), nullable=True),
            StructField('CLARITY_ORDINAL', IntegerType(), nullable=True)
    ]))

    # Make prediction using registered model
    registry_prediction = registered_model.run(test_input_df, function_name="predict")
    print("Prediction from registered model:")
    registry_prediction.select("PRICE").show()
```

Figure 6-42 shows the results of the preceding code.

```
34    # Make prediction using registered model
35    registry_prediction = registered_model.run(test_input_df, function_name="predict")
36    print("Prediction from registered model:")
37    registry_prediction.select("PRICE").show()


=== TESTING REGISTERED MODEL ===
Prediction from registered model:
------------
|"PRICE"   |
------------
|4631.8    |
------------
```

Figure 6-42. Model inference using the model saved in the registry

The predicted price I get here is the same as the predicted price I got before when inferring directly from the model. This is pleasant news for me since I can trust that the correct model is saved in the registry. Now, the final step is to log the registry in a table as well. This is not something that you need to do, but these are best practices defined by ML practitioners in order to track things back. A very simple code, shown here, can help us achieve that:

```
    # Save model registry information
    registry_info = [
        (model_name, model_version, "Random Forest", "Production", model_comment)
    ]
    registry_df = session.create_dataframe(
        registry_info,
        schema=StructType([
```

```
        StructField("MODEL_NAME", StringType()),
        StructField("VERSION", StringType()),
        StructField("MODEL_TYPE", StringType()),
        StructField("STATUS", StringType()),
        StructField("DESCRIPTION", StringType())
    ])
)

    registry_df.write.mode("overwrite").save_as_table("MODEL_REGISTRY_LOG")
```

Once this is done, we have completed training and saved an ML model on Snowflake. Isn't it amazing that you were only in one environment, and you could do so much with your data? And you didn't only work with your data; you could also perform all the governance and work around it to deliver a best-in-class type of data product.

Summary

This brings me to the end of this hands-on example, and this chapter. You will find the notebook, dataset, and setup script in this book's GitHub repo (*https://oreil.ly/ advanced-snowflake-repoch6-2*). One thing to note here is that there are several other ways to achieve the same task. The purpose of this tutorial was not to build the best machine learning model with the best programming practices, but rather to showcase some of the fantastic capabilities of Snowflake and show you how easy it is to manage everything from just one interface. I hope you enjoyed reading it and walking through the example!

## CHAPTER 7

What's Next?

In this chapter, I will walk you through some of the new offerings from Snowflake and briefly look into their functionality and how they come together to help you boost your data workloads in Snowflake. Several of these were announced at the Snowflake Summit 2025 and may still be in preview features when this book is published. For the most updated information on these features, please refer to the Snowflake documentation (*https://docs.snowflake.com*).

Without further ado, let's dive into some of the most exciting announcements.

Snowflake Generation 2 Warehouses

Snowflake has announced a performance boost for its standard warehouses, a significant upgrade known as Snowflake's generation 2 (Gen2) standard warehouses. It is a considerable leap forward, combining faster underlying hardware with intelligent software optimizations. The practical impact is that most queries will run faster, and you can handle more concurrent workloads without the performance degradation you might see on the equivalent standard warehouse.

For example, if your ETL pipeline previously struggled with large MERGE operations that took hours to complete, you might find these same operations finishing in a much quicker time on Gen2 warehouses. Similarly, complex analytical queries that scan large datasets could see significant speedups, especially when multiple users are running queries simultaneously. However, the actual performance gains vary considerably based on your specific workload patterns and warehouse configuration. Some of you might see dramatic improvements while others might only experience modest gains.

To create a Gen2 warehouse in Snowflake, all you need to do is simply add a resource constraint to the SQL statement for creating a warehouse:

```
create or replace warehouse my_gen2_wh
    resource_constraint = standard_gen_2
    warehouse_size = small
;
```

I'd highly recommend that you test it out on your data workloads. Run your benchmarks and see if there are some performance gains (cost- and time-wise). In general, the faster the queries finish, the cheaper it should be, as Snowflake follows a consumption-based model, but the credit consumption (*https://oreil.ly/Z40ED*) for Gen2 warehouses is slightly higher compared to the standard warehouses. Gen2 warehouses are being rolled out to all regions slowly. You must check Snowflake's region availability page (*https://oreil.ly/HZ-5o*) to get the latest updates.

Snowflake Adaptive Compute

On a similar topic, also relating to Snowflake compute and warehouses, Snowflake has also announced its support for Adaptive Compute. Adaptive Compute is Snowflake's solution to the constant warehouse resize issue. That means you will no longer have to worry about resizing warehouses for different data workloads. Adaptive Compute will handle these decisions automatically, routing queries intelligently to clusters of the appropriate size. For example, if your team typically runs a mix of quick dashboard queries and heavy ETL jobs, Adaptive Compute would automatically provision smaller clusters for the dashboards and larger ones for the ETL work, all from a shared resource pool within your account. Exciting, isn't it?

Snowflake Openflow

If you ask me personally, Snowflake Openflow is perhaps my favorite announcement from the Snowflake Summit 2025. Snowflake Openflow is a managed Apache NiFi service that handles connecting different data sources to destinations at scale. Openflow can handle everything from traditional database tables to images, videos, audio files, and sensor data streams, making it a key component in enabling the use of generative AI for your organization.

If you zoom out here a little bit and think about Snowflake's journey from being a data warehousing organization to becoming the AI Data Cloud, this announcement of Openflow comes from the heart of that transformation. The power to move your data fast, in a secure way, all within your governed data environment without extra infrastructure? Sign me up!

The service runs in your cloud environment, giving you complete control over data movement while eliminating the operational overhead of managing NiFi clusters yourself. You get Snowflake's security, compliance monitoring, and observability out of the box. The list of connectors (*https://nifi.apache.org/components*) is huge. Let's quickly look at how you can get started with Openflow in Snowflake. Figure 7-1 shows where you can find Openflow in Snowsight and launch it.

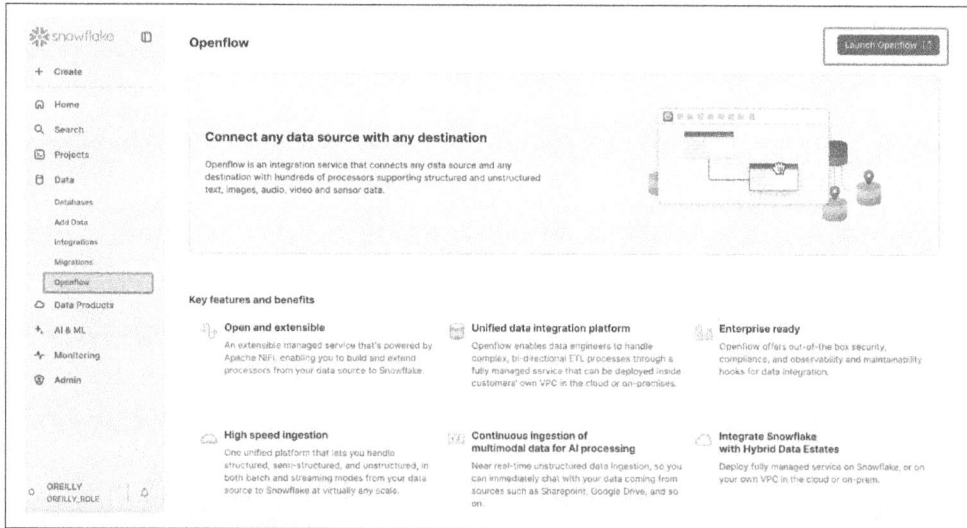

Figure 7-1. Openflow in Snowsight

The next step is to create a deployment for Openflow (Figure 7-2). Currently, it is deployed on AWS; after completing all the steps in Snowflake, you need an AWS account to be able to deploy the Openflow deployment pool.

Figure 7-2. Creating an Openflow deployment in Snowsight

Now that you have started creating a deployment, you need to decide how it will be deployed: on a virtual private cloud (VPC) managed by Snowflake or one that you supply, the Snowflake role that owns the deployment, and the roles that have access to it. Figure 7-3 shows the setup I used.

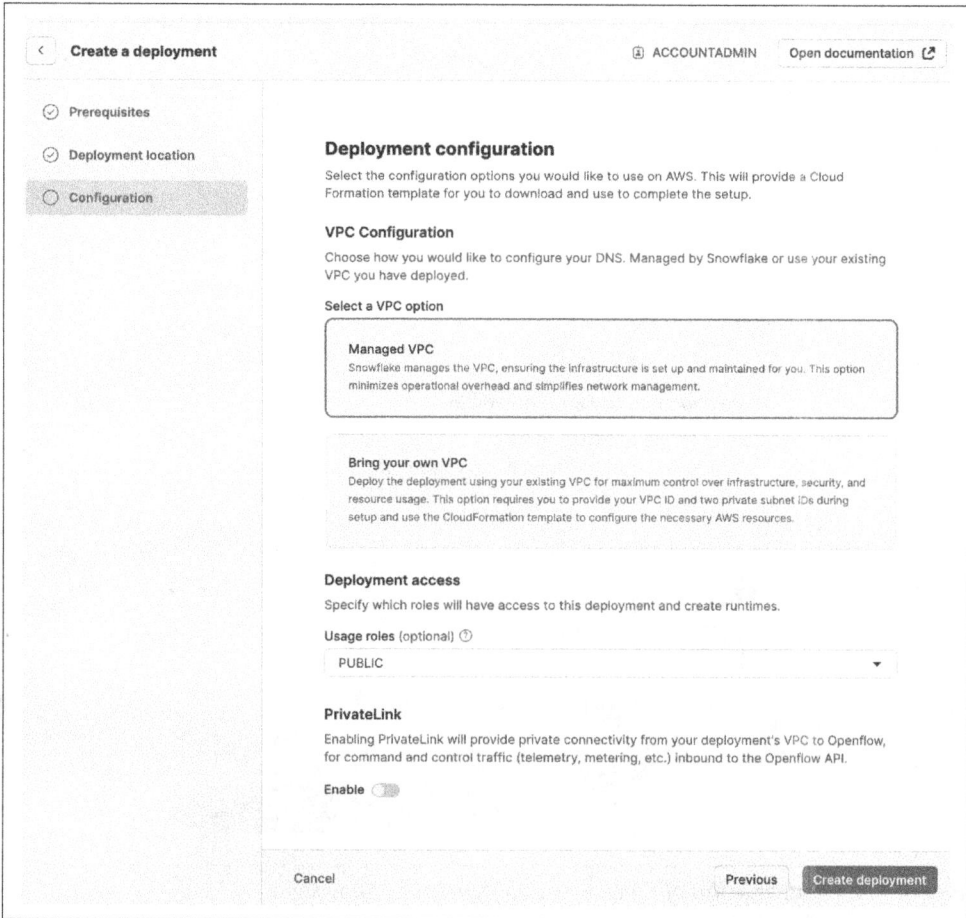

Figure 7-3. Choosing the VPC and roles for deploying Openflow

And voilà! As you see in Figure 7-4, the deployment is created, and it will generate an AWS CloudFormation script that you need to upload to your AWS account in order to get it up and running there. It's a YAML file that you can download.

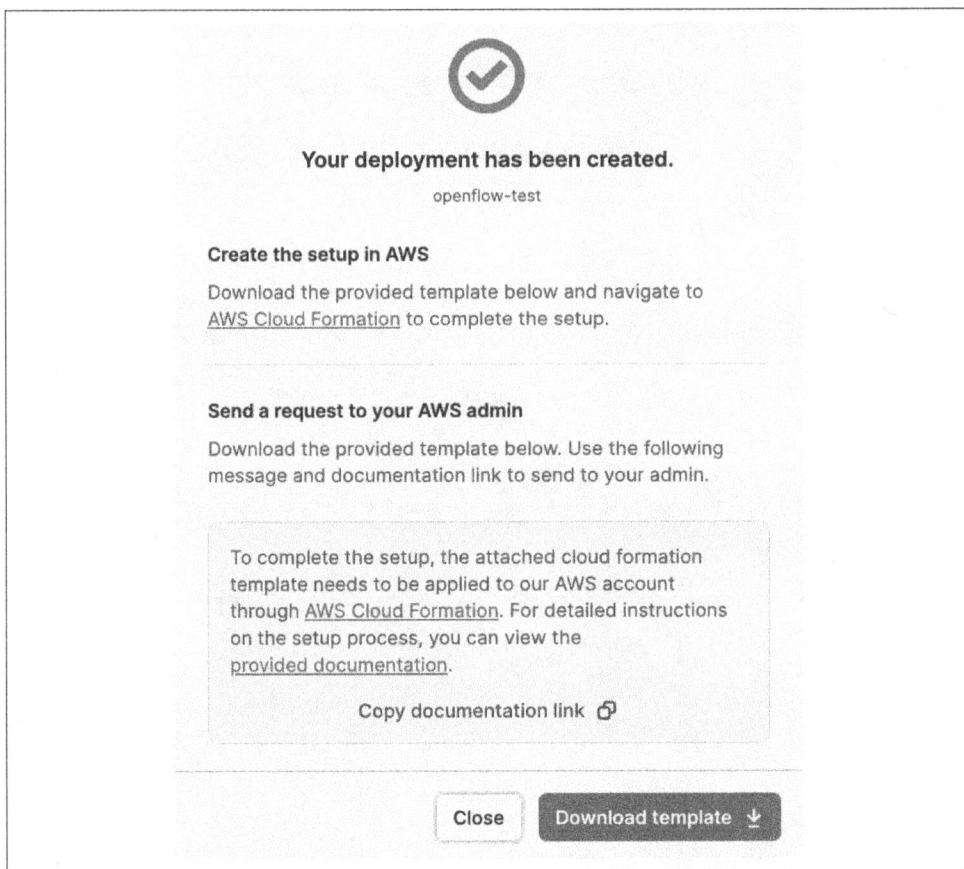

Figure 7-4. Confirmation of Openflow deployment in Snowsight

Now, all you need to do is navigate to your AWS account and create a new CloudFormation stack, select "Choose an existing template," then upload the file that you downloaded from Snowflake, give it the details, and that's it. Figure 7-5 shows how it looks in AWS.

The script will do its magic and create the AWS resources needed for Openflow's setup. It will take a couple of minutes before everything is ready in AWS, and once that's done, you're prepared to go to Snowflake. The next step in Snowflake is to create runtimes.

> I won't go further into the Openflow setup for the scope of this book. You may refer to the Snowflake documentation (*https:// oreil.ly/LgUGW*) and forums for documentation, motivation, and details on the connectors.

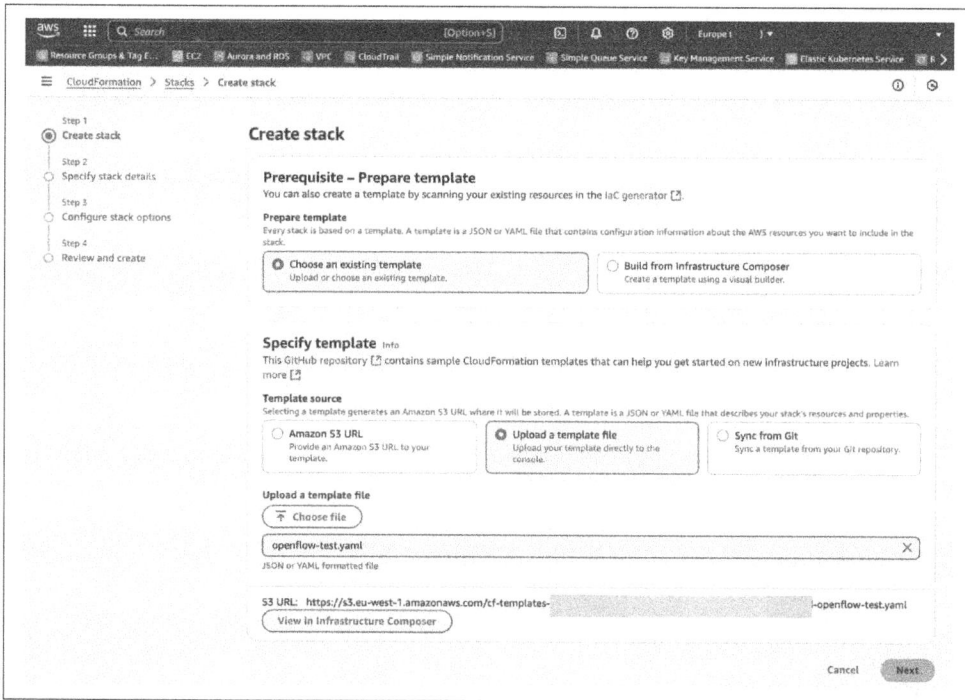

Figure 7-5. Openflow deployment on AWS

Snowsight Workspaces

Snowsight Workspaces give you a proper development environment within Snowflake that functions more like what you expect from a modern IDE, rather than the typical SQL editor experience. Instead of working with isolated queries or notebooks, you get a unified interface where you can create and manage multiple files across different languages and formats, whether you're writing SQL transformations, creating Python scripts for data analysis, or building complex data pipelines. In Workspaces, everything is file-based; you can connect your workspace directly to Git repositories, enabling proper version control and collaboration with your team. You might have a workspace containing SQL files for your data transformations, Python scripts for machine learning, and configuration files for your pipeline orchestration, all organized in folders and tracked in Git just like any other software project, all within Snowflake. Workspaces make it possible to bring software engineering best practices to your data work, and the native Git integration by Snowflake helps you version control everything, including SQL worksheets, Streamlit dashboards, Native Apps, and any configuration files.

Even though it's a preview feature right now, it is generally available on all Snowflake accounts. Figure 7-6 shows how the Workspaces section looks within Snowsight.

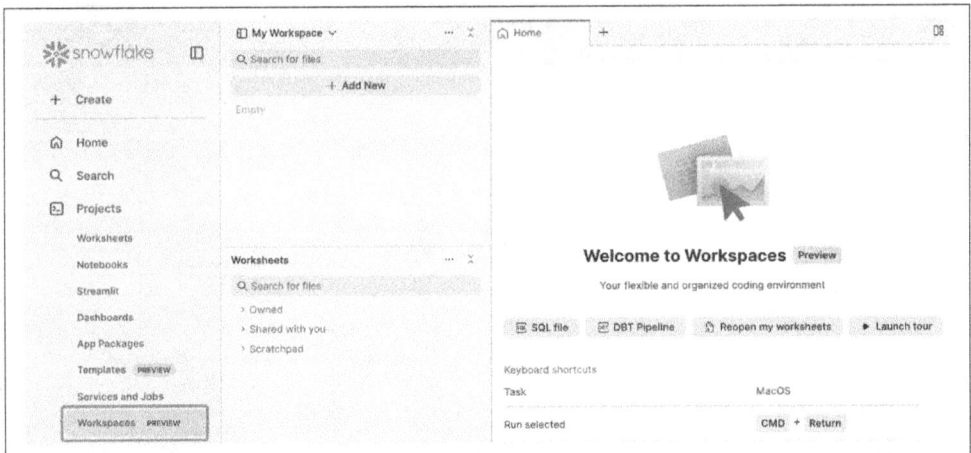

Figure 7-6. Snowsight Workspaces

dbt Projects on Snowflake

If you are a data practitioner, you've probably heard about data build tool (dbt) (*https://getdbt.com*). It has gained enormous popularity in the past few years. If you're already using dbt or considering it, Snowflake's announcement is going to simplify how you work with dbt and data transformations in general. We now know that Snowsight Workspaces is bringing an integrated IDE to Snowflake, and to give it fuel, Snowflake also announced the ability to run and govern dbt natively within Snowflake. You can now create new dbt projects or import existing dbt projects into Snowflake, eliminating additional infrastructure management. You can run your dbt projects using Snowflake virtual warehouses. Figure 7-7 shows the new drop-down menu in Snowflake Workspaces where you can choose "dbt Project" as an option.

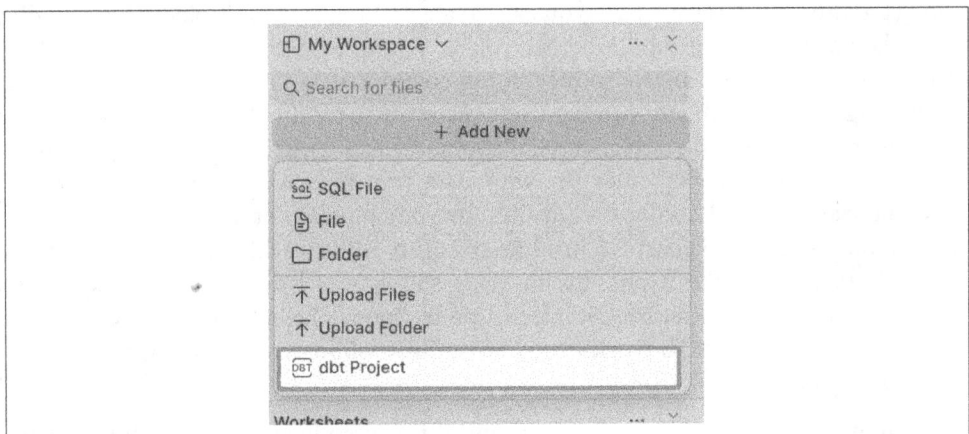

Figure 7-7. dbt projects in Snowflake Workspaces

Snowflake Cortex AISQL

Snowflake Cortex AISQL represents a significant advancement in data analytics by integrating powerful AI capabilities directly into Snowflake's SQL engine, enabling organizations to analyze multimodal enterprise data using familiar SQL commands. This innovation addresses the challenge of extracting insights from diverse unstructured data sources like documents, images, and audio files, all with your favorite SQL flavor.

Snowflake has introduced a new data type for unstructured data called FILE. The FILE data type is a pointer to a file in an internal or external Snowflake stage. This new data type helps Snowflake SQL become truly multimodal and allows you to run AISQL functions. You can read more about it in the Snowflake documentation (*https://oreil.ly/MyPNC*). Let's now look at some of the AISQL functions that Snowflake offers:

AI_CLASSIFY allows you to classify text or images into the list of labels provided.

AI_COMPLETE allows you to generate a response from your given prompt. Here's a good example query for it:

```
SELECT AI_COMPLETE(
    'snowflake-arctic',
    'In 20 words, why is O Reilly learning platform so highly ranked?'
    );
```

In Figure 7-8, we can see the response to the query.

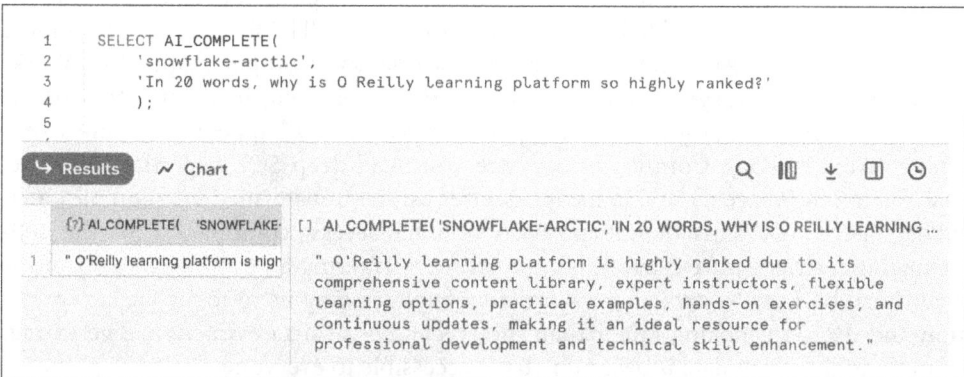

Figure 7-8. Using the AI_COMPLETE SQL function

AI_FILTER currently supports text and image, and returns your prompts as a Boolean output. Given its nature, you can use it within the WHERE clause of your query and have limitless possibilities with advanced SQL. A fun little query to test it out could be the following:

```
SELECT AI_FILTER('Is O Reilly an American company?')
;
```

In Figure 7-9, you can see the result of this query.

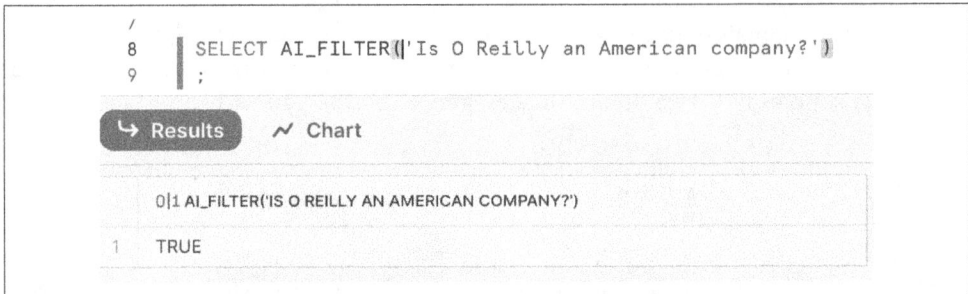

Figure 7-9. Result of the AI_FILTER query

AI_JOIN allows you to join two tables or views using a prompt, eliminating the need for predefining keys and allowing you to join the tables using semantic understanding. As its name suggests, the AI_AGG function aggregates the given column according to your given instructions, e.g., you can give it customer reviews and ask it to summarize the overall sentiment of the reviews.

Closing Remarks

With that, it is time to wrap up this chapter, and the book. As you've seen throughout this book, Snowflake continues to evolve at a remarkable pace, constantly pushing the boundaries of what's possible in the data platform space. The features we've explored in this final chapter—generation 2 warehouses, Adaptive Compute, Openflow, Workspaces, native dbt integration, and Cortex AISQL—represent just a snapshot of the innovation happening right now, and the pace at which it is happening is quite astonishing. We're moving from a world where you need deep SQL expertise to extract insights to one where natural language queries can be transformed into complex analytical operations. This democratization of data access, combined with the self-managing infrastructure capabilities, means we're entering an era where many of the traditional barriers to data analysis are dissolving, freeing us to focus on interpretation and decision making rather than the mechanics of data extraction. The extraction of insights from data is becoming truly accessible to everyone.

The key to thriving in this rapidly changing landscape is maintaining a mindset of continuous learning and experimentation, especially as AI becomes increasingly integrated into every aspect of the data platform. Start experimenting and get your hands dirty with the new features coming out, and you'll understand the implications of these new innovations on your data architecture. The AI capabilities in Cortex aren't just about making queries easier to write anymore; they're about fundamentally changing who can work with data and how quickly insights can be generated. Consider how AISQL generation might affect your team's skill requirements, or how Cortex's machine learning functions could enable new types of analysis that were previously too complex or time-consuming. The organizations that will get the most value from Snowflake are those that embrace this culture of experimentation and aren't afraid to challenge their existing approaches, whether that's rethinking warehouse sizing with Adaptive Compute, exploring new data integration patterns with Openflow, or reimagining how business users interact with data through AI-powered interfaces.

Remember that mastering advanced Snowflake in the AI era isn't just about understanding the technical features anymore; it is much more than that. It is about developing the judgment to know when and how to apply them effectively while understanding their broader implications for data democratization and organizational change. The convergence of AI capabilities with enterprise data platforms represents one of the most significant shifts in our field since the move to cloud computing.

Stay curious, keep experimenting, and most importantly, never stop questioning whether there's a better way to solve the problems you are facing. The future of data platforms is being written right now, with AI as a central theme, and by staying engaged with these emerging capabilities, you're positioning yourself to be part of that evolution rather than just a passive observer.

Index

area of geospatial objects, 60
artifacts
    of ML model saved with each version, 169
    no path to Streamlit UI in, 113
artificial intelligence (AI)
    increasing integration into Snowflake, 182
    Snowflake as AI Data Cloud, 174
    Snowflake Cortex AISQL, 181
    Snowflake for, 119
        Snowflake Cortex, 124-135
audio, 20
Avro, 20
AWS (see Amazon Web Services)
Azure, 18, 22
    using OpenAI's GPT models through, 130

B

Billing & Terms section (Snowsight Admin), 11
BOOLAND_AGG function, 42
BOOLOR_AGG function, 43
BOOLXOR_AGG function, 45

C

caller and owner rights (stored procedures), 31
call_udf function, 86
chaining dynamic tables, 26
change data capture (CDC), 26
CI/CD (continuous integration and continuous
    delivery) pipelines, 99
classify_text function, 128
CLI (command-line interface), Snowflake, 95
    adding path to Streamlit UI for Snowflake
        Native App (example), 113
    creating app from, using Snowflake CLI
        project templates, 108
    downloading and installing on local
        machine, 107
client-side versus server-side Snowpark, 66
clones, zero-copy clones of Snowflake objects,
    21
closing remarks, 182
closing sessions, 82
cloud services layer, 17
    features of, 22-24
cloud storage layer, 17
cloud-agnostic layer, 18
col function (snowflake.snowpark.functions),
    82
collaboration

features in cloud services layer, 23
    (see also shares and secure data sharing)
collect function, 82, 84
Complete API (Snowflake Cortex), 124
complete function (Python), 124
    comparison of output to SQL COMPLETE,
        125
COMPLETE function (SQL), 125
    comparison of output to Python complete,
        125
compute layer, 17
    compute pools of VMs for container execu-
        tion, 99
    features of, 21
conda package manager, 72
    activating conda virtual environment, 83
    using to set up Python environment, 15
connection to Snowflake instance, 107
constructor functions, 54-58
Contacts tab (Snowsight Admin), 11
container images, storing on Snowflake image
    registry, 99
Container Runtime, 120
    advantages of, 120
    Snowflake Notebook creation dialog box
        for, 121
Container Services (Snowpark) (see Snowpark
    Container Services)
containers
    executing on Snowpark Container Services,
        99
    Snowpark Container Services, 98
    using Python packages in for Snowflake
        Container Services, 74
continuous learning and experimentation,
    mindset of, 182
Copilot (see Snowflake Copilot)
COPY command, 33
Copy History subsection (Monitoring in Snow-
    sight), 10
correlation matrix of numerical variables, 150
Cortex (see Snowflake Cortex)
Cortex Agents API, 124
Cortex Complete API, 124
Cortex Embed API, 124
Cost Management tab (Snowsight Admin), 11
CPUs
    Container Runtime for Snowflake Note-
        books, running on, 121

infrastructure management in cloud services layer, 23
internal stages, 33
intersection of geospatial objects, 59, 61

J

Java
    stored procedures in, 31
    use in Snowpark, 65
    user-defined functions in, 29
JavaScript
    stored procedures in, 31
    user-defined functions in, 29
job service model, 99
JSON, 20
Jupyter notebooks, 5
    loading dependencies into, 83

K

knowledge definition format (KDF), 20

L

LAG and LEAD functions, 52
lambda functions, 70
    defining named temporary UDF as, 86
LAST_VALUE and FIRST_VALUE functions, 51
learning and experimentation, continuous, 182
LIMIT clause, 37
LineString type, 54
    ST_MAKEPOLYGON function taking, 57
listings, 32
Llama LLM models, 130
LLMs (large language models)
    Document AI, 8
    fine-tuning in Snowflake Cortex, 130
    LLM-powered features in Snowflake Cortex, 124
    searching with Snowflake Cortex Search, 131
    Snowflake Cortex LLM functions, 124-129
    in Snowflake Cortex, 119
log_model method, 79

M

machine learning (ML)
    AI & ML section of Snowsight, 8
    custom ML workflows in Snowflake, 71

datasets in Snowflake, 77-78
end-to-end machine learning with Snowflake (example), 135-171
    artifacts of model with each version saved, 168
    checking stats of datasets, 146
    creating new Snowflake Notebook, 138
    creating prediction function for new diamonds, 164
    examining correlations of different variables in dataset, 150
    loading diamonds dataset, 144
    loading needed Anaconda libraries in Notebooks, 143
    plotting feature importance, 160
    restarting Notebooks session and loading dataset, 143
    saving model registry information, 170
    saving model to Snowflake ML Model Registry, 165
    saving results and predictions to Snowflake, 163
    splitting dataset into training set and test set, 157
    starting Snowpark session and loading dataset, 144
    table with feature engineered dataset in the database, 155
    test set performance and evaluation metrics, 159
    testing registered model, 169
    training ML models, 158
    visualizations of distributions and relations in dataset, 147
    visualizing predicted versus actual price values, 161
features, 74
ML modeling API in Snowpark, 72
Snowflake Feature Store, 74-77
Snowflake ML, 71
Snowflake ML components, 72
Snowpark ML support, 66
manifest file (application package), 97
Markdown, 120
Marketplace, 96
    in Data Products section of Snowsight Data tab, 7
materialized views, 29
Matplotlib, 121

pipes, 33
POINT type, 54
Polygon type
    creating using ST_MAKEPOLYGON, 57
Private Sharing section (Data Products tab in
    Snowsight), 7
privileges, 98
    (see also permissions)
    granting to ML_DEV role, 135
productivity enhancement with Snowpark, 66
programming languages
    stored procedures support in, 31
    user-defined functions in, 29
project definition file (application package), 97
Projects tab (Snowsight), 5
prototyping, rapid, with Streamlit in Snowflake,
    102
Provider Studio subsection (Data Products tab
    in Snowsight), 7
publishing applications, 115
Python
    Anaconda open source distribution, 72
    installing packages using Container Run-
        time, 121
    LLM functions in, 124
        complete function, 125
        extract_answer, 126
        sentiment and classify_text functions,
            128
        summarize function, 127
    packages offered by Snowflake, 72
    PySpark API for Apache Spark, 67
    in Snowflake Notebooks, 120
    snowflake-ml-python library, 71
    Snowpark/Python environment, setting up,
        14
    stored procedures in, 31
    use in Snowpark, 65
    user-defined functions in, 29
    using interchangeably with SQL in Snow-
        flake Notebooks, 121
    worksheets in Snowflake, 13

Q

QUALIFY clause, 35
    use with WINDOW clause, 37
Query History tab, 69
query optimization

role of metadata stored in cloud services
    layer, 23

R

RAG (retrieval-augmented generation), 131
RANK and DENSE_RANK functions, 49-50
    creating temporary table as dataset, 49
    sample query ranking savings, 50
rank-related window functions, 46
rapid prototyping, using Streamlit in Snow-
    flake, 102
RBAC (see role-based access control)
refreshes
    automatic, in dynamic tables, 26
    of downstream dynamic tables, 27
registering permanent UDFs, 90
register_feature_view function, 76
Registry constructor function, 79
registry of ML models, 78-80
relationship functions, 59
    (see also measurement and relationship
        functions)
REST API, fetching Cortex LLM SQL function
    results from, 124
result-level clauses (SQL), 37
retrieval-augmented generation (RAG), 131
role-based access control (RBAC)
    containerized applications and, 98
    creating APPLICATION role, 108
    creating new ML_DEV role, 135
    creating role to access virtual warehouse
        and create an application, 106
    in Snowflake Notebooks, 121
ROW_NUMBER function, 47-48
    parameters of, 47
    sample query using, 47

S

Scala
    stored procedures in, 31
    use in Snowpark, 65
    user-defined functions in, 29
scalar functions, 29
    ST_COLLECT, 58
scaling
    compute layer of Snowflake, 17
    containerized applications, 98
    Snowpark allowing apps to scale, 66
    storage layer in Snowflake, 17

setting larger size for initialization of
dynamic tables, 27
Snowflake's generation 2 (Gen2) standard
warehouses, 173
Snowpark-optimized warehouses, 22
standard virtual warehouses in Snowflake,
21
Warehouses tab (Snowsight Admin), 11
web interface for Snowflake (see Snowsight)
well-known text (WKT), 58
WHERE clause, 35
AI_FILTER function in, 181
HAVING clause and, order of execution, 36
use with FROM and QUALIFY clauses, 37
WINDOW clause, 37
window frame functions, 46
window functions, 37, 46-53
categories of, 46
FIRST_VALUE and LAST_VALUE, 51
LAG and LEAD, 52
RANK and DENSE_RANK, 49-50
ROW_NUMBER, 47-48
window_frame parameter, 49

worksheets, 12-14
creating new worksheet for ML example,
135
Python, 13
SQL, 12
Worksheets (Snowsight), 5
Workspaces (Snowsight), 179
dbt projects in, 180

X
XML, 20
XOR operator, BOOLXOR_AGG function, 45

Y
YAML
manifest file, 97
semantic models, 129

Z
zero-copy clones, 21
zero-shot extraction, 132

About the Author

Muhammad Fasih Ullah is the head of data and analytics for NordicFeel Group, the leading Nordic beauty ecommerce group. His current work focuses on developing resilient and high-functioning data organizations that manage scalable data and analytics needs. He has helped teams design and build scalable data layers that process millions of rows daily and prepare data for analytical use across multiple brands and markets.

As a four-time Snowflake Data Superhero, the platform's highest community recognition, Fasih has leveraged his in-depth knowledge of Snowflake to help save his organization and clients hundreds of thousands of dollars in data warehousing costs while dramatically improving performance and capabilities. With over eight years of experience in data, analytics, data architecture, and AI, Fasih has built his expertise across diverse industries at companies including Voi Technology and Afiniti.

Colophon

The animal on the cover of *Advanced Snowflake* is a Haida ermine (*Mustela haidarum*), a member of the weasel family that is native to and named for the Haida Gwaii archipelago off the coast of British Columbia. Haida ermine are endemic to islands along North America's Pacific Northwest coast.

The fur coat of the Haida ermine turns reddish-brown in summer and white in winter. Even though it rarely snows at the low elevations of their island habitat, these creatures are very difficult to spot in all seasons. Haida ermines are carnivores capable of hunting prey many times their size (about 7 to 13 inches).

Haida ermine were designated as a unique species in 2013 and have not been assessed by the IUCN Red List of Threatened Species. Conservationists have concerns about the decreasing populations of many species in the genus *Mustela*. Many of the animals on O'Reilly covers are endangered; all of them are important to the world.

The cover illustration is by José Marzan Jr., based on an antique line engraving from *Lydekker's Royal Natural History*. The series design is by Edie Freedman, Ellie Volckhausen, and Karen Montgomery. The cover fonts are Gilroy Semibold and Guardian Sans. The text font is Adobe Minion Pro; the heading font is Adobe Myriad Condensed; and the code font is Dalton Maag's Ubuntu Mono.

O'REILLY®

Learn from experts.
Become one yourself.

60,000+ titles | Live events with experts | Role-based courses
Interactive learning | Certification preparation

**Try the O'Reilly learning platform
free for 10 days.**

©2025 O'Reilly Media, Inc. O'Reilly is a registered trademark of O'Reilly Media, Inc. 718900_7x9.1875

www.ingramcontent.com/pod-product-compliance
Lightning Source LLC
Chambersburg PA
CBHW061420210326
41598CB00035B/6282